Open Source Library Solutions (OSLS)

Open Source Library Solutions (OSLS)

Edited By

Aditya Tripathi
H N Prasad
Rajani Mishra

Open Source Library Solutions (OSLS)

ISBN : 978-81-7000-623-7

Price : Rs. 850/-

First Published 2010

Published by:
Ess Ess Publications
4831/24, Ansari Road,
Darya Ganj,
New Delhi-110 002.
INDIA
Phones: 23260807, 41563444
Fax: 41563334
E-mail: info@essessreference.com
www.essessreference.com

Cover Design by *Patch Creative Unit*

Printed and bound in India

Contents

FOREWORD

Libraries and Information Centres (LICs) are facing unprecedented challenges due to changes in form and access to their collections on one hand and also due to an ever increasing demand from the clientele for more refined services. It is indeed a long cherished objective of LICs to bring pinpointed information to users rather than information resources that may only be indicative of the sought information. However the task is by no means trivial or easily accomplished given the varied IT tools available and expected services in an intensively IT oriented environment.

Another issue pertains to economics where libraries have to make services cost effective. As is evident, most finances are consumed for manpower, infrastructure and building collections and often enough it is found that there is a financial crunch when new services and IT infrastructure has to be put in place. Against this scene is the increase in patron expectations of the library through demands for e-resources, web based services, multimedia resources and such.

With this background, in the Indian scenario, the profession is really at crossroads. Library personnel are often from schools (which they might have attended long back) where they were taught traditional librarianship. There have been efforts such as those through University Grants Commission (UGC) Academic Staff Colleges to upgrade the knowledge and skills in a continuing education mode but it had scant impact with many of the courses only running as a formality because of very little practical and hands-on component in the curricula. The point really is that the profession needs to quickly adapt to the challenges through more practical and hands-on training of in-service professionals on an immediate basis. On the other hand, Indian library and information schools have to go back to the drawing board and come up with more meaningful and pertinent curricula that in effect nurtures NextGen library and information professionals.

Given all these challenges, it is indeed gratifying that we have atleast a few points in favour of where we are headed. One is the appreciable interest and zest that library and information professionals have in them to try and test new tools in order to offer new services. Often enough it is true that library staff is doing some extra work and research on their own in the interest of their clientele though they do not stand to gain any monetary benefits. This indeed is a commendable effort.

The other major fillip comes from the availability of Open Source Software (OSS) for library and information field. There are today very useful OSS starting from the Debian platform and Apache Web Server in general to LIS-specific software like, Library Management Software (LMS) such as Koha and Digital Library (DL) software such as DSpace, Eprints, Fedora, GSDL, CDSware, etc. No doubt the hardware costs have to be borne by libraries but the availability of efficient OSS has considerably cut down the software costs. OSS have also given reliable and robust tools for several LIS applications that have made implementation of institutional repositories, availability of Web-based Online Public Access Catalogs (OPACs) on open source LMSes a possibility. In addition, it is only apt to acknowledge the active communities around each of the OSSes that have formed self and community help groups that offer advisory, managerial and technical support.

The essays, research articles, comparative studies and case studies in this book are testimony to the efforts of the library professionals in offering refined information services to their clientele. It is hoped that the contents will enthuse more professionals in adopting OSS for their library services which will ultimately result in content becoming 'open' as we march towards realizing the grand dream of truly achieving 'Open Access to Information'.

A.R.D. Prasad
Documentation research and training Centre,
Indian Statistical Institute, Bangalore

PREFACE

Libraries have limited finance for serving the users. Against the increasing user base and demand for quick service the budget of libraries appears to be shrinking day-by-day. The technology has come up as a tool for librarians though the affair appears to be costly in terms of expenditure over hardware and software. The price of hardware is going down while the price of software is increasing day-by-day. Open Source Movement has come up as a big solace for those who wish to incorporate technology to their work. There are solutions from simple word processor to the complex Library Management Systems (LMSs) in the public domain. These software can not only be used but also can be modified as per the individual needs. The source code of the software is available for modifications and any other adaptions.

The OSS movement has liberated librarians from the paws of unscrupulous vendors who wish to monopolize library market. OSSs follow community based development model where inputs are shared in form of experiences of library professionals for further growth of software. During last 7-8 years we have witnessed growth of such solutions and there increased implementation all over the world. It is encouraging to note that the website of White House, United States is developed over Drupal, an open source Content Management System (CMS).

The implementation of OSS has been seen in e-learning,

e-governance, e-publishing and so on. The libraries can very well adopt these new technologies for its patrons to improved access to the materials acquired by the library. Users of libraries can be educated before they use the library and its collection. The library education program can be delivered for users anytime as per their comfort. However such commercial applications are very costly and sometimes beyond the limits of library. The open source CMS like Joomla, Drupal, Plone etc. can be very well fit in with no additional cost except the existing hardware. The areas where libraries can see the implementation of OSSs are:

- Library Management Systems
- Digital Libraries
- E-publishing
- Federated Searching
- Consortium Management etc.

Librarians have to keep on scratching their head to have cheapest solution with maximum features for library automation. Koha is a 'Free and Open Source Software' (FOSS) automation tool to automate all the activities of a library. Another area where OSSs have made mark is implementation of digital libraries. The solutions like Dspace, Eprints, Greenstone etc. are widely being used by the library community all over the world. It is observed that many of the libraries are involved in publishing the journals using tools such as Open Journal System (OJS). The tools like Open Archive Harvesters are very handy for developing customized federated search.

However, still it has been observed that many of the libraries hesitate to work with the OSSs. They find it difficult to adopt OSS model with a fear of handling such systems. Apart from this many a times the library professionals find themselves uncomfortable with new technologies and want someone else to handle on their behalf. This dependency creates monopoly in favour of vendors and often leads to a kind of blackmail situation where library professionals find themselves into a fix situation.

The librarians have to stand head straight and say no to this kind of dependencies and rise to the stature so that they can dictate the situation on their terms. There is no dearth of professional competency when it comes to handle OSSs and other ICT tools. The professional forums both online and offline are good platform to discuss the difficulties and share mutual experiences. The present book demonstrates the capabilities of librarians acquired on various categories of FOSS based tools like, Digital Library Systems, Library Management Systems, Content Management Systems, E-learning Systems etc. It is the high time to say "no" to proprietary products as there are several FOSS based solutions available for library activities. Now it is the zest and the zeal of library community which has to be tested against the time.

This volume is an outcome of National Seminar on Open Source Library Solutions held at Department of Library and Information Science, Banaras Hindu University, Varanasi in 2009.

EDITORS

1

Open Source Software @ DLIS-BHU

H. N. Prasad
Professor
Department of Library and Information ScienceBanaras Hindu University, Varanasi
hnprasad.bhu@gmail.com

Aditya Tripathi
Assistant Professor
Department of Library and Information Science
Banaras Hindu University Varanasi
aditya@bhu.ac.in
adityatripathi@hotmail.com

ABSTRACT

States that OSS has added a new chapter in library administration and services. Various OSS solutions are available under public licensing for download and use for libraries. Discusses Content Management System, e-learning software, digital library software. Presents successful test of cross lingual Sanskrit digital library called Saraswati.

Keywords : Open Source Library Solutions, Digital Library, Content Management System, E-learning System

1. INTRODUCTION

Open Source Software are talk of the town now a days in the parlance of librarianship. The dependency on software organizations have reduced due to the introduction of the products in open source domain. The librarians are not required to depend on software firms only thing they have to be little techno savvy. The open source movement has revolutionized the scenario. The Open Source Software are often delivered free under public licensing system like GNU. However, one must abide with the license statement attached with the software. It was Richard Stallman who first gave the idea of free software later on Tim O' Reilly first coined the term Open Source Software (OSS) and kicked off the Open Source Movement. It is a normal understanding that an open source software is also free. However, it is not always true. The OSS can be normally distributed free cost and a person who has distribution can redistribute it. The source code can be read and modified by anyone. Out of source code one can derive a new software and further that can be redistributed. However, in the licensing of open source software author can restrict the re-distribution of source code if someone has modified the source code. As per the OSS philosophy there should not be any discrimination among people who want to use it. The license of OSS does not show any bias towards a product, software or technology.

In the library parlance OSS are available for almost all kind of activities from word process to library automation. The Department of Library and Information Science, Banaras Hindu University test several OSS technologies in order to identify their potential. The areas on which experiments are done are as follows,

2. CONTENT MANAGEMENT SYSTEM @DLIS-BHU

Content can be anything including audio, motion pictures,

text and graphics. But often content is understood as textual content which is not always true. With the advent of web the mode of service delivery has changed to online from offline. Web has become a medium for quick access and delivery of service. Content management systems are tools for managing web pages over WWW. These software allow online publication and manipulation of web content. Hence, CMS is a system comprising hardware and software that allows an organisation to manage its content "usually web content" by automating business and other processes and providing an authoring environment for web publishers. The web content can be of following types,

- Static webpage
- Dynamic webpage
- Emails
- Bulletin Boards
- Forum
- Blogs
- News
- Articles
- Movies
- Songs
- Databases
- Graphics

CMS is good for publishing web content in a standardized way. Hence, the content would have one kind of theme and behaviour for all the web pages or web objects. Implementation of CMS reduces human labour and time towards modifying the websites. CMS follow modular approach for content design. A single modification at one place will be visualized within the entire website wherever that particular data is viewed. It reduces data redundancy and duplication of work. These systems have good scalability that means the system supports large number of web pages with larger size. These systems are backed up by a database management system.

CMS are compliant with existing web standards like HTML Document Type Definition, metadata standards. The webmaster or content designer does not have to worry about these standards it is taken care by the CMS itself. The content designer need not to know the HTML for designing the webpage. In an Open source environment CMS can adopt several widgets like bulletin board, chat rooms etc. as third party products. Widgets are utilities towards a service. In an open source environment the implementation of upgrades of CMS can be easily done online as well as offline.

These CMS software are free and no cost. The cost which is involved is only on the hardware and content design. In a CMS content can be developed in a distributed manner. That means software is loaded at one place and content designer can feed in their data seating on different locations. Since, the system is in distributed environment and content can be generated simultaneously by many designers it takes less time and cost to develop the system.

One of the drawbacks of distributed environment is lack of control. But the implementation of CMS solves the problem and a webmaster can have full control on his web content whatever is being published. A workflow of content generation can be defined where there can be different levels of checks including editorial support and publishing authority.

Almost all the available Open Source CMS have following features,

- Importing and creating multimedia materials
- User authentication and their roles
- Category definition and their roles

- Workflow definition with messaging for communication
- Archiving and tracking multiple versions of a single instance of content
- Inherent repository to support archiving
- Publishing the content for quick access
- Enterprise search and retrieval

The major open source software are,

- Joomla
- Plone
- Postnuke
- Xoops
- Drupal

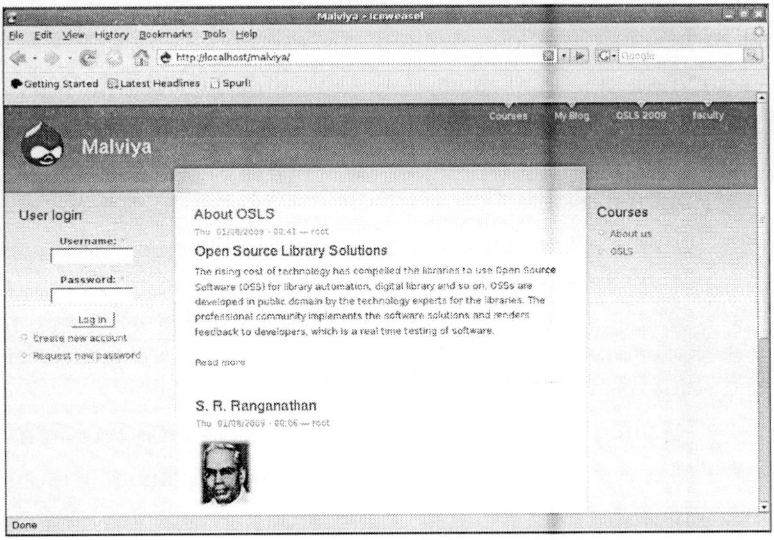

Fig. 1: Malviya designed using Drupal

3. E-LEARNING @DLIS-BHU

Web has revolutionized the mode of production and delivery of services. Now it is not necessary that one should go to college in order to attend the classes. It has shaped the concept of virtual class-rooms and virtual college supporting the distance education. It has become boon for those for whom it is not possible to attend the college due to distance and are already working. Lectures and examinations can be taken any time. Many of these systems are supported by open source online software. The features of these software are as follows,

- Real-time synchronus communication between learner and instructor through chat.
- Threaded discussion boards or forums can be created for sharing views on subject matter
- Participants for each course can be defined.
- Teachers for each course can be defined.
- Courses can be created having several lessons
- Lessons can be appended with exercise
- Students can be given online assignments or offline tasks with a restricted time period.
- These systems support method of assessment declaration of final result.
- Online examination can be conducted. The questions can be framed with mode of answer of true-false, multiple choice, short answer, matching question, random questions, numerical questions, embedded answer questions with descriptive text and graphics.
- Result is declared with grade or marks as it is required
- Many of such system support creation of individual blogs
- Teachers and Students can enroll or removed from a course
- Backup and Restoration of course can be done

Some of the software which support e-learning are as follows,

- ATutor
- Claroline
- Dokeos
- eFront
- KEWL
- LON-CAPA
- Moodle
- OLAT
- Sakai Project

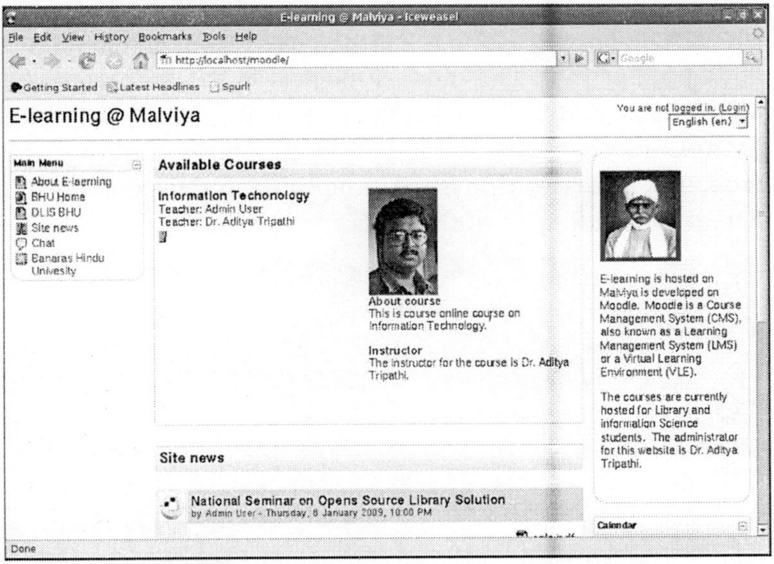

Fig.2: Malviya: an E-learning environment using Moodle

4. DIGITAL LIBRARIES @DLIS-BHU

Digital libraries are collection of digital objects available over networked environment where objects are read with help of a digital reading device. The trend among the libraries are to store documents in digital format as much as possible so that these documents can be delivered to the users over their desktop within no time. Digital libraries can be searched full text as well as through metadata. There are a number of open source digital library software available free of cost for download and use. Hence, Digital library software are Digital Object management system to support storage, search and retrievable of digital objects.

The current trend is to establish federated digital libraries. Federated digital libraries are kept a part from each other at different geographical locations. This architecture of establishing federated digital library is reduces traffic load on one server and distributes it over other systems.

Digital preservation is another area where digital library plays a major role. The physical objects in the library can be digitized and kept inside a digital library. One way it facilitates the use of informational content of the object and on other hand it reduces the physical tangibility to the object and increases the life span of the object.

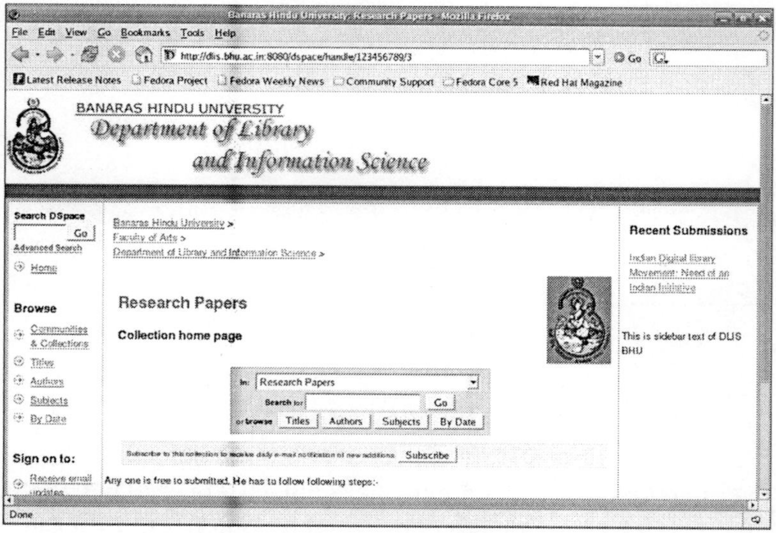

Fig. 3: Digital library using Dspace

Institutional repositories are being established all over the world where authors can submit their research reports and articles online for others to read. The OSS based Digital Object Management System like Dspace, Eprint etc. Support online submission and reviewing the objects. These OSS solutions for libraries provide better control for system administrator with additional power in the hands of users and authors. Some common features of Digital library software are:

- Low cost, including all hardware and software components
- Technically simple to install and manage
- Robust
- Scalable
- Open and inter-operable
- Modular
- User Friendly
- Multi-user (including both searching and maintenance)
- Multimedia digital object enabled
- Platform independent (including both client and server components) interoperable

Some of the software which are used to create Digital libraries are as follows,

- GreenStone Digital Library (GSDL)
- Dspace
- Eprint

5. DIGITAL LIBRARY - SARASWATI

Saraswati is a test-bed digital library in Sanskrit language designed at Department of Library and Information Science. Banaras Hindu University. The system exploits the feature of reading Sanskrit in different scripts. The system successfully demonstrates searching of document in one script and retrieving the documents written in different Indic scripts. The system is successfully tested with two north Indian language scripts i.e Hindi and Bengali and two south Indian language scripts i.e Telugu and Kannada.

Fig. 4: Saraswati test-bed Sanskrit Digital Library

6. CONCLUSION

OSS has come up as movement in library function and administration. It has revolutionized the library services. There are number of OSS solutions available for download and use. For library automation solutions like KOHA, EverGreen and NewGenLib are available. However, there are other ready made PHP and MySQL based tools are also available for different automation activities. Much specialized tools like Digital Library Solutions, Content Management Solutions, E-learning Solutions could be used as and when the need of use arises. Solutions are there for use, only a feel has to be developed within the library community for using OSS solutions.

7. REFERENCES AND RESOURCES

1. Open Source Initiative. *http://www.opensource.org/*
2. GNU Operating System *www.gnu.org*
3. Richard Stallman's Personal Home Page. *http://stallman.org/*
4. Drupal. *http://drupal.org/*
5. Joomla. *http://joomla.org*
6. Plone CMS. *http://plone.org*
7. Moodle.org: open-source community-based tools for learning. *http://moodle.org*
8. DSpace Digital Library Software. *http://www.dspace.org*
9. GreeStone Digital Library Software. *http://www.greenstone.org*

2

Application of Open Source Software (OSS) in Development of Libraries and Information Centres

Ram Kumar Dangi
Assistant Librarian
Faculty of Law, BHU, Varanasi
rkdangi05@rediffmail.com
Santosh Kumar
Professional Assistant
Faculty of Law, BHU, Varanasi
ksverma99@yahoo.co.in
Manoj Kumar Verma
Senior Technical Asistant
DLIS , BHU, Varanasi
manojdlisbhu@gmail.com

ABSTRACTS

Defines the concept of Open Source Software (OSS) amidst the rising cost of technology for library automation in the digital era. Explains the role of OSS in the development of library and information centres (LICs). Narrates the selected OSS for integrated library system and its application in the digital environment.

Enumerates the basic commandants of OSS, advantages and its limitations at the operational level. Highlights how OSS improves the library system and on-line services in the LICs.

Keywords: Free Software Foundations (FSF), Digital Library, Open Source Library Network (OSLN), GNU General Public License (GNU GPL), etc.

1. INTRODUCTION

Open Source Software (**OSS**) is one of the most visible ways of taking technologies to the common people and ensuring that disadvantage section of the society is also a part of the technological advancement which is taking place around the world. OSS has two basic properties (a) the 'source code' or the program itself is available free of cost for use, modifications, as well distribution; and (b) it is illegal to convert an OSS into a proprietary version by virtue of stipulation contained in the licensed with the respect to OSS.

OSS can be described both as a philosophy and a process. As a philosophy it states the intended use of software and method for its distribution with the following goals:

- free to run the software for any purpose
- free to modify the software to suit their needs
- free to redistribute of the software gratis or fun
- free to distribute the modified version of software

Apart from the above, OSS is also a process for the creation and maintenance of software. It is not a formalized process, rather than a process of conversion with common characteristics between software projects. The developer of a software project always is trying to solve the specific problems commonly called 'scratching an itch'. The developer assume that other people may also have same problems and consequently the developer makes the project's source code available on the net in anticipation that other people can also use it. The success of the software depends on the developers' ability to foster communications and some of the community members for which the software is being developed.

2. DEFINITION OF THE OPEN SOURCE SOFTWARE (OSS)

OSS can be defined from different viewpoints to reflect a string of ideas in the field. According to Chudnov:

- An OSS is typically created and maintained by developers crossing constitutional and national boundaries, collaborating by using internet based communication and development tools.
- Output is generally a certain kind of 'free', often through a license that specifies that applications and source code are free to use, modify, and redistribute it as long as all user, modifications are similarly licensed.
- Quality, not profit, drives open source developers who take personal pride in seeing their working solution adopted.

According to Free Software Foundation (FSF) in open source software (OSS), the users' should have freedom to run copy, distribute, study, change, and improve the software.

3. THE TEN COMMANDMENTS

The Open Source Initiative (OSI) identified ten criteria for a software product to be called open source. The OSI certifies a software license as an 'OSI Certified License' on the basis of the following 'Ten Commandments.'

1. Free Redistribution: The license shall not restrict any party from selling or giving away the software as a component of an aggregate software distribution containing programs from several different sources. The license shall not require a royalty or other fee for such sale.

2. Source Code: The program must include source code, and must allow distribution in source code as well as compiled form. Where some form of a product is not distributed with source code, there must be a well-publicized means of obtaining the source code for no more than a reasonable reproduction cost–preferably, downloading via the Internet without charge.

3. Derived Works: The license must allow modifications and derived works, and must allow them to be distributed under the same terms as the license of the original software.

4. Integrity of the Author's Source Code: The license may restrict source code from being distributed in modified form only if the license allows the distribution of "patch files" with the source code for the purpose of modifying the program at build time. The license must explicitly permit distribution of software built from modified source code.

5. No Discrimination against Persons or Groups: The license must not discriminate against any person or group of persons.

6. No Discrimination against Fields of Endeavor: The license must not restrict anyone from making use of the program in a specific field of endeavor.

7. Distribution of License: The rights attached to the program must apply to all to whom the program is redistributed without the need for execution of an additional license by hose parties.

8. License Must not be Specific to a Product: The rights attached to the program must not depend on the program's being part of a particular software distribution.

9. The License must not restrict Other Software: The license must not place restrictions on other software that is distributed along with the licensed software. For example, the license must not insist that all other programs distributed on the same medium must be open-source software.

10. The License must be Technology-Neutral: No provision of the license may be predicated on any individual technology or style of interface.

4. ADVANTAGES OF OSS

The biggest advantage of OSS is that this software can be converted into local languages for the benefit of local people, as the source code of this software is made available to user's alongwith the programs. Some other advantages are as follows when the source code of a program is made available:

i. Anybody can read the source code provided they have the requisite know how to use technology.

ii. Anyone can contribute by modifying the code by adding the new features, correcting errors and by creating a new code super structure on the available hail structure and platform.

iii. It saves time, money, and efforts in reinventing the wheel. This also brings down the cost of development and the time involved in upgrading the software. Thus, it satisfies the canon of library and information science as propounded by S R Ranganathan.

iv. Unlike the proprietary software hidden trapdoors cannot be introduced kit the source code is available for the security at large.

v. Due to rising cost of automation of Library and Information Centre (LICs), OSS can be used an alternate to modernize the LICs as the this is very cost-effective project.

5. LIMITATIONS OF OSS

The following limitations can be enumerated while implementing the OSS in LICs

i. OSS can lack formal support making it difficult for libraries without significant capacity in their systems department to participate in OSS development or to use OSS.

ii. OSS needs to develop a participatory organizational model that allows many to contribute perhaps in different ways to OSS development.

iii. OSS is not always easy to use. It is therefore largely inaccessible to the many libraries and library system departments that require plug-and-play software that is well documented and supported and can be easily installed (and uninstalled).

iv. OSS initiatives do not always do enough to get non-systems librarians and library patrons involved in design and testing of OSS. As such, they are seen as being something that exclusively offers benefits to and holds interest for library systems staff and not for the wider library community.

6. APPLICATION OF OSS IN LIBRARY & INFORMATION CENTRE (LICS)

The use of OSS in library and information centre is not only the set of computer software, but it covers the socio-economic infrastructure in which the software is intended to use. OSS in LICs can bring many changes and in services provided to the users community. Daniel Chudnov has done a lot to raise awareness of OSS in libraries. In the current network environment the affinity of OSS development to librarianship the currently available OSS has best chance to develop. The library related applications such as Z39.50, koha, clients and server, system to manage collection, MARC record readers and writers and integrated library system are directly related to users.

There are number of open sources for library application which fulfills the specific needs of the user's within the library.

OSS can be applied successfully in housekeeping operation of libraries, workshop and training, national leadership, economic viability and open source data, repositories, etc. The concept of OSS in national leadership was propounded by the David Dorman as OSLN (Open Source Library Network). The OSS can provide ample instructions during workshop and training, staffing, installation and maintenance of library software. The activities would describe and demonstrate the OSS in libraries. The main streaming process would include presentation, workshop and training at local, regional and national level. OSS needs to be demonstrated as an economically viable method of supporting software and system. During the last several years library have spent a lot of time, efforts, and money on resource sharing. The pools of these resources sharing together are satisfying the users' need of the professionals as well as common users in the LICs. Likewise selected URL's to internet spider to create scientific subject index. In brief the importance of OSS in libraries can be as follows:

i. OSS is an economical alternative to libraries' reliance upon commercially supplied software. That is, despite the real costs involved in the development, maintenance, and use of OSS software but these are lower than those associated with library reliance upon commercial software..

ii. OSS is very useful if libraries are to develop software and systems that meet their patrons' needs. With OSS the IT infrastructure that is essential to library operations and services can be:

   - open (that is, built according to open standards and as such potentially inter operable with other essential software and systems);
   - ubiquitously available to libraries;
   - capable of being tailored to suit the needs and circumstances of individual libraries

- documented (and documentation must be available); and
- errors can more effectively be identified and corrected.

iii. OSS ensures that library systems and online services will be more functional for libraries and their patrons. OSS motivates and empowers systems librarians and related technical staff by encouraging creativity and positioning them to make a difference in the services.

7. SELECTED OSS

There are several OSS available in the market for the development of libraries and open source software for other commercial use. Selected OSS for library and information centre in general, a house keeping and digital library is as follows:

7.1. KOHA (http://www.koha.org/): Koha is the first open-source integrated library system (ILS) developed in 1999. Koha is a full-featured open source ILS. Developed initially in the New Zealand by the Katapo Communications, it is currently maintained by a team of software providers and library technology staff from around the world. To install Koha for immediate use following configuration is required. It requires a Linux Server, Apache, MySQL, Perl, Root on the Server, a reasonable level of command with command line and database administration skill. The Koha ILS includes catalogue, OPAC, circulation, member management, and acquisitions package. Koha is used by public libraries, private collectors, not-profit organizations, churches, schools, and corporate. Some of the key features are:

- Simple clear interface for librarians and members (patrons) to search right from the front page.
- Customizable search - you choose which fields you want on your search forms when you set it up.

- Reading lists for members - now you can find the name of that great book you read last year.
- Full acquisitions including budgets and pricing information (including supplier and currency conversion), being kept so that you can see what you've ordered and received - so handy at end of year and audit time.

7.2. NewGenLib (www.newgenlib.com) : NewGenLib, an Integrated Library Management System, is now freely available as open source under the most widely used free software license, GNU General Public License (GNU GPL) v3. NewGenLib is the result of collaboration between specialists in library automation and software specialists. The software was developed over a 4-year joint effort between a professional charitable trust, Kesavan Institute of Information and Knowledge Management (KIIKM) and a fledgling software development company, Verus Solutions Pvt. Limited (VSPL), both in Hyderabad, India.. NewGenLib is complaint with OAI-PMH and thus it is possible for NewGenLib libraries to create OA repositories of their institutions. NewGenLib software can perform the following functions:

i. NewGenLib is a web-based library automation and networking solution. As a result a metadata database created by a library using NewGenLib is searchable on the web, the platform which digital libraries worldwide are using.

ii. NewGenLib allows the description and storage of data of not only on the conventional material types such as print-on-paper textual materials but also digital content such as images, audio, video, web pages and full text. Such content may not necessarily be 'owned' by the library. These could be anywhere but accessible on the web. They can actually see full text, view images, and play video and audio clips from their desktops.

iii. The above is possible because NewGenLib allows any

metadata record in its database to have digital content attached to it. For instance, a record could have images, full text (e.g., a PDF file of the full text of the book), a video clip, or an audio clip. All digital content in NewGenLib is stored as a repository on the web server side of the NewGenLib application.

iv. NewGenLib uses international standards, notably the MARC-21 standard which is used in over 70 countries of the world. Many digital library initiatives and library automation software in the world are based on using such standards. In addition, NewGenLib uses UNICODE 3.0 so that it will be possible to create metadata records in non-Roman scripts, including Indian languages.

v. NewGenLib allows browser-based access to its database from anywhere as long as the user is connected to the Internet. The user can not only see digital content on his desktop, he can download it, listen to it, or view it as long he has authorization to do so. The delivery could be as streaming content or via file transfer.

vi. NewGenLib provides extensive search, display, retrieval and formatting features, enabling users to easily find information from the library's metadata database and link to other databases that a library could identify as being useful to its clients.

7.3. Greenstone (http://www.greenstone.org/): Greenstone is produced by the New Zealand Digital Library Project at the University of Waikato, and developed and distributed in cooperation with UNESCO and the Human Info NGO. Greenstone is a suite of software for building and distributing digital library collections. It provides a new way of organizing information and publishing it on the Internet or on CD-ROM. Greenstone runs on Apache, Perl and GDBM and it can be associated with UNIX, Windows, Linux, Marcos X. Some of the important features are:

- Support for image, video, and text collection
- Support for multilingual collection building
- Z39.50 client available on Linux systems

7.4. DSpace (http://www.dspace.org/) : DSpace is a specialized type of digital asset management or content management system: it manages and distributes digital items, made up of digital files and allows for the creation, indexing, and searching of associated metadata to locate and retrieve the items. It is designed to support the long-term reservation of the digital material stored in the repository. DSpace was developed out of collaboration between MIT Libraries and Hewlett-Packard Company. The important features of DSpace are:

- DSpace is organized to accommodate the multidisciplinary and organizational needs of a large institution.
- DSpace Supports for a Variety of Digital Formats and Content Types including text, images, audio, and video.
- DSpace allows contributors to limit access to items in DSpace - at the collection and the individual item level.
- DSpace provides long-term physical storage and management of digital items in a secure, professionally managed repository
- The DSpace submission process allows for the description of each item using a qualified version of the Dublin Core metadata schema.

7.5. Fedora :(http://www.fedora.info/) : Flexible Extensible Digital Object and Repository Architecture (Fedora) is a toolkit to build a digital object repository management system. The system, designed to be a foundation upon which interoperable web-based digital libraries, institutional repositories and other information management systems canbe built, demonstrates how distributed digital library architecture can be deployed using web-based technologies, including XML and Web services. It was jointly developed by the University of Virginia and Cornell University the Fedora project was funded by the Andrew W. Mellon Foundation. The interface to the system consists of three open APIs that are exposed as web services:

- **Management API (API-M)** – defines an interface for administering the repository. It includes operations necessary for clients to create and maintain digital objects and their components. API-M is implemented as a SOAP-enabled web service.
- **Access API (API-A)** – defines an interface for accessing digital objects stored in the repository. It includes operations necessary for clients to perform disseminations on objects in the depository and to discover information about an object using object reflection. API-A is implemented as a SOAP-enabled web service.
- **Access-Lite API (API-A-Lite)** – defines a streamlined version of the Fedora Access Service that is implemented as an HTTP-enabled web service.

7.6. iVia (http://infomine.ucr.edu/iVia/) : Based on Apache, MySQL, and Berkeley DB iVia is an open source Internet subject portal or virtual library system. As a hybrid expert and machine built collection creation and management system, it supports a primary, expert-created, first-tier collection that is augmented by a large, second-tier collection of significant Internet resources that are automatically gathered and described. The iVia system is an INFOMINE creation generously funded by the National Leadership Grant Program of the U.S. Institute of Museum and Library Services, the Fund for the Improvement of Post-Secondary Education of the U.S. Department of Education and the Library of the University of California, Riverside. Some of the major features of the iVia system include:

- A core system that is fast, robust, reliable and scalable to millions of records and users for internet resources.
- Classifiers that enable semi-automated metadata content creation providing expert/machine interaction throughout the record building process.
- Search/browse interface options that provide users with great flexibility in finding resources and which support all levels of user search skills.
- Support for single or multiple subject virtual library projects which can share data and efforts on any of several levels of cooperation.
- Support for the following standards: OAI Protocol for Metadata Harvesting (OAI-PMH), Dublin core, MARC (Machine-Readable Cataloging), Library of Congress Subject Headings (LCSH), and Library of Congress Classifications (LCC).

7.7. Dienst (http://www.cs.cornell.edu/cdlrg/dienst/software/DienstSoftware.htm) : The distributed Dienst software is configured to handle textual resources (documents) in a variety of formats on Apache, Perl, mod_perl, ImageMagic, PerlMagic, freeways-sf. However, the Dienst architecture includes a sophisticated document model that accommodates a wide variety of digital resources. Using the Dienst software for these other resources will require some programming. Dienst is a project of the CDLRG - Cornell Digital Library Research Group. Work on Dienst sponsored by the Defense Advanced Research Projects Agency (DARPA) on behalf of the Digital Libraries Initiative. Additional work on Dienst is sponsored by the National Science Foundation Digital Libraries Initiative. Their supporting platforms are Supported Platforms are UNIX, Linux, MacOS X, Windows (not tested).

7.8. DjVuLibre (http://djvu.sourceforge.net/) : DjVu (pronounced "deja vu") is a compression technique, a file format, and a delivery platform that is specifically designed to enable the creation of digital libraries of printed material, either scanned from paper or digitally. DjVu documents are displayed within web browsers through a very lightweight plug-in (available for all major platforms). Server-side full-text search can easily be provided using free indexing tools and a few Perl scripts. The DjVu project was started by Yann LeCun at AT&T Labs-Research in 1996. Much of the research and innovations behind DjVu were the work of Leon Bottou, Yann LeCun, Patrick Haffner, Paul Howard, and Yoshua Bengio, with some contributions from Pascal Vincent, Patrice Simard, and Steven Pigeon. DjVuLibre is a GPL implementation of DjVu maintained by the original inventors of DjVu. Go to http://djvu.sourceforge.net/credits.html to know the historical details of the project.

7.9. Net::OAI::Harvester (http//search.cpan.org/author/ESUMMERS/OAI-Harvester-0.5/) : Net::OAI::Harvester is a Perl extension for easily querying OAIPMH repositories. OAI-PMH allows data repositories to share metadata about their digital assets. Net::OAI::Harvester is a OAI-PMH client, so it does for OAIPMH what LWP::User Agent does for HTTP. At the moment this module supports only Dublin Core (oai_dc) schema handling through XML::Handler. Some of the features are:

- It is able to handle memory-crazy requests like list Records and list Identifiers
- XML::SAX filters are used which will allow interested developers to write their own metadata parsing packages, and drop them into place
- It has built in support for unqualified Dublin Core, and has a framework for dropping in one's own parser for other kinds of metadata

7.10. APACHE (http:apache.org) : This is most popular web (HTTP) server on the internet and a standard open piece of software. It is 'a patchy' server, and it made up of many modular parts to create a coherent whole. Apache is currently a version of 2.0. There are others modules dealing with logging transactions and CGI (Common Gateway interface) scripting others modules allow to rewrite incoming request, manage email, implement the title used HTTP put method; write other module on Perl or transform XML file using XSLT.

7.11. CVS (Http://cvshome.org/) : CVS is an acronym of Concurrent Version System. It consists of a client and server application which might prove very useful in the library and information centre as most of software require used in the libraries require client and server module. The server is set up and point to a directory where one or more project are saved. Usernames and passwords are created, and servers sits and wait for connections. CVS client is also a command-line driven. On the command-line location of a CVS server has to be specified. One logged in CVS command used to download remote project. After that source code can be hacked away.

7.12. GNU Tools : GNU is a computer operating system composed entirely of free software. Prominent components of GNU system include GNU Compiler Collection (GCC) and GNUC library (glibe). GNU works as text editor and the GNOME desktop environment. Development of GNU was initiated by Richard Stallman and was the original focus of the Free Software Foundation (FSF). GNU project was launched in 1983 to develop a complete UNIX-like operating system which is free software.

Apart from the above OSS tools, some others can also be enumerated such as Rapid Visual OAI Tools (RVOT), OAI/ODL Harwester template, ARC search service on OAI-PMH protocol, VTOA/OAI PMH Perl implementation, CDSWare for on-line library catalogue, hypermail for creating mailing list archive, E-print to create open access services, and D-like software for archiving for digital documents which can be used for database and information retrieval in the library and information centre.

8. CONCLUSIONS

There are numbers of positive impact of OSS, when it is applied at operational level in libraries it can boost the services in library and information Centres. OSS has also provided new ways and means to the library and information centre in the era of information explosion to organize their library database, services and facilities without too much expenditure on infrastructure development in the libraries. The small and unaided library are using the OSS freely to automate their library house-keeping operations to fulfill the informational needs of their users. OSS has also provided opportunity to users to modify the software by using the source code for the better services. As the cost of reading materials and software for library automation are increasing in leaps and bound, OSS is the right and ultimate solution to automate the services in the libraries to serve the maximum users and the minimum cost. Mahatma Gandhi's messages of 'weave your own cloth'. The spirit behind this messages is 'self-reliance' which is the guiding factor behind propagation of open source code in OSS which is being advanced by developers of OSS and various governments.

REFERENCES

1. Amin, Saiful 'Open Source Software for Libraries : a Trend Report' a Project Report submitted in partial fulfillment of Award of AIDS, at DRTC, Bangalore, https://drtc.isibang.ac.in/bitstream/handle/1849/190/OSS_for_libraries.pdf?., visited on 27 December 2008.
2. Open Source Software in libraries, http://infomotions.com/musings/ossnlibraries-lita/, visited on 27 December 2008.
3. http://www.fsf.org/licensing/essays/free-sw.html, visited on 23 December 2008.
4. Shah, Ajay 'What Open Source software means to India, http://www.mayin.org/ ajayshah /MEDIA/1998/free-sw.html, visited on 23 December 2008.
5. Suri, Priti & Associates .Open Source and the Law. New Delhi: LexisNexis Butterworths, 2006.

3

Open Source For Libraries and Research Community : Presenting the Case of Gist Find

Amit Jha
Manager – Research & Development
Global Information Systems Technology Pvt. Ltd. (GIST)
ajha@gist.in

Collin D'mello
Vice President, Sales & Publisher Relations
Global Information Systems Technology Pvt. Ltd. (GIST)
collin@gist.in

Preeti Chaturvedi
Manager – Business Development
Global Information Systems Technology Pvt. Ltd. (GIST)
preeti@gist.in

Tarun Arora
Chief Operating Officer
Global Information Systems Technology Pvt. Ltd. (GIST)
tarun@gist.in

ABSTRACT

There has been a significant development in terms of information access as more and more libraries invest in IT infrastructure and gravitate towards electronic content. In the face of unlimited information options/ resources, limited budgets and increasing customer demands, librarians are looking for innovative ways to leverage technology in tackling the issues of Cost and Collaboration while ensuring speedy information discovery and management. Open source applications like Meta Search; Library 2.0; Citation Management; Serials Management; Integrated Library Systems; Digital Repositories etc. offer some of the best solutions towards dealing with such issues. The paper presents the case of GIST FIND, a meta search service, which is powered by various open source initiatives, and how it can address some of the most urgent needs of the library and research community.

Keywords: GIST Find, Meta Search Services, Library 2.0, Integrated Library Management System.

1. CURRENT SCENARIO OF LIBRARY AND RESEARCH COMMUNITIES

As education becomes more competitive and the number of institutions rapidly increases, libraries can be a distinguishing factor in establishing the identity of institutions. The knowledge infrastructure of libraries determines the quality of research output of an institution's academic community. There has also been a significant development in terms of information access as more and more libraries invest in IT infrastructure and gravitate towards electronic content. In order to facilitate and encourage the digitization of libraries, the government has taken many initiatives like forming consortia (like INFLIBNET, INDEST) which ensure that all academic institutions across India have access to international content at competitive costs; the Digital Library of India (DLI)- the biggest national level digital library project in India whereby leading Indian institutes like IISc, CMU, NSF, ERNET and MCIT are collaborating with Carnegie Mellon to facilitate digitization of more than 1 million books; the ERNET project whereby the Department of Electronics seeks to create expertise R&D and education in the country in the area of networking and internet.

Challenges of Librarians and Researchers in India

In the face of unlimited information options/resources, limited budgets and increasing customer demands, librarians are looking for innovative ways to leverage technology in tackling the following issues:

- Maximizing ROI on resources and drive usage
- Ensuring speedy information discovery at barest minimum costs
- Managing multiple authentications by different publishers
- Building an environment of academic research and collaboration around the resources available

While on the one hand, institutional authorities are looking for ways to make research and learning more efficient, researchers are faced with an overload of information and paucity of time. They are also dealing with some critical challenges like:

- How to maximize research efficiency?
- How to get desired results in the least possible time?
- How to collaborate and share with other researchers?

2. THE SOLUTION: OPEN SOURCE

The answer to most of these problems comes in the form of Open Source Solutions for information discovery and management. Open Source Software refers to software that provides freedom…

- Freedom 1: The freedom to use the software for any purpose.

- Freedom 2: The freedom to access and study the source of the software.
- Freedom 3: The freedom to make changes to the software using its source code.
- Freedom 4: The freedom to share the software (original or modified) with others, under the same conditions.

From the perspective of the academic community, Open Source comes loaded with the advantages of the two **Cs- Cost** and **Collaboration.** Not only are open source solutions highly cost effective and customizable, they are also based on the concept of community which facilitates larger collaboration between academic groups and institutions. Below is a brief definition of the different forms of Open Source:

Open Source: While Open Source Software refers to software that includes the source code and is available for free, one of the key distinctions of OSS is that it can be modified as well as improvised upon with great ease.

Open Access: Open access helps to ensure long-term access to scholarly articles. Unlike articles that are licensed in traditional article databases, libraries and others can create local copies and repositories of these resources. Libraries, by working together to make repositories of open access literature, can ensure continued access to these scholarly publications into the distant future.

Open Standards: Open Standards are defined by Pountain as "[a] standard that is independent of any single institution or manufacturer, and to which users may propose amendments." The use of Open Standards implies greater freedom to institutions because the standards can be acquired for free and customized according to the institute's own requirement. They also lend themselves to extended collaboration amongst academic communities and groups.

Using Open Source to deal with the Challenges of Information Management in Libraries

We have all heard about Web 2.0. A recent development in this context is Library 2.0. What it essentially entails is a user driven and user developed virtual repository of resources and information. Open Source technologies are helping libraries in creating new services and opportunities that were not available earlier, such as virtual reference, personalized OPAC interfaces, or downloadable media that students and researchers can use whenever, wherever they want. This increase in available technologies gives libraries the ability to offer improved, customer-driven service opportunities and makes them a critical component of the information architecture of institutions. The key technical trends being witnessed amongst the library community are:

Library 2.0: The concept of Library 2.0 first made its conference debut at Internet Librarian 2005. It entails the following characteristics:

- Providing full featured comprehensive Open Public Access Catalog
- Harnessing the library user in both design and implementation of services
- Involving the Library users in crafting and modifying library provided services
- Harvesting and integrating ideas and products from peripheral fields into library service models

Full Featured OPAC: The evolution of Open Public Access Catalogs is both interesting as well as relevant from our research and information delivery perspective. As open public access catalogs graduate from being desktop inventories to browser applications, they are becoming more and more feature rich and customer focused. What this means is that they are using more and more evolved search technologies like meta search and are also involving the user in greater interaction with the system through tagging, RSS and peer reviews and networking.

Meta Search: Open Source meta search engines are highly cost effective and customizable because the user can get access to the code itself and can modify it according to his own standards- a possibility which would not exist with other commercial solutions.

Citation management: Open Source Services have taken citation management note sharing to the next level. Not only do they incorporate the best features of older reference management systems-the ability to store author, title, and publication fields and to export that information as formatted references, they also incorporate the latest features of social media applications like tagging, interacting and community.

Serials Management: Open source applications like CUFTS provide electronic resource management services, allowing the library to centralize all of the details about electronic collections, including licensing terms, renewal dates, contacts, and more. They also provide direct links to full text articles in the library's database.

Integrated Library Systems: We are also increasingly witnessing the growth of enterprise level ILS wherein libraries of all sizes can collaborate to achieve their technology goals. ILS like Koha include modules for circulation, cataloging, acquisitions, serials, reserves, patron management, branch relationships, and more.

Digital Repositories: Newer systems like DSpace are successfully using open source for digital preservation. As faculty and other researchers develop research materials and scholarly publications in increasingly complex digital formats, there is a need to collect, preserve, index and distribute them: a time-consuming and expensive chore for individual faculty and their departments, labs, and centers to manage themselves. The DSpace system provides a way to manage these research materials and publications in a professionally maintained repository to give them greater visibility and accessibility over time.

3. A STUDY IN OPEN SOURCE SERVICE FOR LIBRARIES: THE CASE OF GIST FIND

i. Why we chose meta search?

As the leading information management and services provider with a majority of its clientele in the education sector, GIST had an in-depth insight into the problems of the research community. Researchers and librarians alike were faced with the problem of information overload wherein the online resources, both paid as well as free, were multiplying thereby placing an increasing premium on research time.

GIST analyzed the market scenario and realized that there was an urgent need to amongst the research community for a search service which could simplify access to multiple resources by various publishers while integrating various applications which would make the process of research more manageable and cost effective. GIST realized that this service would also enable librarians to move from information management towards information consulting. It would also save the researchers the trouble of mastering search on different publisher platforms before using their resources.

ii. Why we chose to build it on open source technologies?

After identifying the problem of search and information management and delivery, GIST decided to use Open Source applications to develop a meta search service. The main reasons for opting for open source applications while developing the service were:

- **Highly Customizable and Cost Effective Solution:** GIST realized the significance of developing an Open Source Service which would serve the dual purpose of:
  - Incorporating indigenous insights and highly customized solutions to local problems of Indian researchers.
  - Offering a cost effective service to cater to the demands of the Indian academic community.
- **Overcome challenges of maintaining IT teams for information management:** Besides helping libraries to maximize their return on resource investment, GIST felt that the meta search service would offer the ease of use which comes with Software as a Service (SaaS) solution. By offering a hosted service along with a strong backend support team, the meta search service would enable institutions to focus on their core competence of information and knowledge dissemination while taking care of their IT hassles.

As a response to the pressing needs of the research community, Global Information System's Technology, India's leading information management company, has created GIST FIND- a customizable, open source, meta search service that allows researchers to search across multiple resources through a single user interface. These resources can be subscribed, non-subscribed, open source, patent databases and other such resources relevant to the institution. GIST FIND has been developed by GIST Pvt. Ltd, India's leading information consulting company. The organization developed this service after an in-depth analysis of the education ecosystem.

Features of GIST FIND

Based on its decades of experience and extensive research, GIST has incorporated some critical and exciting features in GIST FIND....

- **Subscription Identifier helps utilize the library's resources :** Libraries make a sizeable investment in resources, and it is of utmost importance that users get to know what resources are available to them. GIST FIND's subscription identifier legends help researchers see the availability of resultant resources in their library.
- **Setup Resources helps users save time by making highly specific searches :** Irrelevant searches and scanning reams of data which is not pertaining to their information needs, takes up most of the valuable time of researchers, leaving little room for the actual value addition. GIST FIND has designed a unique feature of "Setup Resources" through which users can narrow down the universe of the databases that they will search through on various parameters like subscription type, subject area, resources type even down to specific named resources.
- **Clustering and Author Federated Searches ensure that users don't waste time going through unnecessary results:** GIST FIND organizes the results of the users' searches according to Topic, Author and Year. This helps users in better managing and organizing their results. One of the most striking features of the service is the federated search by author's name. Through this feature, users can sort the results of their desired author.

Some Technical Facts about GIST FIND

- **Open Source Technology:** GIST Find has been developed by integrating many open source initiatives to bring to libraries the integrated functionality in a single window.
- **W3C Standards:** GIST Find is built on W3C standards i.e. XHTML, DOM, XML which makes the applications very robust, Interoperable and customizable
- **NISO Metasearching Initiatives:** GIST Find follows the meta-searching standards set by NISO and uses Z39.50

protocol, XML Gateway, HTML Parsing which ensures results integrity between GIST Find and Original Source.

- **Harvests Usage Statistics using NISO Protocol:** GIST Find uses NISO Protocols to harvest usage statistics providing the ability to extract data in acceptable formats like Excel, CSV etc.
- **Generates Counter Compliant Reports and Customized Reports:** GIST Find has built usage statistics platform which provides libraries with counter compliant reports and also ability to develop customized reports for consortium and institution.

The main objective behind developing a service like GIST FIND is to help the library in strengthening its information dissemination thereby enhancing the quality of research produced by its users

NOTES AND REFERENCES

(i) Enterprise Search Summit; November 6-7 2007; San Jose McEnery Convention Center, San Jose, CA

(ii) Contemplating Federated Search, Melissa Rethlefsen, Library Journal, 7/15/2008

Synopsis

- There seems to be a feeling that the existing search solutions have made zombies out of researchers. There is a lack of strategic approach while searching. One of the challenges is that researchers do not apply too much critical thinking while using keywords or other parameters for search
- Google-like relevancy is the end goal of quick information searches but not necessarily the end goal of research.
- While federated search might have its limitations, it does help researchers discover new sources of information.

(iii) Federated Search 101, Alexis Linoski and Tine Walczyk, 7/15/2008

- Google has come out with its own federated search solution in the form of "Google Scholar" However, the limitation is that it does not allow users to narrow down and make their searches niche and specific.
- There are more than a dozen federated search products on the market. Furthermore, many vendors also license their products or connectors to other vendors or resell another product.
- According to a survey, the features librarians desire the most in a federated search solution are limiting results by source, date, range, full text, or peer review; speed of results retrieval; appearance of the interface; sorting of results; and deduplication.
- In terms of hosting options, either the service provider offers a hosted solution whereby the vendor hosts the product on its servers, and access is accomplished via IP authentication; or they offer the option to install their software on your library's server.

(iv) Free your Search with Open Source, Karen Koombs, 7/15/2008

- The advantages of federated search are Built-in application programming interfaces (APIs), highly customizable interfaces, speedy return of search results, and the ability to participate in the development process are all potential benefits
- While many people think the difficulty of implementing an open source federated search tool is in the installation, the real challenge is the configuration of search targets, or "connectors." This means collecting connection information (host, username, and password) from vendors as well as

mapping metadata gathered from each database to fields used by the tool.

(v) Building Bearcat, Lisa A. Ellis, Joseph Hartnett and Michael Waldman, 7/15/2008

- Locating databases by subject isn't very easy when one relies solely on the database's name, as many are totally nondescript or don't lend themselves to subject identification.
- To deal with the problem of multiple databases and access points, libraries need effective federated search solutions.

(vi) Web Links and Resources:-

- http://www.dwheeler.com/oss_fs_why.html
- http://www.dwheeler.com/oss_fs_eval.html
- http://open-source.gbdirect.co.uk/migration/benefit.html
- http://www.osv.org.au/index.cgi?tid=5
- http://sandro.groganz.com/wiki/Category:Open_Source_Marketing
- http://en.wikipedia.org/wiki/Open_source#Terms_based_on_open_source
- http://infomotions.com/musings/ossnlibraries/
- http://en.wikipedia.org/wiki/Library_2.0
- http://www.libraryjournal.com/article/CA6365200.html
- http://connect.educause.edu/Library/EDUCAUSEQuarterly/OpenSourceSoftwareinEduca/46592?time=1230267273
- http://www.degreetutor.com/library/managing-expenses/open-source-library
- http://www.acm.org/ubiquity/views/v4i47_dorman.html

4

An Information Model for A University System Using Dspace

Sneha Tripathi
Assistant Librarian
Sayaji Rao Gaekwad Library
Banaras Hindu University, Varanasi
sneha.tripathi@gmail.com

ABSTRACT

Institutional Repositories are much talked in parlance to Scholarly publishing. This has emerged as one of the best possible ways for the researchers to publish their scholarly work and make it accessible to fellow research community. The present paper explores the possibility of using DSpace as possible option for Institutional Repository for Academic Institutions like Universities and Colleges. An Information Model is proposed and possible communities are identified for a University System.

Keywords: Digital Library, Open Source Library Software, Dspace, Institutional Repository.

1. INTRODUCTION

Scholarly Communication involves the process of sharing and publishing of research works by academicians, scholars and researchers. The present trend in Scholarly Communication seeks for information model which has wider reach and economically viable. Rising costs of scholarly journals have restricted the free flow of scholarly information. Moreover, many of the researchers lack the expertise/resources to preserve/store their datasets, preprints and other valuable scholarly resources. Hence, the concept of developing Institutional Repositories arose where the concerned academic/research fraternity can publish and preserve their research outputs with much ease. This also helps in raising the institutional profile. In India, academic and research institutes such as IISC, Bangalore, All IITs, Indian Statistical Institute and others have their institutional repositories in place while many others are in the planning stages.

2. ABOUT DSPACE

Scholarly publications have brought in a number of research publications in various complex digital formats which are required to be collected, stored, indexed, preserved and distributed which is quite a cumbersome work for researchers and scientific community. DSpace is a digital repository system which manages the research output of an Institution so as to make it accessible to the research community. Developed jointly by MIT Libraries and Hewlett-Packard (HP), DSpace facilitates capturing, storing, indexing, preserving and redistributing intellectual output of an Institution. It is open source and recognizes BSD License for redistribution. DSpace, since after its inception, has been one of the widely used by different Institutions to establish their Institutional Repository system.

The reasons are many. Some of them are:

i. DSpace is freely available under BSD license for institutions to store their scholarly digital materials.

ii. Customization is possible to further extend and enhance the capabilities of DSpace to match with the needs and workflow of the organization.

iii. DSpace is a service model for open access and/or digital archiving for perpetual access.

iv. Support to popular Data Formats: DSpace supports many popular data formats and has the provision of registering new formats.

v. Collections in DSpace are searchable and retrievable through Web.

vi. Provides access to the digital work of the whole institution through one interface.

vii. DSpace facilitates developing a Multilingual Institutional Repository.

viii. DSpace complies with OAI-PMH (Open Archive Initiative Protocol for Metadata Harvesting).

3. INFORMATION MODEL USING DSPACE

The information model of DSpace is carved around the idea of organizational "Communities"—based on their different information management needs. The objective of the information model is to ease the process of submission of research out. For an Academic system like Universities and Colleges, the "Communities" could be defined as Institutes; Study Centers; Faculties (such as Faculty of Arts; Faculty of Science, etc.). The system offers different level of customization that can be stretched to meet the varying needs of the Institution. The digital work from the different sections or departments of the institution can be made accessible through a single web interface. Collections within DSpace are developed under the subhead Communities. Each community and collection retains their identity within the repository.

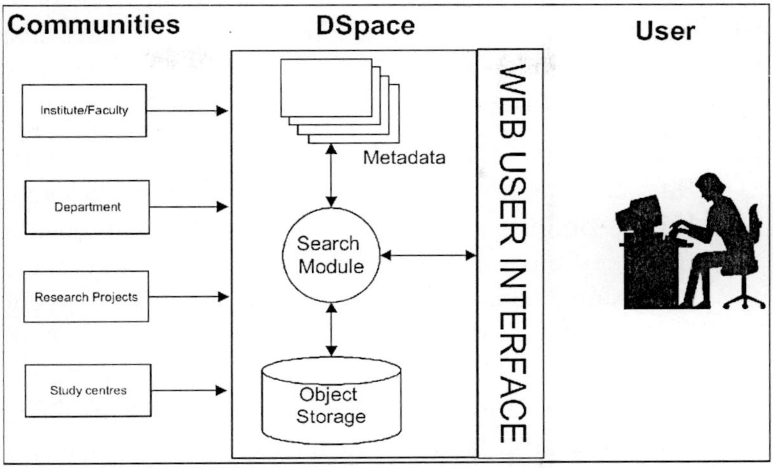

Fig. 1: Information model using DSpace

I. Communities : Each DSpace Repository is categorized into ***Communities.*** A *Community* could be the

a. Name of different departments of an Institute/University. e.g. Department of Physics; Faculty of Performing Arts.

b. Subject Categories. e.g. Sciences; Social Sciences; Arts and Humanities, etc.

Each community can be further subdivided to the level of Sub-communities

II. Collections: Related or similar contents are collated to form several ***Collections*** under each community. A collection may appear in more than one community. e.g. a community could have a collection of

a. Research articles

b. Conference Proceedings

c. Project Reports

d. Image Collections, etc.

III. Items : Items are logical units of content. Each collection is composed of ***Items***, which are the basic archival elements of the archive. Each item is owned by one collection. Additionally, an item may appear in additional collections; however every item has one and only one owning collection. A DSpace Item consists of

a. **Bitstream(s) :** Computer Files having Content. Bitstreams do not have Metadata. For example: a single HTML or Image File. Sometimes an item can have a Bundle of bitstreams e.g. a group of HTML and image bitstreams making up an HTML document. Bitstream format could be MSWord; JPEG encoded image format, etc.

b. **Metadata :** DSpace uses a qualified Dublin Core metadata standard for describing items within a collection. There are three types of metadata that is used by DSpace:

   - **Descriptive Metadata :** Descriptive metadata describes attributes of an object, such as its name, its creator, or its size.
   - **Administrative Metadata :** Administrative metadata helps with the administration of an object. Examples: submission details of the object such as location; date of submission in the repository or the name of the user who created the metadata about the object.
   - **Structural Metadata :** This includes information about how to present an item, or bitstreams within an item, to an end-user, and the relationships between constituent parts of the item. Structural metadata in DSpace is currently fairly basic.

c. License detail related to the item

d. Plain text or thumbnail of the bitstreams in case a filter-media is used (which does full-text indexing or creates thumbnails to images)

4. SUPPORTED CONTENT AND FORMATS TYPES

DSpace accepts all types of digital content such as Text, Images, Audio and Video. The possible types of contents supported are

- Preprints, articles
- Postprints
- Technical Reports
- Conference Papers
- Theses/Dissertations
- Datasets e.g. statistical, geospatial, scientific

The different formats of content supported are

- Images - visual, scientific, etc.
- Audio files
- Video files
- Digitized library collections
- Computer programs
- Visual simulations and models
- Audio, Video Files and Image Files
- Web pages, Multimedia publications

Each institution can determine its own list of supported formats and content types, based on its needs and resources in their DSpace installation.

5. DIGITAL PRESERVATION

DSpace supports the digital preservation of the items stored in it. The different functionalities available with DSpace are

5.1. Format Registry : DSpace facilitate specification of different supported formats as well as the unsupported one in an Institutional Repository. The validation of Formats can also be made through external services such as JHOVE. JHOVE provides functions to perform format-specific identification, validation, and characterization of digital objects

5.2. Bit Intergrity Checker: State of a file can be changed because of manual editing, virus, or a corrupted file format. DSpace can perform Checksum to verify the integrity of bitstreams in the digital file.

5.3. DSpace provides long-term physical storage and management of digital items in a secure, professionally managed repository including standard operating procedures such as backup, mirroring, refreshing media, and disaster recovery.

5.4. DSpace assigns a persistent identifier to each contributed item to ensure its retrievability far into the future. DSpace uses Handle System as a method of identifying digital objects in the repository. The information associated to the digital object can be changed as needed to reflect its current state without changing its identifier, thus allowing the name of the item to persist over changes of location and other related state information.

5.5. DSpace provides a mechanism for advising content contributors of the preservation support levels they can expect for the files they submit.

6. SEARCH AND RETRIEVAL

Each item in DSpace is described using a qualified version of the Dublin Core Metadata Schema during their submission in the repository. These descriptions are entered into a relational database, which is used by the search engine to retrieve items. Dspace uses the Lucene Search Engine for searching and browsing for documents.

7. WORKFLOW

DSpace allows differing submission workflows as per the

requirements of different communities identified for an Institute. One can define the level of complexity for each community. In general, an item goes through following processes before it appears in the digital repository.

Submission à review (workflow 1) à metadata validation (workflow 2) à approval (workflow 3).

The DSpace administrator can decide on how many workflows are to be defined for each collection. For example, if he defines workflow-1 only, the item will be deposited in the repository immediately after a reviewer okays it.

Also, the "role" of a DSpace user could be defined and can be restricted to one or more of the following:

- By whom the submission could be made and with what restrictions.
- Who is allowed to deposit items?
- What type of items one is allowed to deposit in a collection?
- Who can review, enhance, or approve the submission?
- To what collections one have access to deposit material?
- Who all can see the items once deposited?

8. CONCLUSION

An Institutional Repository reflects the research activities of an institute. It could be used as an indicator for performance evaluation of an author on different possible scales. A number of existing digital repositories based on DSpace authenticate it as one of the most powerful software over other available solutions. The robustness and scalability offered by it is best suited to meet the varied and growing demands of a University/ Academic System. The only need is to make aware and encourage the researchers and faculty members to actively participate to enrich the repository.

REFERENCES

1. DSpace at MIT. *http://www.dspace.org*
2. GNU Eprints Archive Software. *http://software.eprints.org/*
3. DSpace Metadata *http://dspace.org/technology/metadata.html*
4. DSpace@MIT. *http://libraries.mit.edu/dspace-mit/technology/features.html*

5

Greenstone: Open-source Digital Library Software

Rajendra Kumar Bharti
Asstt.Librarian
Nehru Library, N.D.University of Agriculture & Technology
Kumarganj, Faizabad (U.P.)

ABSTRACT

The Greenstone is a open source digital library software. It is a suite of software for building and distributing digital library collections with effective full text searching and metadata facilities. It provides a new way of organizing information and publishing it on the Internet or C.D.ROM. It is open source multilingual software. Greenstone incorporates an interface that makes to attractive and easy to use for People.

Keywords : Digital Library, Greenstone.

1. INTRODUCTION

Every Libraries of India are facing challenges due to the budget cut, reduced staff, Devaluation of rupees against major currencies, escalation in the cost of foreign publication and day to day information explosion which affects the research and academics activity. The rising cost of technology has compelled the libraries to use open source software (OSS) for libraries automation, digital library and so on.

OSS are developed by Public domain, Public domain is a charitable Trust of technology expert of libraries .These charitable trust provide or distributed OSS free of cost or minimum cost to the libraries. The professional community implements the software solution and rendered feed back to developers.

Today, there are OSS available for different libraries activities which are better than the commercial solutions .This has made the libraries services more cost effective and least dependent on commercial software and vendors. There are following features of OSS should be:

1.Library automation 2. Digital repositories 3.Digita preservation 4.Consortiam planning 5.Community Education 6.Office management 7.Content development 8.E-Publishing 9.Knowlege Management 10.E-Goverence 11.Community Networks.

The aim of the Greenstone software is to empower users, particularly in universities Libraries and other public Service institutions, to build their own digital Libraries. Digital libraries are radically reforming how information is disseminated and acquired in UNESCO,S Partner communities and institution in the field of the education science and culture around the world, and particularly in developing countries. We hope that this software will encourage the effective development of digital libraries to share information and place it in the Public domain.

Greenstone Digital Libraries software from the New Zealand Digital Library Project provide a new way of organizing information and making a available over the Internet. Collection of information comprise large number of document (typically several thousand to several million), and a uniform interface is provided to them. Libraries include many collections, individual.

The structure of a collection is determined by a configuration file. Existing collections range from newspapers articles to technical documents, from educational journal to oral history, from visual art to videos, from MIDI pop music collections to ethnic folksongs.

Making information available using Greenstone is far more than just putting it on the Web. The information become searchable, brows able and maintainable. Each collection, prior to presentation, undergoes a building process that once established is fully automatics. Searching utilizes various indexes of text and/metadata, while browsing utilizes metadata such as title and author.

To address the broad demands of digital libraries, the system is public, extensible and widely used internationally. Greenstone supports collections in many different languages. Greenstone CD-ROMs have been published by the United Nations and other humanitarian agencies for distribution in developing countries.

Information Collections built by Greenstone combine full-text search with browsing indexes based on different metadata types. There are several ways for users to find information, although they differ between collections depending on the metadata available and the collection design.

Searching is full-Text and depending on the collection-users selects indexes built from different parts of the full text or metadata. Some collections have separatef indexes of full document, sections, paragraph, titles, and section headings, each of which can be searched for particular words or phrases.

Each document may be hierarchically organized into logical sections.

2. THE COLLECTOR

The structure of each collection is determined at set up.

This includes specifying the format of source document, deciding to display the documents on the screen, determining what the source of metadata will be. Choosing what full-text searching and browsing facilities should be provided. And outlining how the search and browsing result should be displayed. Once a collection is in place, new documents in the same format can be added automatically. The collector can be used to:

i. Create a new collection with the same structure as an existing one.
ii. Create a new collection with a different structure
iii. Add new material to an existing collection.
iv. Modify the structure of an existing collection.
v. Delete a collection.
vi. Write an existing collection to a self- contained, self-installing windows C.D.ROM.

3. COLLECTION BUILDING

Greenstone provides GUI based collection building facility. There are two kinds of build i.e. minimal and full collection build. Minimal build takes less time as it does not import all the files unlike full collection build.

4. CONCLUSION

Greenstone has several implementation around India and abroad. The software is being promoted by UNESCO. UNESCO organizes courses for using greenstone digital library software. It is one of the easiest tool for building digital library.

REFERENCE

1. Greenstone website. http://www.greenstone.org
2. Greenstone user manual.

6

Planning of Digital Library Using Open Source Software: Dspace

Vijay Kumar Bharati
Asstt. Librarian, MGKVP, Varanasi
Sunil Kumar Gautam
Banaras Hindu University, Varanasi

ABSTRACT

Open-source is becoming an increasingly popular software development method. Interest in the open source software model as a means of developing software for the library community has developed considerably in the last few years. Fortunately, much of the software that has been developed for libraries can be used to provide extended library services. Massachusetts Institute of Technology (MIT) and Hewlett-Packard Labs have been collaborating on the development of an open source system called DSpace that suitable for building a repository for the digital research and educational material produced by members of a research university or organization. This paper discusses the history, development and technology of Open Source bsoftware DSpace and also elaborate benefits and features of DSpace.

Keywords : Digital Library, Dspace, Open Source Library Solutions.

1. INTRODUCTION

DSpace is a digital repository system that captures, stores, indexes, preserves, and redistributes abn organization's research material in digital formats. The software has been co developed by MIT and Hewlett Packard for use on Windows and Unix/ Linux platforms. This open source software preserves and enables easy and open access to all types of digital content including text, images, moving images, mpegs and data sets.

Digital library (DL) is organized collection of information in electronic format. Electronic object contains images, text, maps, digital catalogue videos and scientific and government data bases etc. Digital library integration work touches many areas of library operation. Based on our experience and approach to develop the DL we have plotted the following planning process:

1. The organizational goals of the Institute and the library should drive digital library initiative work
2. Long-term planning: Based on the continuously evolving nature of digital environment library should make detail technical plans that forecast the feature ahead.
3. Collaborative network: The best practice of social networking with community-wise participation to develop digital library
4. Follow the standards for resources and services of digital library

In the view of functional definition from cooperative educational service agency's website Digital dictionary state "A digital library is collection of documents in organized electronic form, available on the internet or on CD-ROM (compact-disk read only memory) disks. The use of a digital library is enhanced by a broadband connection such as cable modem or DSL. Dial-up connections can be used to access documents. Internet-based digital libraries can be updated on a daily basis. This is one of the greatest assets of this emerging technology. On CD-ROM, the amount of data is limited to several hundred megabytes (MB) per disk, but access is generally much faster than on an Internet connection. Several CD-ROMs can be combined in a set, and because the disks are small, a large library can be accommodated in a reasonable physical space. The main limitation of CD-ROM is the fact that updating cannot be done as frequently as on the Internet. In addition, producing and distributing CD-ROMs involves overhead costs that are largely nonexistent in internet-based libraries. Electronics distribution of intellectual and artistic property has authors, agents and publishers concerned about the possibility of copyright infringement. It is much easier to copy a CD-ROM, or to download an electronic book and make unauthorized copies of it, than it is to reproduce bound volumes and distribute theme illegitimately. Fundamental changes in copyright law - and/or changes in the way in which the laws are enforced - are likely to occur as digital libraries expand and their use becomes more widespread.

"For smooth functioning of digital library work in traditional library system the IT expert can provide a broad base support for a library technical needs such as personal computer and server support and digital library application with insight and training of the open source software. The GSDL software is the best suit to plan and develop the digital library

2. MEANING, HISTORY AND DEVELOPMENT OF OPEN SOURCE SOFTWARE DSPACE

Free Software "is software that comes with permission for anyone to use, copy, and distribute, either verbatim or with modifications, either gratis or for a fee. In particular, this means that source code must be available." Open source resources are shared without cost, provided with the means to customize and enhance them, and are managed through a licensing process that protects the rights of the creators and their collaborators while allowing users broad access. Adopters may evolve into developers, and all belong to a community centered on a product.

DSpace is an open source software package that provides the tools for management of digital assets, and is commonly used as the basis for an institutional repository. It supports a wide variety of data, including books, theses, 3D digital scans of objects, photographs, film, video, research data sets and other forms of content. The data is arranged as community collections of items, which bundle bit streams together. DSpace is also intended as a platform for digital preservation activities.

MIT Libraries and HP Labs started to develop the software in November 2000 as part of the HP-MIT Alliance, an innovative research and development initiative between industry and academia. Two years later, they released DSpace 1.0 as open source digital repository software under the BSD licence. By September 2006, approximately 175 research institutions located in more than 35 countries had registered a live DSpace repository.The first version of DSpace was released in November 2002, following a joint effort by developers from MIT and HP Labs in Cambridge, Massachusetts. DSpace 1.3 was released in 2005, and at around the same time the DSpace User Group Meeting was held at the University of Cambridge. In March 2008, the DSpace Community released DSpace 1.5.The story of DSpace's development and release offers an interesting take on the progress of an open source project. Although the two original partners (HP Labs (UK) and MIT Libraries) undertook the initial development in a proprietary fashion, it was always envisaged that the code would be 'opened up' and an open source community would be encouraged.

3. BENEFITS OF DSPACE OSS

- Access and distribution - Web and CD-ROM Getting your research results out quickly, to a worldwide audience
- Archiving and distributing material you would currently put on your personal website
- Storing examples of students' projects (with the students' permission)
- Showcasing students' theses (again with permission)
- Keeping track of your own publications/bibliography
- Having a persistent network identifier for your work, that never changes or breaks
- Reaching a worldwide audience through exposure to search engines such as Google
- Storing reusable teaching materials that you can use with course management system

3.1. Technology

DSpace was developed to be open source, and in such a way that institutions and organizations with minimal resources could run it. The system is designed to run on the UNIX platform, and comprises other open source middleware and tools, and programs written by the DSpace team. DSpace is written in Java and JSP, using the Java Servlet API. It uses a relational database, and supports the use of PostgreSQL and Oracle. It makes its holdings available primarily via a web interface, but it also supports the OAI-PMH v2.0, and is capable of exporting METS (Metadata Encoding and Transmission Standard) packages. DSpace is open source and freely available, neither MIT Libraries nor HP offer formal support for DSpace adopters. It is our assumption that institutions that use DSpace will have resources to use the system, including adequate hardware that runs the UNIX operating system, and a LNIX systems administrator to install and configure the system

3.2. Features of DSpace OSS

The DSpace system provides a way to manage these research materials and publications in a professionally maintained repository to give them greater visibility and accessibility over time. Open source software is distributed with source code-a licensing condition- and users can alter the product to meet their needs and so contribute to its development. Open source adopters become part of a community, blurring the distinction between users and developers

3.3. Metadata

The end-user or public interface supports search and retrieval of items by browsing or searching the metadata .DSpace uses a qualified Dublin Core metadata standard for describing items intellectually (specifically, the Libraries Working Group Application Profile). Only three fields are required: title, language, and submission date, all other fields are optional. There are additional fields for document abstracts, keywords, technical metadata and rights metadata, among others. This metadata is displayed in the item record in DSpace, and is indexed for browsing and searching the system.

3.4. Built around the idea of organizational Communities

DSpace is designed to make participation by depositors easy. The system's information model is built around the idea of organizational "Communities") "Communities" are defined to be the schools, departments, labs, and centers of the Institute. Each Community can adapt the system to meet its particular needs and manage the submission process itself.

3.5. User Interface

DSpace's current user interface is web-based. There are several interfaces: one for submitters and others involved in the submission process, one for end-users looking for information, and one for system administrators

3.6. Other Features

- Multiplatform availability - Unix, Windows
- Powerful Indexing
- Metadata-based
- Field-based indexing
- Powerful searching and browsing
- Full-text and fielded search
- Boolean and ranked retrieval
- Browsing - Field-based and hierarchical document browsing
- Common interface for different DL collection
- Multilingual support - documents and interfaces
- Access & updating security, activity log
- OAI
- Strong R&D based development group

4. CONCLUSION

The ever-changing digital information environment should continue to provide continues stream of integration and implementation analysis. The digital library initiator will turn these challenges into opportunity for creative solutions in the traditional library environment in India. Planning is both behavior and the process; it is the process of moving on Digital Library from where it is to where it wants to be in a given period of time by setting it on a predetermined course of action and committing its human and physical resources to that goal. Since the software was originally released, a community made up of organisations that either use or develop the DSpace open source software has emerged. Investment in DSpace continues to grow. Adopters employ technical and functional experts to build and expand local DSpace services and pursue various research agendas pertaining to the DSpace platform. For example, adopters gather and manage, for deposit in DSpace, collections of digital material that require long-term stewardship; they provide capital outlays for server, back-up and storage hardware; and they offer technical support to the community and commit resources to develop the DSpace platform further. we anticipate that DSpace will play an important role in the future of academic libraries and archives.

REFERENCES

1. Nickolas,Devid M.,Thomsan Kirsten and Yeats, A Stuart: Usability and Open source software development,New Zealand.

2. Jose,Sanjo: Adoption of open source digital library sofware packages: a survey, Bangalore.

3. Blandford, A., Stelmaszewska, H. & Bryan-Kinns, N. (2001 to appear) Use of multiple digital libraries:

4. Witten, I.H., Boddie, S.J., Bainbridge, D. & McNab, R.J. (2000) Greenstone: a comprehensive open source digital library software

system, Proceedings gfthe FifhACM Coglerence on Digital Libraries, an Antonio, TX. 1] 3-121.

5. www. digitallibrary. ernet. in www. dl ib. org/

6. www. dspace. org www. dspace. irri. org www. wickipedia. org www. cesa8. k12. wi. us/media/digital-dictionary. htm

7

Developing Electronic Repository of Theses and Dissertations of Indian Universities Using GSDL 2.81

Rabindra Nath Mohanta
Librarian, Vasanta College for Women,
Rajghat Fort, Varanasi-221001
rnmohanta@hotmail.com
Rajesh Kumar Mishra
Documentation Officer
Central University of Tibetan Studies, Sarnath, Varanasi
mrkdo@yahoo.com

ABSTRACT

Defines Institutional Repository, Open Source Software and identifies the need for institutional repositories for theses and dissertations in Indian Universities. Suggests for developing institutional repositories of theses and dissertations in Indian university libraries using Greenstone OSS and suggests for continuance of the online bibliographic union database of theses of INFLIBNET

Keywords: Digital Repositories, ETD, GSDL, Indian Universities.

1. INTRODUCTION

Research outcome in all the disciplines in the Indian universities has been increased but due to several reasons the quality has gradually deteriorated during the last few decades. There may be different opinions about the concept of the quality in education but one thing is true that it is a never ending multidimensional process. To improve quality of educational products as well as the quality of the educational service it is required that the quality of teaching in our classrooms and quality of research undertaken by faculty members and research scholars in our colleges and universities must be improved.[1] Electronic repositories of theses and dissertations in Indian Universities can help to maintain the qualities of research in the university and to avoid the duplication of research. Theses and dissertations are very important to the academician and research scholars because these are primary sources of information and are often published in the printed form, moreover it is much difficult to locate and access the printed copy of theses and dissertations. Thus it is very important to have electronic storage and retrieval system to access the theses and dissertations of the Indian Universities.

2. REVIEW OF LITERATURE

The Institutional repositories of academic output of universities and colleges have gained momentum during last 2-3 decades in western countries and now in India. Sri Venkateswar University (SVU) library has a large theses and dissertation (TD) collection that are much in demand by user community. To cater to the growing demand and also to provide open access to the theses and dissertations of SVU, the university launched Electronic thesis and dissertation repository using D-space open source software.[2] IIT Bombay has been accepting on line submission of Ph.D. Theses and M.Tech dissertations by its doctoral and postgraduate students. It allows students upload their theses, to obtain supervisor's approval and finally submit to the library's ETD database. Central library of IIT Bombay supports and maintain the full text database of over 4500 items submitted since 1999 using open source software, GSDL. The database is accessible on intranet through the library homepage.[3] Now few Indian universities and academic institutions are uploading their collection of theses and dissertation on Vidyanidhi. (www.dspacevidyanidhi.org.in). It is the premier national repository for e-theses, developed by Dept. of Lib. & Inf. Sc., University of Mysore, to facilitate the archiving and accessing of doctoral theses online. No doubt this repository enlarges the research and audience for Indian doctoral research works.[4] INFLIBNET Centre is also maintaining and providing access to the bibliographic details of Ph.D. thesis and dissertations awarded by the Indian Universities.[5]

3. INSTITUTIONAL REPOSITORY

Institutional repository is a set of services that the institute offers to the members of its community for the management and dissemination of digital materials created by the institution and its community members. It is most essentially an organizational commitment to the stewardship of these digital materials, including long-term preservation where appropriate, as well as organization and access or distribution.[6]

Libraries of leading research institutions and universities are developing institutional repositories (IR) of research papers of scientists and scholars of their institution. These repositories are of much use to the entire research community. Some institutions in India, like Indian Institute of Science, Bangalore; Indian Institute of Management, Kozikode; Indian Institute of Technology, Delhi ; National Institute of Technology, Rourkela; National Aerospace Laboratories, Bangalore; National Chemical Laboratory, Pune; Information and Library Network

(INFLIBNET), Ahmedabad; National Institute of Oceanography, Goa; Raman Research Institute, Bangalore; Indira Gandhi National Open University (IGNOU) and many more have developed the open access Institutional Repositories (IRs) to disseminate the research outputs and courseware of their institute. Sometimes these are self-archived, otherwise, the administrators of the repositories collect the research documents from different sources and submit them to the IR on behalf of the person concerned.[7]

About 850 such Institutional Repository projects have been initiated by various academic and research organizations these include many Electronic Theses and Dissertations Projects. Online access to the documents will significantly increase the use of theses which in turn lead to greater citation.

4. IMPORTANCE OF THESES AND DISSERTATION IN INDIAN UNIVERSITIES

Theses and dissertations are original work in a specified subject field. One important characteristic of such output is that they may be the results of purely academic pursuit. The subject of a thesis may not have any commercial application yet it may be worth pursuing an idea, process, a technique etc. Out of all the primary sources, these are probably least used because mainly their existence is not known in many cases and secondly they are not easily accessible due to their unpublished nature, so it is very important to have electronic repository of theses and dissertations produced in the Indian Universities to make them accessible among research community and enlarge to speedup the knowledge cycle and to promote the interdisciplinary research.

5. OPEN SOURCE SOFTWARE

Free information is the first principle of the knowledge society. Perhaps this idea given birth to the open source software movement. In case of open source digital library software, the software developed for in house use by leading research institutions are made available under GNU Public User license for free public use. The Open Source Initiative (www.opensource.org) defines open source as a development method for software that harnesses the power of distributed peer review and transparency of process. The promise of open source is better quality, higher reliability, more flexibility, lower cost, and an end to predatory vendor lock-in. The open source software may be used by any university library to create digital library of theses and dissertations. The important open source software available and used in India are: D-Space (www.dspace.org), e-Print (www.eprints.org), Greenstone (GSDL) (www.greenstone.org), Fedora (www.fedora.info) etc.

6. PREREQUISITS FOR DEVELOPING ELECTRONIC REPOSITORY OF THESES AND DISSERTATIONS

Any one could try to understand the process to build digital library of available digital objects using any open-source software, but the development of Institutional Repository of digital objects like thesis and dissertations requires planning, amendments in existing procedures, ICT infrastructure and motivated team to find out the right track.

7. TYPES OF THESES AND DISSERTATIONS

Based on the format, the theses and dissertations of universities may be divided in two types:

i. Born Digital theses: (theses and dissertations submitted in soft copy)

ii. Printed collection of theses and dissertations

It is a labor intensive, time taking and fund consuming to digitize the existing printed collection of theses and dissertations, so universities and libraries should take initiatives to ensure online accessibility of theses and dissertations composed on computers by developing digital repositories.

University libraries should take initiatives to collect the softcopies of the theses and dissertations submitted in various department of the University. It is feasible because the computers have replaced the manual typewriters and almost all the theses and dissertations and being composed on computers. It is only required to finalize and prescribe the standards concerning font, format, and other relevant details by the university. E.g. library willing develop digital library of Hindi theses and dissertations using Greenstone OSS must get the softcopy of theses composed using standard Unicode font.

After collecting the softcopies of theses and dissertations, copy them on hard disk and rename them according to any helpful, logical and uniform pattern. The data entry sheets have to be prepared preferably based on field description of Dublin Core Metadata Set.

7. THE GREENSTONE DIGITAL LIBRARY SOFTWARE

Greenstone is a suite of software for building and distributing digital library collections. It provides a new way of organizing digital objects and publishing them on Internet or on CD-ROM. Greenstone is produced by the New Zealand Digital Library Project at the University of Waikato, and developed and distributed in cooperation with UNESCO and Human Info NGO. It is open-source software, available from www.greenstone.org under the terms of GNU General Public License. The latest version of Greenstone 2.81 is available for download.

7.1. Why to Use Greenstone

- It is accessible via web browser
- Provides full-text and fielded search

- Having flexible browsing facility
- Creates access structure automatically
- Can make use of available metadata
- Plugins extend the system's capabilities
- Supports multi gigabite collection
- Supports documents of all Indian languages
- User interface is available in multiple languages
- Collection can contain text, pictures, audio and video
- Uses advanced compression techniques
- Collections can be published on the Internet or on CD-ROM[8]

7.2. Prerequisits to Install the Greenstone

- Web Browser (Internet explorer or Netscape)
- Java runtime

  j2re-1_4_2_13-windows-i586-p.exe
- Image Magic

  ImageMagick-6.3.0-3-Q16-windows-dll.exe

All the above stated required software's are freely available on respective websites.

7.3. The Process of Collection Building

Install the greenstone on server in client server environment or on a desktop. Create a new collection in Greenstone Librarian Interface using following steps.

Provide a name to the Collection Title / Digital Library, define the description of content.

Gather: This tab facilitates to select the files of theses and dissertations from workspace (left panel) to the collection building area (right panel) just by drag and drop.

Enrich: Enrich tab explains how metadata is created, edited, assigned and retrieved, and how to use external metadata sources. Here you can provide the metadata with the help of pre compiled data entry sheet.

Design: It helps to customize the interface and to specify the searchable fields.

Create: It is used to create the collection. Just click the Build Collection the greenstone will start the building collection as per defined conditions.

After completion of the collection building a message of completion will appear and now the preview of the collection may be seen.

Format: It controls the structure and appearance of the collection. They affect such things as where buttons appear when a document is shown etc.

8. CONCLUSION

Building a digital library of theses and dissertations awarded and accepted by Indian Universities and Institute of Higher learning over past years (with cut-off point of, say ten years or so) will no doubt be a massive work. It needs a lot of resources - computational, as well as financial and others.[9] So it better to have full text electronic repository of these theses and dissertations in individual university libraries and to continue INFLIBNET's present online bibliographic union database of theses. This database covers the bibliographic Metadata of Doctoral Theses submitted to 238 Universities/ Institutes in India. It has over 2,19,074 unique records from all subjects. Indian Universities must take initiative to digitize their theses and dissertation collection so that these can be utilized efficiently and effectively.

REFERENCES

1. TANDON, Pramod. Guest Editorial. Quality and Relevance in Higher Education. University News. 46,46; 2008. p 3-4
2. REDDY, C Aruna Prasad. Open Access to University and Research Assets: Sri Venkateswar University ETD Repository. *IASLIC BULL.*52,1;2007.p35-42
3. JATWANI,D. Best Practice in a modern Library and Information Centre – The Case of Central Library , IIT Bombay. *In* 6th International CALIBER-2008.Ahmedabad: INFLIBNET Centre, 2008. p1-21.
4. SHARMA, Hari Prasad. Moving Beyond Library Automation : Role of E-Resources in academic Libraries. *University News.46,34;2008.*p6-10.
5. http://www.inflibnet.ac.in Accessed on 15th December 2008.
6. LYNCH, C. Institutional Repositories: Essential Infrastructure for scholarship in the Digital Age. ARL Bimonthy Report 226. www.arl.org/newsltr/226/ir.html Accessed on June 26, 2008.
7. RAJASEKHAR,T.B. Improving the visibility of Indian research : an institutional, open access publishing model. *In* Indo-US Workshop on Open Digital Libraries and Interoperability, June23-25,2003 *cited by* Kamila, Kanchan. Impact of ICT Towards Change of Library and Information Science (LIS) Curricula and Information Services Pattern. *In* 6th International CALIBER-2008.Ahmedabad: INFLIBNET Centre,2008. p61-75.
8. WITTEN, IAN H. et al. Greenstone Digital Library User's Guide. www.greenstone.org Accessed on 13th December 2008.
9. CHOUDHARY, G.G. How to make best use of the Intellectual Output of the country? : A Simple approach to the Design of a Digital Library of Theses and dissertations in Indian Universities. *In* CALIBER-2001.Ahmedabad:INFLIBNET Centre,2001.p12-23.

8

Comparative Evaluation of Open Source Digital Library Packages

Vinit Kumar
Junior Research Fellow
Documentation Research and Training Centre
Indian Statistical Institute, Bangalore, India
vinit@drtc.isibang.ac.in

ABSTRACT

In the last decade the way to publish and access information has been changed a lot because of the availability of open access repositories. This became possible because of a varied range of open source repository packages. Other reasons like every year deduction in library budget and increasing urge to show more visibility of their institute, popular institutions also started establishing repositories. This paper starts with giving brief introduction of different open access models, open source philosophy and some of the expectations from a digital library package and tries to evaluate DSpace, EPrints and Greenstone.

Keywords: Dspace, Eprints, Greenstone, Evaluation, OSS.

1. INTRODUCTION TO OPEN SOURCE, OPEN ACCESS ARCHIVES

With the rapid deduction in library budget, crisis in scholarly publication, high cost of dissemination of research and the challenge of preservation caused a convergence of factors and created "a perfect storm" in the library and information world.

This has given rise to aura of open source softwares to provide open access to the research literature/articles.

Open access

According to Peter Suber [14]

"Open-access (OA) literature is digital, online, free of charge, and free of most copyright and licensing restrictions. What makes it possible is the internet and the consent of the author or copyright-holder"

The main aim or value that was associated with the upcoming of open access movement was to provide

- long-term preservation of electronic resources
- widest possible access to research and scholarship
- respect for intellectual property rights

There are two primary vehicles for delivering open access to research articles:

- Open access Archives/Repositories ("Green OA")

  OA archives can contain preprints, postprints(peer reviewed), or both.
- Open access Journals ("Gold OA").

Open Source

The common understanding that is associated with open source software is that it is free, but OSI (Open Source

Initiative) at *www.opensource.org* [10]defines open source comprehensively and highlights the following points:

i. Free redistribution

ii. Source code

iii. Derived works

iv. Integrity of the authors source code

v. No discrimination among person or groups

vi. No discrimination among fields of endeavour

vii. Distribution of license

viii. License must not be specific to a product

ix. License must not restrict other software

x. License must be Technology neutral.

Reason Behind Boost in Open source

Open source DL softwares because of its free access and good level of functionality are being used heavily as an alternative to commercial DL softwares.

Gone are the days when it was only big companies who were producing software products, at present because of good communication system availability of open source softwares and decreasing cost of computing and other requisites, librarians and other persons from different fields are also joining their hands in development of open source softwares.

The availability of the source code in open source softwares gives power to users to modify and make any changes or improvements to it, and such contributions can come from a community of programmers having different talents pools.

2. DIGITAL LIBRARIES AND ARCHIVES

Digital libraries (DLs) facilitate creation, organisation and management of multimedia digital content and collections, and provide search, retrieval and other information services over computer networks and other electronic media.

With the availability of a big list of open source digital library packages it is now too much tough for librarians, and repository managers to decide one out of those. So there is high need for evaluation of these packages. This paper tries to evaluate three most popular DL softwares.

Expectations from a DL software

Evaluation can only be done if and only if we have a detail list of expectations from a DL software. Broadly we can divide our expectations in following categories.

- Content Management:
  - Content Flow
  - Text and multimedia indexing and retrieval
- User Interface:
  - Personalisation and visualization
  - Multilingual support
- User administration:
  - Restricted access
- System administration:
  - Preservation standards support
  - Automatic indexing
  - Persistent document identification
- Other characteristics:
  - Document summarization and categorization
  - Interoperability
  - Complainant with DL standards
  - Documentation

Content management feature is an important expectation from DL software. A DL software should be easy and functional in handling creation of content, submitting, reviewing and organizing. It should be able to provide searching and browsing functions such as metadata search, full-text search, and hierarchical subject browsing, additionally content encoded in various popular formats including text (e.g. ASCII, UNICODE, RTF), image (e.g. TIFF. GIF. JPEG), presentation (e.g. Adobe Postscript and Adobe PDF), structured formats(e.g. HTML and XML), audio and video (e.g. real, MP3. AVI and MPEG) ought to be supported.

Second important feature is User interface. A DL software should provide flexibility in customizing the interface to suit the needs of different digital library implementations as well as the support for multilingual access. With multilingual access, the user is able to specify the language for the DLs user interface as well as the cataloguing information stored within it.

Thirdly digital library deals with a lot of users like a traditional library so the user administration is also an important expected feature. This includes restricting access to content in the DL through password authentication, IP filtering, and proxy filtering. Specially when a particular DL content is in sensitive domain like defence but it is not encouraged in open access philosophy. Also one can monitor and report usage patterns. This usage patterns are analysed, the needs and interests of DL users can be better understood. End users of a system want to be able to organize the information space according to their own profiles based on their interest so we can say that personalisation and visualization is also an expected feature in DL.

As like every software which provides service there is high requirement of back end maintenance same is applicable for DL software also. Functionality of automatic tools is useful particularly for large DLs where maintenance work is labour-intensive. Functions such as automated content acquisition, harvesting and automatic metadata generation, including named entity recognition and automatic subject indexing/ classification, makes DL maintenance much easier. Apart from this a DL needs to support preservation standards as well as persistent document identification, so that the transfer of digital materials from one hardware/software configuration to another would not compromise reference citations and other links. This can be achieved only when a DL can offer functionality of handles and support for various available standards.

Some other expectations would be document summarization and categorization which offers a user to overcome the information overload. A DL should also support interoperability so that it can communicate with other DLs. For this a lot of protocols like Z39.50, OAIPMH, SRU/SRW, SOAP are available among these at least two basic interoperability protocols should be supported, viz. Z39.50 and OAI-PMH(Open Archive Initiative for Metadata Harvesting).

Additionally, the DL must be compliant with standards established for DL collection and services. For e.g. For representation of Information XML; XHTML for web pages so that it can be accessed from small portable devices like Mobile and PDA's, TIFF, GIF and JPEG for images, Unicode for multilingual support and information interchange; and Dublin core and MARC 21 for metadata.

Most importantly the DL package should provide mechanisms for support like documentation, manuals, mailing lists, discussion forums, bug tracking, feature request systems and formal helpdesk support.

3. WAYS TO EVALUATE DL PACKAGES

For effective evaluation there should be some framework to test. Punter[12] points out the following instruments can be used to accomplish this task.

i. Static analysis of code, for structural measurement or anomaly checking
ii. Dynamic analysis of code, for test coverage or failure data;
iii. Reference tools that compare the software product
iv. Reference statistical data; and
v. Inspection with checklists.

Although he further points that the first three are usually looked upon as well founded and applicable to software evaluation, experience shows that the use of checklists are necessary.

Checklist

The checklist which is used to evaluate is heavily borrowed from a work of Goh et. al.[5] They designed a checklist for the evaluation of digital library software using 12 categories. The categories were determined from the literature and each category is assigned a weight which sums up to 100 percent for all categories whereas the items making up a category always sum up 10. An institution which would like to evaluate institutional repository software can adapt the checklist with its items or fine-tune the weights according to their needs.

The checklist consists of 12 categories of items, each with varying degrees of importance: content management, content acquisition, metadata, search, access control and security, report and inquiry, preservation, interoperability, user interface, standard compliance, automatic tools and support. The weights were assigned on the basis of a modified Delphi technique by four people familiar with institutional repositories. If discrepancies in the weight estimates were observed, they were resolved through discussion.

The checklist and usage can be found from appendix 1.

4. SELECTION OF DL PACKAGES FOR EVALUATION

From the heap of available open source DL packages it was really very much tough to choose packages for evaluation. For the purpose of this paper the list available at the Registry of Open Access Repository (ROAR)[13] three packages viz. DSpace, EPrints and Greenstone were taken for evaluation on the basis of these criteria:

- The software package must be available for download and installation at no cost via an open source license to facilitate evaluation.
- The software package should be relatively well known and commonly used, and this was inferred from the number of bases installed, especially in credible organizations such as universities. (taken from ROAR)
- The software must be supported either on Linux or Windows, as these are commonly used platforms.

DSpace

DSpace[1] is an open source software package that provides the tools for management of digital assets, and is commonly used as the basis for an institutional repository. It supports a wide variety of data, including books, theses, 3D digital scans of objects, photographs, film, video, research data sets and other forms of content. The data is arranged as community collections of items, which bundle bitstreams together.

DSpace is also intended as a platform for digital preservation activities. Since its release in 2002, as a product of the HP-MIT Alliance, it has been installed and is in production at over 373 institutions around the globe, from large universities to small higher education colleges, cultural organizations, and research centres. It is shared under a BSD licence, which enables users to customize or extend the software as needed. Version 1.5 has been chosen for the purpose of study.

Greenstone

Greenstone[7] is a suite of software for building and distributing digital library collections. It provides a new way of organizing information and publishing it on the Internet or on CD-ROM. Greenstone is produced by the New Zealand Digital Library Project at the University of Waikato, and developed and distributed in cooperation with UNESCO and the Human Info NGO. It is open-source, multilingual software, issued under the terms of the GNU General Public License. The current installed base is unknown but the number of downloads of the software appear to be large since 11/2000 the average downloads per month since then is 4500. Version 2.81 has been chosen for the purpose of study.

EPrints

EPrints[3] open source software is a flexible platform for building high quality, high value repositories. It is recognised as the easiest and fastest way to set up repositories of research outputs of literature, scientific data, theses and reports or multimedia artefacts from collections, exhibitions and performances. Till today 287 known archives are running EPrints worldwide. Total records in known archives: 519952

EPrints is developed at the School of Electronics and Computer Science, University of Southampton, UK, with the first version of the software publicly released in late 2000. Version 3.1 has been chosen for the purpose of the study.

5. FINDINGS

Table 1: Evaluation result for each categories.

No	*Category*	*DL software packages* *DSpace*	*EPrints*	*Greenstone*
1	Content management	6.51	7*	5
2	Content acquisition	6.49	9.79	5.7
3	Metadata	7	5.84	5.84
4	Search support	13.58	10.72	11.79
5	Access control and privacy	5.83	2.86	2.97
6	Report and inquiry capabilities	1.8	1.8	3*
7	Preservation	5*	2.75	1.25
8	Interoperability	5	5	8
9	User interface	8*	8*	8*
10	Standards compliance	10*	10*	10*
11	Automatic tools	2.66	2.66	4*
12	Support and maintenance	9*	9*	9*
		80.87	75.42	74.55

Note: * indicates the highest category score

5.1. Content Management

This category involves procedure to the submission of content into the DL as well as management of submission workflow. By going through checklist Greenstone lacks some features like sending email notification for users about submission. Whereas EPrints because of providing review of completed contents scored highest, whereas DSpace also scored well because of its stepwise and better review of license statement. Feature of segregated workspaces also adds to the value.

5.2. Content Acquisition

This category involves functions related to import and

export, versioning and supported document formats. Here because of functionality of history and comparison view EPrints again emerged as winner, apart from this the functionality to upload compressed file has added weights to both EPrints and Greenstone whereas DSpace because of its absence lagged behind, but having the ability to approve file formats added. It was found that mostly all DL packages support all popular and established file formats.

5.3. Metadata

For any DL package the support for metadata is important for content indexing, storage , access and preservation. Here DSpace emerged as winner because of having feature of adding and deletion of customized metadata fields and real time updating and indexing of accepted content, whereas all DL packages support by default the core metadata standard Dublin Core. Greenstone because of its availability of various plugins supports a lot of metadata formats. Whereas others have a feature to define new metadata schemas.

5.4. Search Support

Search support refers to a range of searching and browsing functionality such as metadata search, full-text search, and hierarchical subject browsing. All DL packages scored well because it is the most looked feature among developers. As most of them are using same search engine ie. Lucene they have similar functionality of boolean, proximity and truncation search. Apart from this all of them provide full text search and metadata search. In respect of browsing DSpace has better browsing functionality by customised fields which is added. Whereas sorting of results after search also adds to DSpace, while others lack this feature.

5.5. Access and privacy

Access and privacy includes the administration of

passwords as well as the management of user's accounts and rights to specified location in DL. It was found that all DL provide user login and their own space on DL so that better tracking of their tasks can be done whereas EPrints and DSpace provides the facility of retrieval of forgotten password. DSpace because of its IP filtering, encrypted password storage and providing roles to user gained top position. While all the DL packages provided the feature of adding deleting and editing user profiles.

5.6. Report and Inquiry capabilities

Report and Inquiry capabilities category is concerned with usage monitoring and reporting. Here Greenstone emerged as winner because of its functionality of generation of various types of reports. Whereas DSpace and EPrints generates usage report statistics and the presence of functionality of history view adds value to EPrints.

5.7. Preservation

Preservation refers to preservation of metadata and quality control measures to ensure integrity, and persistent document identification for migration purposes. DSpace emerged as clear winner because of support for CNRI handles, better quality control measures and provision of a prescribed digital preservation strategy viz. which file formats are supported, which are unknown and which are unsupported for DL. Others lack this feature but all the packages were found capable of assigning system assigned identifiers.

5.8. Interoperability

Interoperability refers to the function of interaction of DL with other similar kind of system locally or distributed. Results indicated that Greenstone was the best performer because of its added support for z39.50 protocol whereas all the DL packages supported OAIPMH. Greenstone also provides feature of upload of metadata from DSpace repository.

5.9. User Interface

This category refers to the support for multilingual access as well as the ability to customize the user interface to suit the needs of different DL implementations. All DL package secured full score which reflects that these issues were taken care very well. Some peculiar features like availability of themes like Manakin for DSpace helps end user to get a better look and feel. Whereas Greenstone Librarian Interface lacks this feature. On the other hand AJAX enabled EPrints interface is a great boon for low bandwidth users.

5.10. Standards Compliance

Standards are important for the sharing of digital content and a long term digital preservation. All DL packages scored well which confirms that all of them are compliant with the established standards for DLs.

5.11. Automatic Tools

This category refers to tools for automated content acquisition, harvesting and metadata generation. Automatic tools help in reducing the labour cost and valuable time of implementing a DL. Greenstone because of its feature to write plugins and following of CORBA based standards was able to get a better score. While others only have feature of automatic generation of indices and reports.

5.12. System Support and Maintenance

Any open source software can be successful only and only if there is availability of support and maintenance. This category deals with the availability of these.

Experience shows that most open source softwares lack this feature. Here all the chosen packages scored very well, all were backed by well documented manuals, wikis and quick responsive mailing lists. Further all of them have their help desk support also.

6. CONCLUSIONS

The consolidated score [Table 1] shows that DSpace emerged as a good option having best search and browsing support as well good support for metadata and provides more power to administrator to put access restrictions at collection level. The web browser based upload and better user interface. With the option of deployment of themes adds to better look and feel. The back end programming language JAVA makes it platform independent. The lacking points like unavailability to upload compressed files and little bit tough installation put it on backstage.

While EPrints having functionality to upload compressed files and AJAX based interface and very good support for metadata adds value to it. Whereas limited browsing and less implementation of access restrictions are some of the lacking features.

Whereas Greenstone having good report generation, indexing features, availability of a range of plugins, support for Z39.50 adds some feathers to its cap. But lack of embedded interface for Librarians makes it sometimes inaccessible on some machines. The default user interface is also not that much attractive from the user point of view. But the easy installation like one click installation is main reason for increase in number downloads of this software.

The clear indication which is coming out of this study is that all the DL packages are improving day by day and are ready to incorporate new state-of-the-art features.

REFERENCES

1. DSpace visited on December 20, 2008 from *http://www.dspace.org/index.php/Introducing-DSpace/*
2. DSpace wiki Retrieved on December 20, 2008 from *http://wiki.dspace.org/index.php/Main_Page*
3. EPrints visited on December 21, 208 from *http://www.eprints.org/software/v3/*
4. EPrints wiki: Main Page retrieved on December 22, 2008 from *http://wiki.eprints.org/w/Main_Page*
5. Goh, D.; Chua, A.; Kho, D. A.; Khoo, E. B.-H.; Mak, E. B.-T. & Ng, M. W.-M. (2006). A checklist for evaluating open source digital library software. Online Information Review. Vol. 30. No. 4. pp. 360-379. available online at
6. Greenstone manuals: retrieved on December 24, 2008 from *http://www.greenstone.org/manuals/gsdl2/en/html/*
7. Greenstone visited on December 23rd , 2008 from *http://www.greenstone.org/*
8. Greenstone wiki: Retrieved on December 23rd, 2008 from *http://wiki.greenstone.org/wiki/index.php/GreenstoneWiki*
9. Librarians Digital Library: accessed on December 23rd, 2008 at *https://drtc.isibang.ac.in/*
10. Open Source Initiative, The Open Source Definition retrieved on December 23rd, 2008 from *http://www.opensource.org/docs/osd*
11. Punter, T. (1997), "Using checklists to evaluate software product quality", Proceedings of the 8th European Conference on Software Cost Estimation (ESCOM), pp.143-50.
12. Pfister, Joachim and Zimmermann, Hans-Dieter Towards the Introduction of an Institutional Repository: Basic Principles and Concepts available online at *http://edoc.hu-berlin.de/conferences/bobcatsss2008/pfister-joachim-285/PDF/pfister.pdf* pp. 285-293.
13. Registry of Open Access Repositories(ROAR) visited on December 21, 2008 from *http://roar.eprints.org/index.php?action=browse#version*
14. Suber, Peter, Open Access Overview (definition, introduction) retrieved on December 23, 2008 from *http://www.earlham.edu/~peters/fos/overview.htm*.
15. Test repository for EPrints *http://drtc.isibang.ac.in:5555/*

APPENDIX

APPENDIX1: SHOWS CHECKLIST AND USAGE

1. Place a check mark for each item that exists in the software package being evaluated.

2. Within each subcategory,
   a. Multiply the number of check marks by the subcategory weight. This weight also represents the maximum score for that subcategory.
   b. Divide this resulting number by the number of items in the subcategory to obtain the subcategory score.

3. Within each category, sum all subcategory scores, divide the total by 10, and multiply the resulting number by the category weight to obtain the category score.

4. To obtain the consolidated score, sum all category scores.

Table II. Digital library evaluation checklist

	Checklist Categories		Weight	
1.0	**Content Management**			**7.00**
	1.1 **Submission Administration**		**3.00**	
	1.1.1 Allows multiple collections within same installation of system	☐		
	1.1.2 Allows repository administrator to set submission parameters	☐		
	1.1.3 Home page for each collection	☐		
	Sub-category score		☐	
	1.2 **Submission workflow**		**3.00**	
	1.2.1 Segregated submission workspaces	☐		
	1.2.2 Submission roles	☐		
	1.2.3 Configurable submission roles within collections	☐		
	Sub-category score		☐	
	1.3 **Submission support**		**2.00**	
	1.3.1 Email notification for users	☐		
	1.3.2 Email notification for administrators	☐		
	Sub-category score		☐	
	1.4 **Submission review**		**2.00**	
	1.4.1 Allows users to review completed content	☐		
	1.4.2 Allows users to review uncompleted content	☐		
	1.4.3 Allows content administrator to review submissions	☐		
	Sub-category score		☐	
	Category Score			☐

(continued)

Checklist Categories		Weight	
2.0 Content Acquisition			**11.00**
2.1 **Content import/export**		**3.00**	
2.1.1 Upload compressed files	☐		
2.1.2 Upload from existing URL	☐		
2.1.3 Volume import of objects	☐		
2.1.4 Volume import of metadata for existing collections	☐		
2.1.5 Volume export/content portability (to other systems)	☐		
Sub-category score		☐	
2.2 **Document/object formats**		**5.00**	
2.2.1 Administrator ability to limit approved file formats	☐		
2.2.2 Submitted items can comprise multiple files or file types	☐		
2.2.3 Text formats	☐		
2.2.3.1 ASCII	☐		
2.2.3.2 UNICODE	☐		
2.2.3.3 RTF	☐		
2.2.4 Image formats	☐		
2.2.4.1 TIFF	☐		
2.2.4.2 GIF	☐		
2.2.4.3 JPEG	☐		
2.2.5 Presentation formats	☐		
2.2.5.1 Adobe Post Script	☐		
2.2.5.2 Adobe PDF	☐		
2.2.6 Structured formats	☐		
2.2.6.1 HTML	☐		
2.2.6.2 SGML	☐		
2.2.6.3 XML	☐		
2.2.7 Audio and video formats	☐		
2.2.7.1 Wave	☐		
2.2.7.2 Real	☐		
2.2.7.3 MP3	☐		
2.2.7.4 AVI	☐		
2.2.7.5 MPEG	☐		
Sub-category score		☐	
2.3 **Version control**		**2.00**	
2.3.1 Allows past versions of files to be retrieved	☐		
2.3.2 Changes can be identified	☐		
2.3.3 Changes can be compared	☐		
Sub-category score		☐	
Category Score			☐

3.0 Metadata			**12.00**
3.1 **Real time updating and indexing of accepted content**		**1.50**	
3.1.1 Features available	☐		
Sub-category score		☐	

(continued)

	Checklist Categories		Weight	
3.2	**Metadata schemas supported**		**5.00**	
	3.2.1 Dublin Core	☐		
	3.2.2 EAD	☐		
	3.2.3 MARC 21	☐		
	3.2.4 LOM	☐		
	3.2.5 METS	☐		
	3.2.6 MODS	☐		
	3.2.7 VRA Core Categories	☐		
	3.2.8 MPEG-7	☐		
	Sub-category score		☐	
3.3	**Add/delete customized metadata fields**		**1.50**	
	3.3.1 Feature available	☐		
	Sub-category score		☐	
3.4	**Set default values for metadata**		**0.50**	
	3.4.1 Feature available	☐		
	Sub-category score		☐	
3.5	**Supports Unicode character set for metadata**		**1.50**	
	3.5.1 Feature available	☐		
	Sub-category score		☐	
	Category Score			☐
4.0	**Search Support**			**14.00**
4.1	**Full text**		**4.00**	
	4.1.1 Boolean logic	☐		
	4.1.2 Truncation/wild cards	☐		
	4.1.3 Phrase	☐		
	4.1.4 Proximity	☐		
	Sub-category score		☐	
4.2	**Search all descriptive metadata**		**2.50**	
	4.2.1 Boolean	☐		
	4.2.2 Truncation/wild cards	☐		
	Sub-category score		☐	
4.3	**Search selected metadata fields**		**1.00**	
	4.3.1 Feature available	☐		
	Sub-category score		☐	
4.4	**Browse**		**2.00**	
	4.4.1 By author	☐		
	4.4.2 By title	☐		
	4.4.3 By issue date	☐		
	4.4.4 By subject term	☐		
	4.4.5 By collection	☐		
	4.4.6 By customized fields	☐		
	4.4.7 Browse by more than 1 field	☐		
	Sub-category score		☐	

(continued)

	Checklist Categories		Weight	
	4.5 **Sort search results**		**0.50**	
	4.5.1 By author	☐		
	4.5.2 By title	☐		
	4.5.3 By issue date	☐		
	4.5.4 By relevance	☐		
	4.5.5 By other	☐		
	Sub-category score		☐	
	Category Score			☐
5.0	**Access Control and Privacy**			**7.00**
	5.1 **Password administration**		**2.00**	
	5.1.1 System-assigned passwords	☐		
	5.1.2 User selected passwords	☐		
	5.1.3 Forgotten password retrieval function	☐		
	Sub-category score		☐	
	5.2 **User management**		**1.50**	
	5.2.1 Add user profile	☐		
	5.2.2 Edit user profile	☐		
	5.2.3 Delete user profile	☐		
	Sub-category score		☐	
	5.3 **Limit access at different levels**		**1.50**	
	5.3.1 File/object level	☐		
	5.3.2 Collection level	☐		
	Sub-category score		☐	
	5.4 **User roles**		**2.50**	
	5.4.1 Allows definition of different user groups	☐		
	5.4.2 Limits access by role	☐		
	5.4.3 Allows collection to be customized for each role	☐		
	Sub-category score		☐	
	5.5 **Access management**		**1.50**	
	5.5.1 IP source address filtering	☐		
	5.5.2 Proxy filtering	☐		
	5.5.3 Credential-based access	☐		
	Sub-category score		☐	
	5.6 **Security methods**		**1.00**	
	5.6.1Encryption	☐		
	5.6.2 Digital signatures	☐		
	Sub-category score		☐	
	Category Score			☐
6.0	**Report and Inquiry Capabilities**			**3.00**
	6.1 **System generated usage statistics**		**6.00**	
	6.1.1 Feature available	☐		
	Sub-category score		☐	

(continued)

		Checklist Categories		Weight	
	6.2	**Usage reports**		**4.00**	
		6.2.1 Report timeline specification	☐		
		6.2.2 Report fields customization	☐		
		6.2.3 Report templates	☐		
		Sub-category score		☐	
		Category Score			☐
7.0	**Preservation**				**5.00**
	7.1	**Persistent document identification**		**5.00**	
		7.1.1 System assigned identifiers	☐		
		7.1.2 CNRI Handles	☐		
		Sub-category score		☐	
	7.2	**Quality control**		**3.00**	
		7.2.1 Feature available	☐		
		Sub-category score		☐	
	7.3	**Prescribed digital preservation strategy**		**2.00**	
		7.3.1 Feature available	☐		
		Sub-category score		☐	
		Category Score			☐
8.0	**Interoperability**				**10.00**
	8.1	**OAI-PMH**		**5.00**	
		8.1.1 Feature available	☐		
		Sub-category score		☐	
	8.2	**Z39.50 protocol compliant**		**3.00**	
		8.2.1 Feature available	☐		
		Sub-category score		☐	
	8.3	**Research protocols**		**2.00**	
		8.3.1 Dienst	☐		
		8.3.2 SDLIP	☐		
		Sub-category score		☐	
		Category Score			☐
9.0	**User Interface**				**8.00**
	9.1	**Modify interface "look and feel"**		**5.00**	
		9.1.1 Feature available	☐		
		Sub-category score		☐	
	9.2	**Apply a customized header/footer to static or dynamic pages**		**3.00**	
		9.2.1 Feature available	☐		
		Sub-category score		☐	
	9.3	**Supports multi-lingual interfaces**		**2.00**	
		9.3.1 Feature available	☐		
		Sub-category score		☐	
		Category Score			☐

(continued)

	Checklist Categories		Weight	
10.0	**Standards Compliance**			**10.00**
10.1	**Structured document forrmats e.g. XML, SGML**		**3.00**	
	10.1.1 Feature available	☐		
	Sub-category score		☐	
10.2	**Metadata formats e.g. Dublin Core**		**3.00**	
	10.2.1 Feature available	☐		
	Sub-category score		☐	
10.3	**Text document formats e.g. Unicode**		**2.00**	
	10.3.1 Feature available	☐		
	Sub-category score		☐	
10.4	**Image formats e.g. TIFF**		**2.00**	
	10.4.1 Feature available	☐		
	Sub-category score		☐	
	Category Score			☐
11.0	**Automatic Tools**			**4.00**
11.1	**Metadata entry system**		**5.00**	
	11.1.1 Feature available	☐		
	Sub-category score		☐	
11.2	**Generation of**		**5.00**	
	11.2.1 Search indexes	☐		
	11.2.2 HTML pages	☐		
	11.2.3 Reports	☐		
	Sub-category score		☐	
	Category Score			☐
12.0	**System Support and Maintenance**			**9.00**
12.1	**Documentation/manuals**		**4.00**	
	12.1.1 Feature available	☐		
	Sub-category score		☐	
12.2	**Mailing lists/discussion forums**		**2.00**	
	12.2.1 Feature available	☐		
	Sub-category score		☐	
12.3	**Bug track/feature request system**		**1.00**	
	12.3.1 Feature available	☐		
	Sub-category score		☐	
12.4	**Help desk support**		**3.00**	
	12.4.1 Feature available	☐		
	Sub-category score		☐	
	Category Score			☐
	Consolidated Score			☐

Note: Category weights sum to 100, while subcategory weights sum to 10

9

FREE AND OPEN SOURCE SOFTWARE (FOSS) SOLUTIONS FOR CONTENT MANAGEMENT IN LIBRARIES

Dimple Patel
Assistant Professor
Library & Information Science
Osmania University, Hyderabad – 500 007
dimplerp@yahoo.co.in

ABSTRACT

The paper discusses Free and Open Source Software (FOSS) for content management that libraries can use to provide various web-based information services. Librarians are pressed to provide efficient and quick information services with stagnant and ever depleting library budgets. FOSS come to the rescue and allow libraries, to render 24x7, remote and universal access to their information services to the library users even under financial constraints. The paper covers the features of three free and open source content management systems (CMS) i.e. Drupal, Joomla! and Plone. All the three CMS provide numerous add-ons specifically useful for libraries. CMS not only make content management easy for librarians but also allow for collaborative content development, thus allowing library users also to participate, contribute and share content with libraries.

Keywords : Free Open Source Library Software (FOSS), Content Management Systems (CMS), Drupal, Joomla, Plone.

1. INTRODUCTION

Blogs, Wikis, Social networking sites, Twitter, RSS, and other tools termed as Web 2.0 technologies have transformed the way content is created, developed, managed and shared. The emphasis is now on Content Sharing rather than content dissemination. It is no longer a matter of a centralized organization collecting and disseminating information. With the emergence of interdisciplinary subjects, information across various domains needs to be shared by the domain experts and the experts themselves have to stretch their subject boundaries to other disciplines. These developments in technology and subject fields, has led to collaborative content development and sharing across various user groups. Libraries also have adopted these new technologies to reach across to these various groups of users. With these new web-based services libraries can now collaboratively produce, share and disseminate information along with their users. User-participation in content production and sharing help libraries in increasing their information resources base and in turn disseminating it to a wider clientele.

2. WHY CONTENT MANAGEMENT SYSTEM FOR LIBRARIES?

Content management, or CM, is the set of processes and technologies that support the collection, managing, and publishing of information in any form or medium. In recent times this information is typically referred to as content or, to be precise, digital content. Digital content may take the form of text, such as documents, multimedia files, such as audio or video files, or any other file type which follows a content lifecycle which requires management. [1]

A content management system (CMS) is a collection of procedures used to manage work flow in a collaborative environment. These procedures can be manual or computer-based. [2]

The above definition of CMS explains the conceptual model of a CMS. The term CMS is also used for the application software that is used for designing, developing and managing digital content, especially on the Web. A computer software system for organizing and facilitating collaborative creation of documents and other content, especially for loading to a website. [3]. A more explanatory definition is found on the Plone Website [4]:

A content management system, or CMS, is a web application designed to make it easy for non-technical users to add, edit and manage a website. Not only do content management systems help website users with content editing, they also take care of a lot of "behind the scenes" work such as:

- Automatically generate navigation elements
- Making content searchable and indexable
- Keeping track of users, their permissions and security settings
- And much more.

The greatest advantage of using CMS for content management lies in the fact that the user(s) are not required to have any knowledge of Hypertext Markup Language (HTML) to create websites or post content on the website. [5]

3. ADVANTAGES OF USING CMS IN LIBRARIES

CMS provide a new dimension to the way services can be

provided by the libraries. CMS can be used in libraries to:

- Develop library websites
- Manage digital content in various formats (text, image, audio, video, software, scientific data, personal information, etc.)
- Allow centralized content to be developed and managed in a decentralized manner at different levels by the library staff
- Provide library users with an interactive interface
- Increase user participation in library activities / services
- Allow development of shared content for the library
- Allow user participation in content development
- Aid in easy storage and retrieval of data
- Reduce repetitive duplicate input

4. FREE SOFTWARE OR OPEN SOURCE SOFTWARE (OSS) OR FOSS OR FLOSS?

4.1 'Free' Software

The term 'free' here does not merely refer to the price aspect. 'Free' here means as described by the Free Software Foundation. [6] It says, a software is free, only when it provides the computer user the following freedoms:

1. The freedom to run the program, for any purpose (freedom 0).
2. The freedom to study how the program works, and adapt it to your needs (freedom 1). Access to the source code is a precondition for this.
3. The freedom to redistribute copies so you can help your neighbor (freedom 2).
4. The freedom to improve the program, and release your improvements (and modified versions in general) to the

public, so that the whole community benefits (freedom 3). Access to the source code is a precondition for this.

4.2 Open Source Software (OSS)

According to the Open Source Initiative (OSI), the Open Source Definition is as follows (*Note*: As the definition is a lengthy one, it has been presented here in a short form. Please refer to the OSI Website for the full and complete definition.) [7]

Open source doesn't just mean access to the source code. The distribution terms of open-source software must comply with the following criteria:

i. Free Redistribution : The license shall not restrict any party from selling or giving away the software as a component of an aggregate software distribution containing programs from several different sources. The license shall not require a royalty or other fee for such sale.

ii. Source Code : The program must include source code, and must allow distribution in source code as well as compiled form.

iii. Derived Works : The license must allow modifications and derived works, and must allow them to be distributed under the same terms as the license of the original software.

iv. Integrity of The Author's Source Code : The license may restrict source-code from being distributed in modified form only if the license allows the distribution of "patch files" with the source code for the purpose of modifying the program at build time. The license must explicitly permit distribution of software built from modified source code. The license may require derived works to carry a different name or version number from the original software.

v. No Discrimination Against Persons or Groups : The license must not discriminate against any person or group of persons.

vi. No Discrimination Against Fields of Endeavor : The license must not restrict anyone from making use of the program in a specific field of endeavor. For example, it may not restrict the program from being used in a business, or from being used for genetic research.

vii. Distribution of License : The rights attached to the program must apply to all to whom the program is redistributed without the need for execution of an additional license by those parties.

viii. License Must Not Be Specific to a Product : The rights attached to the program must not depend on the program's being part of a particular software distribution. If the program is extracted from that distribution and used or distributed within the terms of the program's license, all parties to whom the program is redistributed should have the same rights as those that are granted in conjunction with the original software distribution.

ix. License Must Not Restrict Other Software : The license must not place restrictions on other software that is distributed along with the licensed software. For example, the license must not insist that all other programs distributed on the same medium must be open-source software.

x. License Must Be Technology-Neutral : No provision of the license may be predicated on any individual technology or style of interface.

4.3 Free and open source software (FOSS) / Free, Libre and Open Source Software (FLOSS)

The terms Free and open source software (FOSS) or Free, Libre and Open Source Software (FLOSS) are increasingly being used by users who are either not biased towards any one kind of software or by users who use, to the fullest advantage, both kinds of software. It is an inclusive term which covers both free software and open source software. The Free software movement is more of a social movement focussing more on the philosophical freedoms it gives to its users. While, the OSS concentrates more on the collaborative development model.

5. FREE AND OPEN SOURCE SOFTWARE (FOSS) CONTENT MANAGEMENT SYSTEM (CMS)

While there are many FOSS content management systems available, this paper discusses the features, modules and usage of three CMS, namely, Drupal, Joomla! and Plone. Drupal and all contributed files hosted on Drupal.org are licensed under the GNU General Public License, version 2 [8] or later. That means you are free to download, reuse, modify, and distribute any files hosted on Drupal.org's CVS repository under the terms of either the GPL version 2 or version 3, and to run Drupal in combination with any code with any license that is compatible with either versions 2 or 3, such as the GNU Affero General Public License (AGPL) version 3. [9] [15] The Joomla software and default templates are copyright 2005-2008 Open Source Matters, Inc. If you want to use, copy, modify or distribute Joomla, you may do so under the terms of the GNU General Public License. [10] Plone uses GPL version 2 as its license. [11]

5.1 Drupal

Drupal was created in 2000 by a Belgian student, Dries Buytaert. Drupal is a modular CMS. The standard release of Drupal, known as "Drupal core", contains basic features common to most CMS, which include the ability to register and maintain individual user accounts, administration menus, RSS-feeds, customizable layout, flexible account privileges, logging, a blogging system, an Internet forum, etc. Additional new features and themes can be included to the Drupal core by using contributed modules and themes. Hence, it is called a "Content Management Framework". [12] Drupal uses Apache, MySQL and PHP.

5.1.1 Main Features of Drupal:

- Multi-sites feature: One can create more than one website using one instance of Drupal installation.
- Administrator can create authenticated users.
- User Roles can be created and accorded relevant permissions.
- Drupal allows users to register, login, log out, maintain user profiles, etc.
- Multi-user content creation and editing: This feature can be used by libraries to encourage and involve library users also to participate in content creation.
- OpenID support
- Access statistics and logging
- Advanced search functions
- Caching and feature throttling (i.e. one can disable features not required by the library) for improved performance under load
- Comments, forums, and polls
- Descriptive URLs (for example, "www.example.com/products" rather than "www.example.com/?q=node/432")
- Multi-level menu system
- RSS Feed and Feed Aggregator
- Security/new release update notification

5.1.2 Drupal Modules for Libraries

As mentioned earlier, Drupal can be extended by adding new modules. Drupal has many user-contributed modules for libraries. The currently available library modules are:

Simple remote search module : This simple module allows users to search a remote database (like your OPAC) from your Drupal site.

Z39.50 Search : This module implements the z39.50 Protocol for Information Retrieval using PHP interface to the YAZ toolkit. With this module you can easily search or scan z39.50 targets (servers) in parallel using the standard Drupal search API and present the results.

Bibliography Module a.k.a. Drupal Scholar : This module allows users manage and display lists of scholarly publications.

Features include

- EndNote tagged and XML import/export
- bibTex import / export
- in-line citing of references in "page" or "story" node types (builds a reference list at the end of the node body)
- selectable output styles (CSE, APA and IEEE)
- taxonomy integration: register keywords as taxonomy and/or assign an entry to an existing vocabulary

OAI-PMH Module

This module provides an Open Archives Initiative Protocol for Metadata Harvesting (OAI-PMH), interface to the Bibliography Module. It exposes metadata from the Biblio module.

MARC : This module allows you to import MARC records as nodes, to do things like pre-populating book review sites or even recreating your library's catalog in a rich social environment.

Library : The Library module allows users to manage the availability of nodes as assets. You can create custom content types using CCK and then add those content types to the library. The module supports multiple copies of a library item associated with one node, and each copy may be individually made available or unavailable. The module allows administrators to define their own library actions. Library actions may make an item available, unavailable, or not change an item's status. Every transaction is associated with a library patron. If you use the trigger module (part of core) with the library module, each library action generates a trigger that you can assign further actions to. The module includes a few built-in actions (send an email, extend the due date of an item). The library module is intended to be very flexible and comes with a number of options. You may use unique identifiers on item instances (e.g. barcodes), have library patrons as users, and configure what fields display in the custom library search.

Islandora Fedora-Drupal module : Robertson Library released the Fedora-Drupal module Islandora as open source. There is a Islandora project hosted by Fedora Commons. The Islandora module allows Drupal users to view and manage digital objects stored in Fedora.

Book Post : The Book Post module makes it easy to post information about books. Any 10 or 13-digit ISBN placed between double curly braces {{}} in a post will convert into the book cover, title, author and publication info. All data comes from the Open Library Project (*http://openlibrary.org/*), an open source catalog that allows users to add books and edit metadata. If there is no cover available for the book you want to post, you can go to the Open Library and add one. It is also possible to use the Open Library ID number instead of the ISBN (e.g. OL8378495M). The Open Library has full text available for many titles in the public domain. A "Read Online" link will automatically appear in your post if the full text is available from the Open Library. There are also options to include links to WorldCat, LibraryThing, and Google Books for books that you post. This module is based on John Miedema's OpenBook Plugin for WordPress.

Biblio Facets : Biblio Facets integrates with the Faceted Search module (*see* section 4.2.10) and allows users to browse Biblio types and fields as facets.

Faceted Search : The Faceted Search module provides a search interface for allowing users to browse content. It is an information navigation and discovery tool. The interface exposes metadata in such a way that users can build their queries as they go, refining or expanding the current query, with results automatically reflecting the current query. This interface also combines free-text search, fully leveraging Drupal's search engine. It avoids complex search forms, and never offers facets that would lead to empty result sets. Faceted Search is in fact a bundle of modules.

- *Faceted Search*: Provides the search framework and API.
- *Faceted Search UI*: Provides the search user interface.
- *Faceted Search Views*: Allows using Views to display the search results.
- *Author Facet*: Allows users to refine the current search based on content author.
- *Content Type Facet*: Allows users to refine the current search based on content type.
- *Date Authored Facet*: Allows users to refine the current search based on content creation date.
- *Taxonomy Facets*: Allows users to search content through taxonomy. Any vocabulary can become a facet that can be used to refine the current search.

- *Field Keyword Filter*: Allows users to perform keyword searches restricted by field. Requires the Field Indexer module.

Content Construction Kit (CCK) : The Content Construction Kit allows you to add custom fields to nodes using a web browser.

oai2forcck : This module provides an implementation the OAI V2 Data-Provider for the Drupal CCK module.

Barcode : This module provides a barcode field type for CCK.

Features

- Generate a barcode image on the fly. It supports EAN-13, EAN-8, UPC-A, UPC-E, ISBN, etc.
- You can also display the barcode as simple text.
- You can provide your own font file

CCK Facets : CCK Facets is a bundle of modules that integrate with Faceted Search to expose Content Construction Kit (CCK) fields as facets. This allows users to browse field values and to filter search results with those values.

CCK Taxonomy Fields : Taxonomy vocabularies will show up as field types that can be added to content types using CCK. Field types can be named anything you want and you can even have several different fields from the same vocabulary on one content type.

Field Indexer : The Field Indexer module indexes field data into Drupal's search index. Each field enabled for indexing becomes a type of index entry. Then, with an appropriate search module, users may perform keyword searches restricted by field.

5.1.3 Drupal in Libraries

1. SOPAC (social OPAC), based on Drupal 4.x and

implemented at the Ann Arbor Library (http://www.blyberg.net/2007/01/21/aadlorg-goes-social/).

2. Fish4Info - a next generation library portal is based on the MARC module. (http://fish4info.org/)
3. http://chicagolibrarian.com/node/262
4. tinytax module that allows to navigate into the taxonomy and list the related content, like the MeSH browser (http://sandbox.scratchpads.eu/)

5. BIBLIOSCAPE (HTTP://SUPPORT.BIBLIOSCAPE.COM)

5.2 Joomla!

Joomla! is a free open source content management system for publishing content on the World Wide Web. Joomla (Joomla 1.0.0) was released on September 16, 2005. Joomla version 1.5 was released on January 22, 2008. It won the Packt Publishing Open Source Content Management System Award in two successive years – 2006 and 2007.

5.2.1 Features

- Page caching to improve performance
- RSS feeds
- Printable versions of pages
- News flashes
- Blogs
- Polls
- Website searching
- Language internationalization.

The Joomla package consists of different kinds of modular extensions. These extensions are of three kinds:

1. Plugins (Previously known as "Mambots".)
2. Components

3. Modules

Plugins are background extensions that extend Joomla with new functionality. The WikiBot, for example, allows the author of Joomla content to use "Wikitags" in Joomla articles which will auto-create dynamic hyperlinks to Wikipedia articles when displayed. Components allow webmasters to perform such tasks as build a community by expanding user features, backup a website, translate content and create URLs that are more friendly to search engines. Modules perform such tasks as displaying a calendar or allowing custom code like Google AdSense etc., to be inserted within the base Joomla code. There are 3500+ extensions available for Joomla. [13]

5.2.2 Joomla! Modules for Libraries

Collection : This module manages a collection of books/ CDs/DVDs/games. Features include, categories/subcategories; use Amazon web service to fetch additional information; provide a link to the Amazon product page with your partner-id; JoomFish support; users can manage their own lists of items; module to display lists.

BookLibrary : This module provides a full-featured book library or book collection management environment on a Joomla-based website. It allows you to manage large book libraries. The component can also be used to easily set up a book selling shop using Amazon if you want. With an Amazon Associates ID (as an Amazon affiliate) you can earn credits with book sales through Amazon, while Amazon takes care of the handling and shipping.

- Full category and subcategory support
- BookID for internal administration
- Lend/Return management, with frontend lend request possibility
- Possibility of frontend book reviews by users, reviews

management in the backend

- Book information and covers retrieved from Amazon through ISBN or entered manually
- Import and export options (CSV, XML, MySQL)
- English included, additional language files can be downloaded from the website

Top Listing module for BookLibrary : This module can be used to display the Top books from BookLibrary. Features include, Show/Hide Covers; Set Cover Height; Choose how many books to display in the top list; Choose if only published books or all books; Choose sorting by hits, date, rating; Choose if hits are displayed; Choose if ranking displayed.

"New Books Extended" module for BookLibrary : The "New Books Extended" module for the BookLibrary module is an improved version of the module to display the newest books from the BookLibrary component. Features include:

- Item Count (choose number of books to display)
- Word Count (limit number of words to show from the book description)
- Show or Hide the Book Title
- Show or Hide the Book Authors
- Show or Hide the Book Cover
- Set the Cover Height
- Set the Display Orientation (horizontal or vertical)
- Sort by Last Added or Last Edited

BookLibrary Top 10 : The BookLibrary Top 10 module displays the 10 most visited books from BookLibrary in a list, with the number of hits behind it.

jbook : This module is a component for books management.

- It allows splitting up the classification in categories and subcategories, with a tree structure, without limits in number of sub-children levels.

- For every book it is possible to insert details like the book cover (with automatic size rearrangement). You can navigate even for author, editor.
- Registered users can see and comment every book reviewed. They can also ask for more information on the book by sending an email to the site administrator.
- There is a mambot to integrate the search in the entire site.
- It is presently available in Italian, English and French.

Librarything : Module which displays your library from librarything.com. It uses their javascript code, but allows changing of parameters, such as how many and cover size, from your Joomla! site module admin.

Now Reading : Displays the cover image of the current article or book the site admin is reading

5.3 Plone

Plone is a free and open source content management system built on top of the Zope application server. Plone is released under the GNU General Public License (GPL) and is designed to be extensible. Additional functionality is added to Plone with Products, which may be distributed through the Plone website or otherwise.

5.3.1 Features

- Collaboration and sharing
- Versioning, history and reverting content
- Upgraded visual HTML editor
- Workflow capabilities
- Full-text indexing of Word and PDF documents

- Presentation mode for content
- Support for the search engine Sitemap protocol
- Support for multiple mark-up formats
- Wiki support
- Automatic previous/next navigation
- Rules engine for content
- Auto-generated tables of contents
- Multilingual content management
- Time-based publishing
- Human-readable URLs
- Powerful graphical page editor
- Navigation and updated site maps
- Drag and drop reordering of content
- XML exports of site configurations
- Localized workflow configuration
- Adjustable templates on content
- Standard content types
- Content is automatically formatted for printing
- Standards-compliant XHTML and CSS
- Accessibility compliant
- RSS feed support
- Automatic image scaling and thumbnail generation
- Free add-on products
- Cross-platform
- Comment capabilities on any content
- Installer packages for multiple platforms
- In-context editing
- Backup support

When compared to other CMS, Plone scores above others, in standards conformance, access control, internationalization, aggregation, user-generated content, micro-applications, active user groups and value. Plone's Web-based administrative interface is optimized for standards, allowing it to work with most common web browsers, and uses additional accessibility standards to help users who have disabilities. All of Plone's features are customizable, and free add-ons are available from the Plone website. [14]

5.3.2 Plone Add-ons for Libraries [16]

Custom Search : Custom Search aims to making custom search queries for Plone sites as easy as possible. The search result listing can be customized to be more descriptive than with the standard Plone search. Powerful search features help to target searches better.

Classification Scheme : A product enabling definition and edition of classification schemes ; these help managing, cataloging and searching big collections of arbitrary content types.

PloneFacetedClassification : A system to classify site contents (by any AT content types) by different attributes (facets) so the user can browse them in a very effective way and easily retrieve what (s)he is looking for.

CatalogBrowser : CatalogBrowser provides a Plone interface to browse into metadata of a Catalog. So it is another way to view a catalog that Topics / Smart Folders.

Collective.categorizing : collective.categorizing aims to add hierarchical categorizing to Plone with Category content type.

Faceted Navigation : Collective Faceted Navigation provides an user interface which lets an user browse items of a Plone site by selecting amongst pre-defined criteria.

icSemantic Thesaurusic : Semantic Thesaurus uses pyThesaurus to manage a multilingual thesaurus that can be used in a Plone site in order to add semantic metadata to the website.

Plone Glossary : Plone Glossary is a product to manage glossaries in your Plone.

Plone Ontology : PloneOntology is an ontology based replacement for the existing keyword mechanism in Plone.

Remote File Index : A tool that indexes content of documents on remote servers

ATAmazon : ATAmazon is a product to display books in your Plone site. It retrieves the metadata from Amazon.com, and auto-populates the form fields so you don't have to type it in manually.

Collective.indexing : Abstract framework for queueing, optimizing and dispatching index operations for portal content.

EEA Faceted Navigation (FacetedNav) : A powerful product to effectively find content in large collections.

Plone Keyword Manager : Plone Keyword Manager allows you to change, merge and delete keywords in Plone and updates all corresponding objects automatically. It uses a similarity search to support you in identifying similar keywords. Keywords can be cleaned up from time to time by a site manager to create a consistent vocabulary.

slc.mindmap : Adds export, viewing and editing support for mindmaps in Plone, with an embedded editor from mindmeister.com

PloneKeywordTools : Tools to manage keywords for content types, could be used for adding keywords to a selection of objects or recursive to all objects in a folder.

Smart Keyword Manager : is a Plone product making it

easy to manage keywords ("tags") using smart folders. On any smart folder, a new tab will appear for Managers, allowing them to do either batch edition of keywords, or massive addition/removal on all objects displayed by the smart folder.

bibliograph.rendering: Render bibliographic information from Plone content.

6. CONCLUSION

Selecting a Content Management System for a library requires a study and plan that will review the type of library, types and formats of content being handled, services being provided, technology skills of the library staff to handle the CMS software, training required for the library staff, training and orientation required for the users, etc. A study to evaluate the CMS software against each other for features like, ease of installation, management, administration, user interface, support, documentation, provision of extensions or add-ons, frequency of upgradations, ease of upgrading, etc (*Note:* similar to the comparison table with a list of features compared against Drupal, Joomla! and Plone given in Appendix – I.) will go a long way in selection of the best suited CMS for specific libraries.

REFERENCES

1. Content Management – Wikipedia http://en.wikipedia.org/wiki/Content_management
2. Accessed on: 09th February, 2010
3. Content Management – Wikipedia http://en.wikipedia.org/wiki/Content_management_system
4. Accessed on: 09th February, 2010
5. content management system - Wiktionary *http://en.wiktionary.org/wiki/content_management_system* Accessed on: 09th February, 2010
6. What is a CMS? *http://plone.org/documentation/faq/what-is-a-cms* Accessed on: 09th February, 2010
7. HTML 4.01 Specification *http://www.w3.org/TR/html401/* Accessed on:

09th February, 2010

8. The Free Software Definition http://www.gnu.org/philosophy/free-sw.html Accessed on: 09th February, 2010
9. The Open Source Definition | Open Source Initiative (OSI) *http://www.opensource.org/docs/osd* Accessed on: 09th February, 2010
10. The GNU General Public License *http://www.gnu.org/licenses/gpl.html* Accessed on: 09th February, 2010
11. GNU Affero General Public License *http://www.fsf.org/licensing/licenses/agpl-3.0.html* Accessed on: 09th February, 2010
12. About the Joomla! Project *http://www.joomla.org/about-joomla/the-project.html* Accessed on: 09th February, 2010
13. Plone License FAQ *http://plone.org/foundation/copyrights/license-faq* Accessed on: 09th February, 2010
14. drupal.org: Community plumbing http://drupal.org/ Accessed on: 09th February, 2010
15. Joomla! Extensions Directory http://extensions.joomla.org/ Accessed on: 09th February, 2010
16. Plone (software) http://en.wikipedia.org/wiki/Plone_(software) Accessed on: 09th February, 2010
17. Licensing FAQ http://drupal.org/licensing/faq#q1Accessed on: 09th February, 2010
18. Downloads | Plone Open Source Content Management *http://plone.org/products* Accessed on: 09th February, 2010

APPENDIX – I

Table : Comparison of features of Drupal, Joomla! and Plone

Features	*Drupal*	*Joomla!*	*Plone*
Ease of Installation	Easy	Easy	Not very easy for those who are not technology-savvy
O/S	Windows, GNU/Linux		Windows, GNU/Linux Windows, GNU/Linux
Web Server	Apache 2	Apache 2	Zope
DBMS	MySQL / PgSQL		MySQL / PgSQL Integrates with SQL
Multisites	Yes	Yes (with extensions*)	Yes
Blogs	Yes		
Wikis	Yes*	Yes	Yes
Social networking	Yes*	Yes*	Yes
Polling	Yes	Yes	Yes*
User Interfaces (Administration and End-user)	Easy to use	Easy to use	Complicated. Requires lot of practice to get used to the interface.
Library-specific modules	Yes	Yes	Yes
Online Documentation	Yes	Yes	Yes
Online Support	Yes	Yes	Yes
Frequency of Updations	Every 3 months (approx.)	Every 3 months (approx.)	Every 3 months (approx.)
Ease of Updation	Easy	Easy	Not very easy for those who are not technology-savvy

* These features are not available with the core system, but can be added with the help of extensions or add-on modules.

10

Organize and Disseminate Free Information Available in the Internet by Using Content Management Software Joomla

Sudip Ranjan Hatua
Assistant Professor
Department of Library & Information Science
Rabindra Bharati University, Kolkata
e-mail: s_hatua@indiatimes.com

ABSTRACT

To find relevant information within huge distributed environment like Internet is not an easy task. The Human being has a limited capability, he cannot browse or read thousand hundreds of pages/ article of his interest though all may be very relevant to the concerned topic. Internet puts a burden on its users by providing millions of pages relevant as well as billions of pages irrelevant and all scattered in an unorganized manner. Search engines come with solutions claiming that they are making powerful automatic indexing systems to provide better results to the users and 'google' is today's most popular search engine. For a given query it retrieves millions of pages. Among them most are irrelevant and duplicate pages. In this situation a semi-automatic system with content management software may be a positive effort to locate, organize and disseminate information to the users specially those less funded academic and public libraries.

Keywords: Content Management Systems (CMS), Joomla, Internet, Information.

1. INTRODUCTION

Since 1980s libraries adopted lots of revolutionary steps from access to disseminate, from processing to services. These trends have been enabled by technological development in the areas of networking, file storage and management and implication of GUI [1]. Most of the ICT enabled libraries now-a-days giving less importance for the materials they collect or house but giving more emphasis on the kind of materials they can obtain in response to the user requests. Internet or specifically www become the best weapon and having most attention to the librarians since its inception. It treated as the biggest source of information as well as medium of publication and communication.

The access to information is not always an easy task, neither from the part of the information provider, nor on the part of the end user. Problems of authoring, presentation, security and performance have to be resolved on the part of the former, whereas problems of data location, relevance and credibility have to be resolved on the part of the latter. Search engine technologies are employed to simplify the process of seeking meaningful content in the WWW, yet the result is not always satisfactory.

The Web provides a new medium for storing, presenting, gathering, sharing, processing and using information. It brings us to a new information age. There is tremendous amount of documents or materials, such as newspapers, movies, music, journals, and many other products and services available in the web. Conceptually, the Web may be viewed in present days as a large and searchable virtual library now –a- days [2].

It is also found that libraries with sufficient supportive fund and equipment may subscribe lots of commercial information packages, they may become member of various associations and consortium and provide information to their users. But what will happen to those libraries facing serious budget scarcity to subscribe online source of information or any costly documents? Internet may be the best alternative. Lots of authentic source of information are freely available which can be identified and represented to it's users in an organized way. However there are many organizations providing reach information of the concerned subject worldwide but do not suffice for information needs arising at local and regional levels and in universities, colleges and other such organizations where there are different practices and research trends.

2. INFORMATION GROWTH IN THE WEB

While talking about identification most of the people are dependent on search engines. How far people gets satisfaction with those search engines is a million dollar question. The Internet is growing at an exponential rate - 7.3 million unique pages are added every day. This rapid growth means it is imperative for institutes, organizations and companies to proactively manage their presence on the Internet and to ensure online success [3]. The study produced by the faculty and students at the school of Information Management and Systems at the University of California shows that print, film, magnetic storage and optical storage media produced about 5 exabytes (equivalent in size to the information contained in 37,000 new libraries the size of the LC book collection) of new information in 2002. 92% of the new information is stored on the magnetic media primarily in hard disks. Film represents 7% of the total whereas paper contains 0.01% and optical storage media contains 0.002%. According to the population research bureau the world population is 6.3 billion thus almost 800mb of recorded information is produced per person each year. The Web contains 170 terabytes of information on its surface; in volume this is 17 times volume of LC print collection [4].

3. ROLE OF SEARCH ENGINES

As the Internet is expanding rapidly, the role of Internet search engines in retrieving information is becoming more important. Search engines vary in size and coverage of their database and functionality. Many users are aware of differences in functionality features like search options and presentation characteristics, but many do not know about differences in the way search engines index web documents. Which elements of a web documents are indexed? An end user is always looking for the appropriate search engines to get a result with the desired recall and precision. The indexing behaviour of search engines is not always consistent. Different results are obtained for the same question, even with the same engine. There are many findings on functionality of Internet indexes [5] and their coverage. Despite all its promises of mechanized efficiency, search engines has remained unsuccessful. As per one analysis, the coverage of the largest search engines, have indexed not more than about 16% of the Web [6]. The limitation of wholly computerized Internet indexing systems is that the automated spider robots that crawl through Websites retrieving data can only read open-text formats, such as HTML files, and cannot record any more that the basic file attributes of non-text format files. Even most search engines cannot survey frame-based sites or dynamic pages, such as those in a database pulled with cgi or perl scripting, and have problems with pages in XML format.

One best alternative may be inclusion of human expertise with automated system by using the content management software. This may be the useful alternative for the so called less funded libraries specially small academic and public libraries to provide lots of latest information and online documents to its users.

4. CONTENT MANAGEMENT SYSTEM

A content management system (CMS) supports the creation, management, distribution, publishing, and discovery of information. The wikipedia defines it as 'a software system used for content management. This includes computer files, image media, audio files, electronic documents and web content.' A content management system has various forms like web content management, workflow for articles, document management system etc. A web content management system is a software system used to manage and control a large, dynamic collection of web material [7].

A Web Content Management strategy is a repeatable method for-

- Identifying content requirements
- Creating consistently structured content for reuse
- Managing content in a definitive source
- Ensuring content complies with standards and guidelines
- Assembling content on demand to meet customers' needs

Components of CMS

A CMS basically has four parts [8]

I. Content creation

II. Content management

III. Publishing

IV. Presentation

CMS Modules

There are various modules which should be available with or can be configured in any CMS, which makes it simple, more attractive and acceptable.

Address Book : Manages a list of contacts, storing information like names, addresses, emails, phone numbers and more. It should also give permissions to allow users to update their own contact details.

Calendar Module : Allows posting of events to a calendar, which can be displayed in a typical calendar view or as a list of events. Allows posting of time, date and event description, and allows to add recurring events.

Content Rotator : Randomly displays a piece of text (which may contain images) to the user every time the page is refreshed.

Form Module : Allows the creation of forms that can be emailed and/or stored in the database. Can create forms with fields including checkboxes, radio buttons, text fields, dropdown boxes, date-time pickers and more.

Image Manager : A tie-in module that allows images to be uploaded and then used in the text editor.

News Feed System : Manages news / announcements on your website.

Private Message Centre : Allows users (currently for Intranet sites only) on the site to send and receive private messages.

Resource Manager : Allows you to upload Resource files such as pdf, MS word and Excel documents and other.

Search Module : Allows users to search the content of your site.

Text Module : This is a core module for the CMS that allows you to edit blocks of text on the site.

Blog Module : Manages a blog or online journal.

4.1. Types of CMS

There are several recognized types of content management systems [9]

Web content management systems (WCMS): These assist in automating various aspects of web publishing, such as wikis.

Integrated content management systems (I-CMS): These assist in managing enterprise documents and content

Digital Asset Management systems (DAM): These assist in managing the lifecycle of digital media (video, graphics, marketing materials, photos, multimedia presentations).

Publications management systems (P-CMS): These assist in managing the publications (manuals, books, help, guidelines, references) content life cycle.

Learning management systems (L-CMS): These assist in managing the web based learning content life cycle.

4.2. The open source CMS

A good number of open source content management softwares are freely available in the Internet. Each has especially of its own. Few of them are as follows-

i. Apache Lenya [http://lenya.apache.org/] : This is written in Java and based on open standard such as XML and XSTL. One of its core component is Cocoon from the Apache software foundation.

ii. ARIADNE [http://www.ariadne-cms.org/] : is an Open

Source, Multilingual Web Application Server and Content Management System built on PHP. Ariadne has a rich user interface which includes wizards, pulldown menus, and an extremely flexible and easy to use WYSIWYG editor.

iii. Back-end [http://back-end.org/]: based on PHP/ MySql and using phplibs templates.

iv. BiolinOS [http://www.bolinos.com/com/] : is a reliable Open Source Content Management System. BolinOS is a modular publication and communication platform for Internet / Web, developed in order to enable simple management of complex portals.

v. Cascade [http://sourceforge.net/projects/cascade] : perl driven web based CMS.

vi. DBPrism [http://www.dbprism.com.ar/index.html] : is an open source framework to generate dynamic XML from a database.

vii. e107 [http://e107.org/news.php] : a PHP/MySQL Website System

viii. EasyPublisher [http://easypublisher.com/] : Easy Publisher is a new system for Internet Content Management that allows to add content to the website or to the intranet which hasWYSIWYG editor.

ix. Jahia CMS and Portal Server 3.0 [http:// www.jahia.org/jahia/home.html] : Jahia is an integrated web content management and portal server; Written completely in the Java programming language; Multilanguage and I18N support.

x. Joomla [http://www.joomla.org/] : is one of the most powerful Open Source Content Management Systems.

xi. Jpublish [http://www.jpublish.org/] : JPublish is a powerful web publishing system designed to ensure a clean separation of developer roles.

xii. Kumera [http://www.cyber4.org/kumera/index.html]: is an Open Source Content Management System written in Perl and using XML for data storage, designed for small to medium web sites.

xiii. Metadot Portal Servre [http://www.metadot.net/] : Open Source Portal Server software for content management and virtual community, news and personalization.

xiv. PHPNuke [http://www.phpnuke.org/] : it is an Advanced Content Management System and is a news automated system specially designed to be used in Intranets and Internet.

xv. Silva [http://infrae.com/products/silva] : Silva is a powerful CMS for organizations that manage complex websites.

xvi. warp [http://www.romanianbusiness.info/warp/] : php/mysql open source content management system, e-commerce, WYSIWYG online HTML/RTF editor.

Among all the CMS, Drupal [http://drupal.org/] is one of the popular open source content management platform. Equipped with a powerful blend of features, Drupal can support a variety of websites ranging from personal weblogs to large community driven websites. It can also be combined with a number of freely available add-on modules like

- Blogs,
- Collaborative authoring environments,
- Forums,
- Peer-to-peer networking,
- Newsletters,
- Picture galleries,
- File uploads and downloads etc.

5. JOOMLA

Joomla is an award-winning Content Management System (CMS) that will help to build websites and other powerful online applications. Most important point is that Joomla is an open source solution that is freely available to everybody. Joomla is used all over the world to power everything from simple, personal homepages to complex corporate web applications. It can be used to easily manage every aspect of the website, from adding content and images to updating a product catalog or for online reservations etc. The actual power of Joomla is inherent in the application framework to create powerful add-ons and extensions. Joomla is flexible, simple, elegant, customizable and powerful CMS software.

System requirement

The following are the minimum requirements before installation of Joomla! 1.0.12 in a linux based system: [9]

- PHP 4.2.x or above - *http://php.net*
- MySQL 3.23.x or above - *http://mysql.org*
- Apache 1.13.19 or above - *http://apache.org*
- Joomla 1.0.12 – *http://developer.joomla.org*

Prior to beginning process of Joomla it should ensured that MySql database is functioning and Apache server is running. Then only, one should start installing and configuring Joomla.

Joomla Installation

- Unzipping the Joomla Core distribution file to a local directory on the local computer
- Then to FTP the files to the host server placing them either directly under, or in, a directory under the web server root.

- After uploading the files and folders, go to homepage i.e. http://www.yoursite.com or http://yoursite.com/ joomla_folder .

A pre-installation check page will be generated by Joomla to verify the following :

- Was everything uploaded to the web site?
- Did it remove (and back up) the old web site?
- Does it really have an Apache / MySQL / PHP Web server?
- Does it have a configuration.php file in the Joomla directory?

If everything runs fine then it will ask for licensing agreement. If agreed, then automatically it will open the page for configuring MySql Database. This way the setup will be completed and Joomla will be ready to function. The content management system Joomla acts as finder for all sources such as repository, harvester, news feeds and also provides user interface for search, harvester and retrieval.

Application

To see how Joomla creates an interface for its main menu and its items work, we need to visit the prototype page by typing the URL as: *http://192.168.1.129/joomla/* which is shown in figure-1

Where (1) is main menu, (2) is user menu, (3) is top menu, (4) shows the various display modes and (5) shows the alphabetical browsing facilities.

We can view all web resource items in a single window, as shown in 4 (fig.1). If one select display mode as Alpha grouped it will display as in figure-2

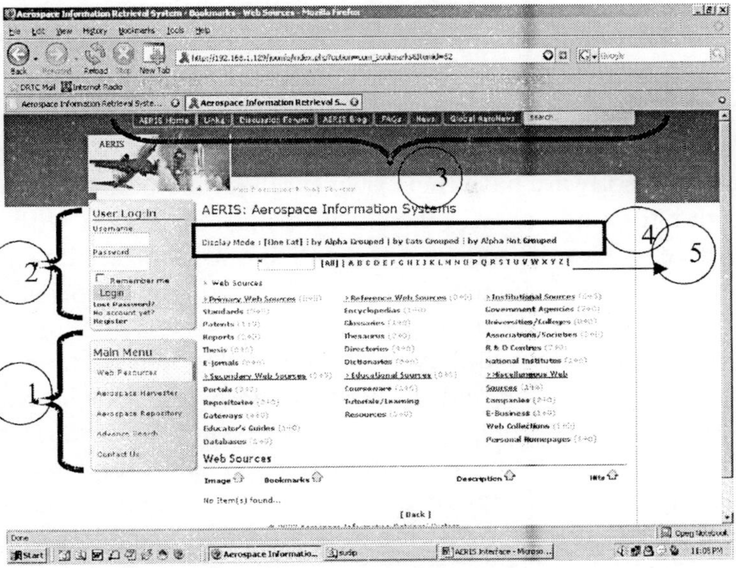

Fig. 1 : AERIS Interface [*http://192.168.1.129/joomla/*] (locally configured)

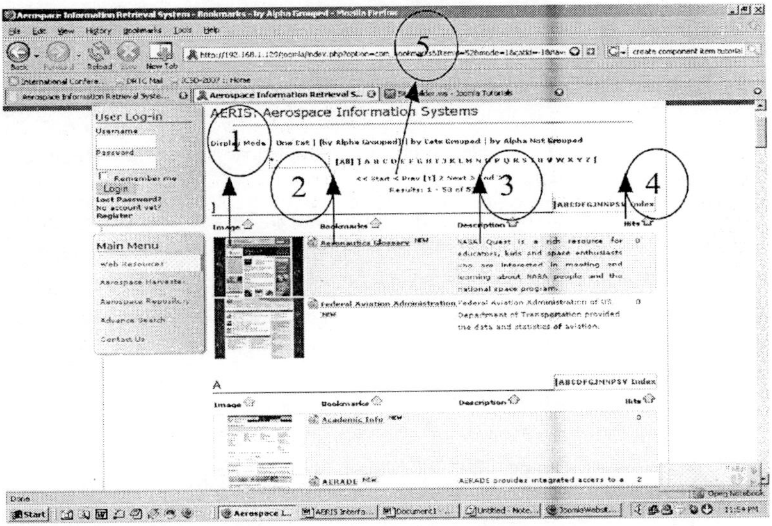

Fig. 2: List by alpha grouped

CONCLUSION

AERIS is an integrated system based on Joomla Content Management Software. We have integrated two more different types of software (1) DSpace digital repository and (2) PKP Metadata Harvester to provide value added services to the users. All these software have there own excellent features that help to put together an web based information system with a comprehensive collection. The CMS Joomla is also allowing 'integration' of document like resources (repositories + ejournals) with non-document like resources such as discussion forum, news, blogs and events in the concerned domain of AS&T. The idea behind developing these tools for storing information was to help users in easy access and quick retrieval of relevant documents in the library. This is a prototype work and illustrative data have been used for Aerospace Science and Technology, however this method can be applicable to any individual subject or universe of subject as a whole.

REFERENCE

1. Besser, Howard. From Internet to Information Super Highway. In James Brook and Iain A Boal (eds), Resisting the virtual life: the culture and politics of information, San Francisco: CityLights, 1995. 59-70p.
2. SAUNDERS (L. M.) (Ed.). The Virtual Library: Visions and Realities, Meckler Publishing, 1993.
3. Sizing The Internet is a site that presents the full text of many essential works in the literature of Internet (*http://www.cyveillance.com/resources/library.asp*).
4. Su (Louise T.). Developing a comprehensive and systematic model of user evaluation of Web-based Search Engine. In: Proceedings of 18th Annual National Online Meeting, New York. Learned Information. Medford, NJ. 1997. 335-344p.
5. LAWRENCE (Steve) and GILES, (C. Lee). Searching the World Wide Web. Science, Vol. 280, April 1998. 98-100p.
6. LAWRENCE (Steve) and GILES, (C. Lee). Searching the World Wide Web. Science, Vol. 280, April 1998. 98-100p.

7. Wikipedia : a free Online Encyclopedia. (2006). Content management system. Retrieved January 15, 2007, from Wikipedia : a free Online Encyclopedia on the World Wide Web: *http://en.wikipedia.org/wiki/Content_management_system*

8. James, Robertson. (June 3, 2003). So, what is a content management system? KM Column. Retrieved January 15, 2007, from *http://www.steptwo.com.au/papers/kmc_what/index.html*

9. System requirements is a site that presents the specification and requirements to build Joomla. *(http://help.joomla.org/content/view/34/132/)*

11

Open Source Software and Koha

Dr. Rajani Mishra
Assistant Professor
Lecturer, Deptt. of Lib. & Inf. Sc. BHU
rajanimishra5@gmail.com

ABSTRACT

Paper discusses the features of advanced version of 'KOHA' the very first open source software. States, various features of koha like Koha-ZOOM, OpeNCIP, and OpenTranslator (a powerful tool for web based federated search. Also states the benefits of Open Source Software.

Keywords : Koha-ZOOM, OpeNCIP, OpenTranslator.

1. INTRODUCTION

Library automation has become must in the changing world scenario. 20th century saw the emergence of ICTs and their use in the libraries. Application of the computers has led to the changed services and sources in the libraries. To provide services to their vendors quickly and efficiently librarians resorted to library automation. Currently Library management Software are integrated systems based on relational database approach, in which system files are integrated in such a way that any change in a single file can activate appropriate change in the related files. These software, being developed by the vendors were very costly and incur a huge sum of their financed money and also make them vendor dependent for any fault. This led the professional to think differently and the product was the **Open Source Software**.

2. WHAT IS OPEN SOURCE SOFTWARE?

LMSs are of two types closed source commercial and open source free to use products. The prerequisite for any program to be called "free" is if it can be used for any purpose, can be adopted for the individual need, source code and the program can be redistributed to others so that any one who wants may get it easily. In other words any software is supposed to be free if it gives user the freedom to share study and modify it. [1]

According to OSI (Open Source Initiative, 2003a) "Open source promotes software reliability and quality by supporting independent peer review and rapid evaluation of source code. To be certified as open source, the license of a program must guarantee the right to read, redistribute modify and use it freely" states Mukhopadhyay P. S. [2]

Open source movement was started by Richard Stallman in 1983. And the term "Open Source" was given by Christine Peterson of the Foresight Institute in 1997.

There is a clear cut division between Open Source Free software and "freeware" which is proprietary software made available free of charge, users usually cannot study, modify, or redistribute freeware whereas in open source software users are free to do such jobs. A free program can potentially be included in a free operating system such as Linux system. [3]

The open source products has a capability of being

tailored to suite the needs and circumstances of individual libraries. Its documents are accessible by all who need them. Easy debugging is another feature. Open source software is not covered under individual "Intellectual Property Rights."

3. WHY OPEN SOURCE PROGRAMS?

Since libraries or facing a steep financial crunch, the use of the library materials have increased manifold, the information explosion and more importantly the dependency upon the vendors for any fault in the proprietary software has led the development of open source programs. OSS licenses allow libraries to cut budget on software and use it to other areas that require more funds; OSS product is not locked into a single vendor says Mukhopadhyay P. S. "Closed source programs continue to suffer security and performance vulnerabilities and skyrocket in prices." [4]

Some of the open source software are **Apache**, which means anyone can access the source code of **Apache** and make changes in the source code, **Linux** (an operating system), **Mozilla**, a web browser derived from Netscape, **Open Office**, (in place of MS Office); and "**Perl**", a very powerful programming language, **MySQL** and **Postgre SQL** for database management.

Open source programs either, can be downloaded and run for free or can be taken from the vendors (Red Hat and SuSE) who have developed pre-packaged versions of open source software at a comparatively lower cost. Due to availability of code principles and universal open standards, libraries and library projects can develop open source software. In fact, one of the Keystone Principles of the U.S. Association of Research Libraries states, "Libraries will create interoperability in the systems they develop and create open source software for the access, dissemination, and management of information." (Keystone Principles, 2003, section 2.4).

4. BENEFITS OF OSS

1. OSS helps libraries to be self reliant.
2. Libraries can develop the software according to the need of their clients.
3. It helps libraries to manage their finances in a cost effective manner i.e. they can use the leftover fund in some other useful and productive services.
4. In OSS debugging of the fault is an important application.
5. More effective and useful in the research and development activities.
6. Provides new dimension to the services and status of the library professionals.
7. OSS is independent of the type and size of the library.
8. It upgrades the skills of the librarians who implement, manage and support the immense variety of constantly developing information products and services.

OSS- Koha: "KOHA" the first open source integrated library solution was developed by Katipo Communications Limited of Wellingoton, NewZealand for the Horowhenua Library Trust, a regional library system located near Wellingoton. Its first version came out in 2000. Now it is in its third version. Koha uses open source tools like Pearl, MySQL and Apache that runs under Linux and uses Telnet to communicate. It supports multiple book budgets and suppliers, real time budget information for Acquisition. Catalogue updates fast and slick, Supports MARC 21 and UNIMARC bibliographic format for cataloging. One can get all member information on one page. Advanced version of Koha has features like Koha-ZOOM, OpenNCIP and OpenTranslator.

Koha ZOOM: Koha-ZOOM is meant for very large integrated library system. Its search engine is based on "Zebra plugin" which can read structured records practically in any input format (e.g., email, XML, MARC) and allows access to the records through exact Boolean search expressions and relevance ranking, field weighting, truncation, stemming, use of fuzzy operators, language-specific indexing, sorting, etc. Zebra is a high-performance indexing and retrieval engine. It is also suitable for nested searching, by language, year and library type, thus very large business libraries can adopt Koha Zoom. In the Advanced search section, it has features like sub-type limits based on audience, content, and format which utilizes coded values in the MARC record.

It supports large data sets (tens of millions of records) and includes support for SRU, Z39.50 and several query languages: CCL, CQL, and PQF. Indexes are updated in real-time with circulation transactions, enabling limits by availability and statuses. [5] Those libraries which do not want to use Zebra they can opt for noZebra option in which bibliographic and authority data is indexed in the RDBMS.

Koha-3 supports a number of important library search and retrieval standards, and micro formats, such as SRU/W, Z39.50, UnAPI and COinS/OpenURL.

ZOOM'S OPAC is user friendly. Users can sort their results by: author, title, date published and any other field the library chooses. If they further want to narrow their search results, by Branch (of the library), Series title, currently available items on particular subject in a particular library and group of libraries? Koha-ZOOM's users with the help of OPAC can integrate content from external web services to expand and improve the information one needs. [6]

OpeNCIP is an open source implementation of the Standard Interchange Protocol (SIP) used by self-check terminals and public internet terminals in libraries, uses the ANSI/NISO Z39.83-2002 NCIP Standard for circulation interchange protocol. NCIP is a protocol for the exchange of borrower and circulation data between library systems. It allows libraries with disparate database and information management systems to share and control access to resources. Since it was available freely on the net with its source code and was included by the Liblime in Koha-3, made the software more powerful. [7]

OpenTranslator is a powerful tool for web based federated search service using SRU/SRW/Z39.50 protocol allows the database access. It does not accesses the database itself but uses another open source service called Pazapar2 for licensed database, free databases catalogs, Z39.50, Telnet and proprietary databases.[8]

5. CONCLUSION

Libraries are resorting to the automation based on Open source software. There is a long list of software in this group both indigenous as well as developed by west. “KOHA” the first in the list of OSS is now in its third version. It has developed a number of features over its predecessor and is widely available on the net for its use.

REFERENCES

1. http://en.wikipedia.org/wiki/Free_software definition#See_also downloaded on 18-02-09
2. Mukhopadhayay Parthsarathi. (2006). Five Laws and Ten Commandments: The Open Road of Library Automation in India. Proceedings of the National Seminar on Opne Source Movement-Asian Perspective, XXII, IIT Roorkee, 2006. IASLIC, Kolkata. 2006. p. 27-36.
3. http://www.fsf.org/licensing/essays/categories.html downloaded on 18-02-09
4. Same as ref. no. 2.
5. http://www.koha.org/about-koha/news/nr1206253557.html downloaded on 16-02-09
6. http://liblime.com/products/koha/koha-zoom downloaded on 16-02-09
7. http://openncip.org/ downloaded on 16-02-09
8. http://en.wikipedia.org/wiki/Liblime downloaded on 16-02-09

12

A Study of Open Source Software (Newgenlib) And Application of RFID Technology in Libraries

Satish Kumar Arya
Assistant Librarian, FJS,
Mody Institute of Technology & Science
Deemed University, Laxmangarh-332 311
aryasatish83@gmail.com

Radha Krishna Kishore Patnala
In-Charge Librarian, FET,
Mody Institute of Technology & Science
Deemed University, Laxmangarh-332 311
rkkissore@gmail.com

ABSTRACT

This article attempts to describe the concept of Open Source Software and RFID Technology. It highlights the features of NewGenLib open source software, and shows position of RFID in an OSS. Article also covers application of RFID in libraries, its benefits, limitations and emphasis to develop free open source software for RFID.

Keywords: Library Automation, NewGenLib, Open Source Software, RFID.

1. INTRODUCTION

Open source is a software development model as well as a software distribution model. In this model the source code of programs is made freely available with the software itself so that anyone can see, change, and distribute it provided they abide by the accompanying license. In this sense, Open Source is similar to peer review, which is used to strengthen the progress of scholarly communication. The open source software differs from the closed source or proprietary software which may only be obtained by some form of payment, either by purchase or by leasing. The difference between the two is the freedom to modify the software. An open system is a design philosophy antithetical to solutions designed to be proprietary. The idea behind it is that institutions, such as libraries, can build a combination of components and deliver services that include several vendors' offerings. Thus, for instance, a library might use an integrated library system from one of the major vendors in combination with an open source product developed by another library or by itself in order to better meet its internal or users' requirements.

2. DEFINITION

According to Open Source Initiative (http://www.opensource.org/):

"Open source promotes software reliability and quality by supporting independent peer review and rapid evolution of source code. To be certified as open source, the license of a program must guarantee the right to read, redistribute, modify, and use it freely."

The GNU website <www.gnu.org/philosophy/free-sw.html> offers the following definition of OSS:

i. The freedom to run the program, for any purpose (freedom 0).

ii. The freedom to study how the program works, and adapt it to your needs (freedom 1). Access to the source code is a precondition for this.

iii. The freedom to redistribute copies so you can help your neighbor (freedom 2).

iv. The freedom to improve the program, and release your improvements to the public, so that the whole community benefits (freedom 3). Access to the source code is a precondition for this.

3. CHARACTERISTICS OF OPEN SOURCE SOFTWARE

The Open Source Initiative (OSI) identified ten criteria for a software product to be open source:

i. Be freely distributable : The software license cannot restrict anyone from selling or giving away the software as part of a larger system or aggregation of programs. The license cannot require royalties or fees for such sale.

ii. Includes the source code: The source code for the program must be freely available, and it must be possible to distribute the source code as well as the compiled form of the program. Deliberately obfuscated source code is not allowed.

iii. Allows for derived works : The license must allow modification of and derived works from the original. In addition, it must allow these modifications and derivatives to be distributed under the same terms as the original software license.

iv. Maintains the integrity of the original source code: The license may restrict source code from being distributed in a modified form only if the license allows the distribution of patch files with the source code to allow for program modifications at build time. This allows the consumer to know who made what changes to the code without impinging on the rights of the original creator.

v. Not discriminate against persons or groups: The license must not discriminate against any person or group of persons.

vi. Not discriminate against fields of endeavor: The license must not restrict anyone from making use of the program in a specific field of endeavor.

vii. Provides for the distribution of the license: The rights attached to the program must apply to everyone the program is distributed to, without their having to execute additional licenses.

viii. Not be specific to a product: The rights attached to a program must not depend on the program being part of a particular software distribution package. This does not mean that one program cannot depend on another program to enable functionality.

ix. Not restrict other software: The license cannot place restrictions on other software that is distributed along with the licensed software. That is, one piece of software cannot prevent another piece of software from being used.

x. Be technology neutral: No provision of the license may be predicated on any individual technology or style of interface.

4. NEWGENLIB

NewGenLib is library automation software. It has functionalities that enable a library to manage its housekeeping operations, viz., acquisition of books and other materials, creation and maintenance of its catalogue database, circulation of its holdings, etc. In addition, however, NewGenLib allows a library to define its own network of libraries. One library in the network called the Host library installs the software on its public-domain server and then configures other libraries as Associate libraries on its network. NewGenLib becomes an open source product at the end of 2007. But before becoming an open source product, it was already in use in 122 libraries, mainly in India but also including installations in Syria (3), Sudan and Cambodia. It is now freely available as open source under the most widely used free software license, GNU General Public License (GNU GPL) v3. Since becoming open source under GNU GPL, considerable interest has been shown in the software.

A. Salient features of NewGenLib Software

i. Freedom: Available under GNU GPL v3

ii. Functional modules are completely web based. Uses Java Web Start™ Technology

iii. Compatibility - Complies with international metadata and interoperability standards: MARC-21, MARC-XML, z39.50, SRU/W, OAI-PMH

iv. Uses chiefly open source components

v. Scalable, manageable and efficient

vi. OS independent - Windows and Linux flavours available

vii. z39.50 Client for federated searching

viii. RFID integration

ix. Networking – Hierarchical and Distributed networks

x. Automated email/instant messaging integrated into different functions of the software

xi. Form letters are configurable and use XML-based Open Office templates

xii. Extensive use of set up parameters enabling easy configuration of the software to suit specific needs, e.g., in defining patron privileges

xiii. Supports multi-user and multiple security levels

xiv. Allows digital attachments to metadata

xv. Internationalized application (I18N)

xvi. Unicode 3.0 complaint

xvii. Arabic version available

xviii. Easily extensible to support other languages

xix. Data entry, storage, retrieval in any (Unicode 3.0) language

B. Functional modules of NewGenLib

i. Acquisitions

ii. Technical processing and database development

iii. Circulation Control

iv. Online Public Access Catalogue

v. Serials Management

vi. Administration and system setup

C. Position of RFID in a Circulation Module of NewGenLib

RFID, that stands for Radio Frequency Identification technology is the latest technology, used for library transaction, inventory functions and theft detection system. It uses radio waves to identify individual items automatically and can be used anywhere that needed a unique identification. The protocol named, Radio Frequency ID (RFID) protocol is available with NewGenLib software for implementing RFID in library. But access to this protocol is provided specifically on payment to those libraries that need this. A folder called NewGenLibFiles and several sub-folders within this basically contain files required by the NewGenLib application. Under this folder NewGenLibFiles, the sub folder called NCIP Schema contains schema related to RFID security and several XML files specifying the messages that are exchanged between NewGenLib and the RFID workstations and gates.

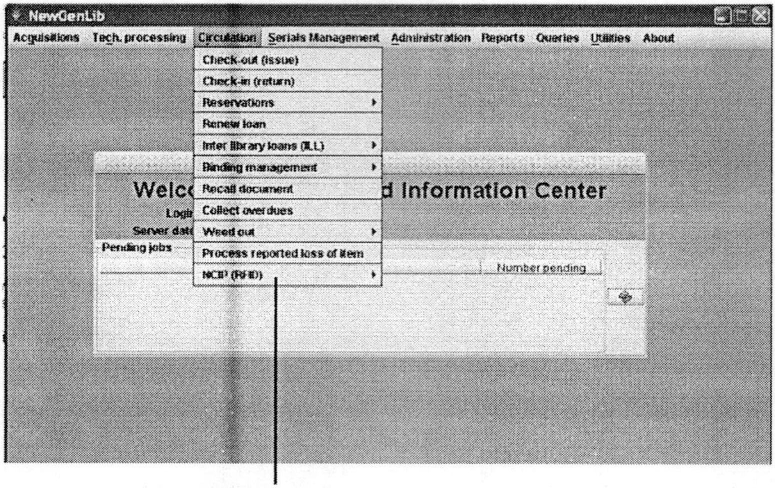

Option of RFID in NewGenLib

Fig. 1: Position of RFID in NewGenLib Software (Circulation)

5. COMPONENTS OF AN RFID SYSTEM

An RFID system plays an important role within the library. A comprehensive RFID system has four components:

i. RFID tags that are electronically programmed with unique information;

ii. Readers or sensors to interrogate the tags;

iii. Antenna; and

iv. A server or docking station on which the software that interfaces with the automated library system is loaded. It is also possible to distribute the software among the readers and sensors.

6. RFID APPLICATION IN LIBRARIES

Library security system : The library security system through RFID can be ensured through Electronic Article Surveillance (EAS) Gate, which is the anti-theft part of the RFID Library Management System using the RFID tags. RFID tags provide enhanced security as instant alarms can designate if patron passes through security gates with documents that has not been checked out and alarm sound will alert library.

Book Drop or Return : The book identified at RFID reader unit, which is located inside the book return slot and then placed in a bin. It automatically checks in documents.

RFID checkout or borrowing station: Without any assistance from library staff, it permits patrons to follow the touch screen menu and checkout documents. The patron's cards and their stack of documents are read simultaneously.

Smart and quick inventory : This is basically used to take inventory and locate missing items without closing the library. The RFID inventory control system consists of two parts, first a hand-held RFID reader that can use for stocktaking of books on the shelves and second is the software that uses to generate inventory repots about the collected data.

7. BENEFITS OF RFID IN LIBRARIES

i. Easier and faster scanning of data, than the old barcode technology.

ii. 100% read detection rate.

iii. Automated return and sorting of items (book drop machine).

iv. High-speed inventory (accuracy).

v. Simplified patron self-checking.

8. LIMITATIONS OF RFID IN LIBRARIES

i. Higher cost than barcodes.

ii. No international Standards.

iii. There is a possibility that user may return book in damage condition in case of self-check in/ Book Drop system.

iv. Removal of tags circumvents RFID system.

v. Existing library building may not be suitable for the RFID System.

vi. Library become full of radiation and it may cause various health problems, especially for staff.

9. CONCLUSION

In conclusion it can be said that, today libraries need to adopt latest technologies available to upgrade there present traditional system. These technologies would help libraries to reduce the workload and to provide the faster and easy services to the library users. There are number of technologies available to update our library system. RFID is the one, which help us to reduce our workload a lot. It helps not only in reducing the workload but also in identifying the thefts, which reduce the loss of books. But, however every new technology comes at a cost. In order to premeditate those cost, efforts must be undertaken to guide its development and implementation. One way to deal with this cost issue is to create and promote free open source software for RFID. The transparency, openness and affordability of free open source software for RFID will allow consumers to have more control over this technology; and will allow the creation of certification programmes to control the usage of the information generated by the ubiquitous computers. On the commercial side, the availability of free open source software for RFID will allow the massive adoption of this revolutionary technology by all supply chain partners, significantly reducing adoption costs. NewGenLib, an Integrated Library Management System, which is now freely available, is providing the facility of RFID technology, but access to RFID protocol is provided specifically on payment to those libraries that need this. This study concludes that there is need to develop free open source software approach for RFID.

REFERENCES

1. Arya, Satish (2007). 'Open source software for libraries: A trend report' (Pages 29-33) submitted project work at Department of Library & Information Science, University of Delhi.
2. *NewGenLib Available at:* http://www.verussolutions.biz/web/, *Access on 09/12/2008*
3. NewGenLib Available at:*http://www.verussolutions.biz/web/node/3* Access on 09/12/2008
4. NewGenLib Available at *http://www.verussolutions.biz/web/node/4* Access on 09/12/2008
5. NewGenLib Available at *http://www.verussolutions.biz/web/node/18* Access on 09/12/2008
6. Ebenezer, Catherine (2002). 'Trends in integrated library system'. *Vine*, 32 (4).
7. Zaheeruddin, Asif (2005). 'Integrating the supply chain with RFID: A technical and business analysis'. *RFIDjournal.com.*
8. RFID Journal Available at *http://www.rfid-library.com/default.html* Access on 09/12/2008
9. Parthasarathi, Mukhopadhayay (2006). 'Five laws and ten commandments: The open road library automation in India'. *XXII IASLIC National seminar. IIT Roorkee,* (2006).
10. Moran, Humberto (2006). 'Open source software: The right IPR approach to RFID'.*RFID Workshop*, June (2006).
11. Bhardwaj, Rajesh Kr. (2000). 'A practical approach to library automation'. Library progress (International), 20 (1).
12. NewGenLib user manual Available at *http://downloads.sourceforge.net/newgenlib/UserManualAllModules.pdf* Access on 01/12/2008

13

Managing Leader and Control Fields of Marc21 Bibliographic Format in Floss Based LMSS: Benchmarking of Koha and Newgenlib

Parthasarathi Mukhopadhya
Assistant Professor
Department of Library and Information Science
The University of Burdwan, Burdwan – 713 104
psmukhopadhyay@gmail.com

ABSTRACT

This paper deals with implementation of MARC 21 bibliographic framework in general and treatment of Leader and Control fields in particular in two advanced level FLOSS based LMSs namely Koha and NewGenlib. It also traces out the advantages and benefits of FLOSS based LMSs in comparison with commercial close source LMSs available in India. Finally put side by sides the utilities provided by Koha and NewGenLib in managing Leader and Control fields of MARC 21 bibliographic format.

Keywords : Free Library Open Source Library Software (FLOSS), NewGenLib, KOHA, LMS, MARC21.

1. INTRODUCTION

Free/Libre Open Source Software (FLOSS) is not a new initiative (remember the efforts of R M Stallman) but the term "open source" itself has been a relative latecomer. Christine Peterson of the Foresight Institute proposed the term *open source* in late 1997 during a meeting of small group of open source movement gurus (Raymond, 2001). There are many people and agencies who provided definitions and features of FLOSS e.g. according to OSI (Open Source Initiative, 2003a) - "*Open source promotes software reliability and quality by supporting independent peer review and rapid evaluation of source code. To be certified as open source, the license of a program must guarantee the right to read, redistribute, modify, and use it freely*". Analysis of definitions given by Chudnov (1999), Raymond (1996), Moody (2001), and Morgan (2002), identifies following attributes of OSS –

- OSS is typically created and maintained by developers crossing institutional and national boundaries, collaborating by using Internet based communications and development tools;
- OSS development process follows the famous Linus's law – "Release early, release often and listen to users";
- Quality, not profit, drives open source developers who take personal pride in seeing their working solutions adopted; and
- Intellectual property rights to open source software belong to anyone who helps to build it or simply use it and is not locked to any single vendor or institutions.

Libraries and open source software are a natural fit. Both promote learning and understanding through the dissemination of information. One of the *Keystone Principles* (Association of Research Libraries, 2004) of Association of Research Libraries (ARL) states, "Libraries will create interoperability in the systems they develop and create open source software for the access, dissemination, and management of information". Library automation is an important event from which future benefits will emerge. It is centered on Library Management Software (LMS). A typical LMS supports selection, ordering, acquisition, processing, circulation, serials control, dissemination of information services and also extend help in library administration, planning and decision making process as a management tool. Chudnov (1999) identified three factors – fund, freedom and fraternity, which are advancing the use of FLOSS in libraries:

- OSS licenses allow libraries to cut budget on software and use it to other areas that require more funds;
- OSS product is not locked into a single vendor. Thus even if a library uses an open source system from one vendor, it might choose to buy technical support from another company or get it from in-house experts; and
- The entire library community might share the responsibility of solving information systems accessibility issues.

2. LIBRARY AUTOMATION: COMMERCIAL OR OPEN – WHICH WAY?

Digital Library Federation (2004) of USA considers and advocates use of OSS in libraries in its draft report on the basis of following reasons. These are as follows:

- OSS is an economical alternative to libraries' reliance upon commercially supplied software. It means that the real costs involved in the development, maintenance, and use of OSS software are lower than those associated with commercial software (license, upgrading and maintenance fees);
- OSS is essential if libraries are to develop software and systems that meet their patrons' needs. With OSS the IT infrastructure for library operations and services can be:

- Open (that is, built according to open standards and as such potentially interoperable with other software and systems);
- Ubiquitously available to libraries;
- Capable of being tailored to suit the needs and circumstances of individual libraries;
- Documented (and documentation is accessible to all); and
- Modified and corrected more effectively ("many eyeballs make bugs shallow").

• OSS ensures that library systems and online services will be more functional (Open Source Initiative, 2003b) for patrons because libraries, through OSS movement, -

- Are reinserted into the research and development process that results in new systems and software;
- Can share a stake in software development and thereby have greater influence over (and as a result take a greater interest in specification of) the functional and performance requirements associated with particular software tools and systems;
- Can motivate and empower systems librarians and related technical staff by encouraging creativity and positioning them to make a difference; and
- Are able to collaborate more easily with experts of other similar domains engaged in common research and development activities.

• OSS democratizes the use of software applications in libraries irrespective of the type or size of the library (Haravu, 2004; Mukhopahyay, 2005).

Certainly OSS provides new opportunities in the development of library system and services in an economic way (Mukhopadhyay, 2006, 2008; Dasgupta, 2005). But at this point it is too early to say that FLOSS based LMSs are all set to replace proprietary software. In fact the issue is more whether FLOSS based LMSs can provide a viable alternative and obviously there remain a number of obstacles to its wider adoption. First of all, FLOSS based LMSs generally demands higher level of technical knowledge to install and maintain it. Users who migrate to open source applications face a steep learning curve and owing to this reason, the implementation of open source solutions today tends to be restricted to infrastructure and other "invisible" applications such as servers, where technical personnel are responsible for their installation and management. Currently, for instance, around 60 percent of the world's Web sites run on Apache web server (NUA, 2006, Open Source Initiative, 2007). FLOSS based LMSs, then, offers new opportunities but also raises a number of challenges for the library and information community (Mulhopadhyay, 2008). Many library automation software vendors say (Poynder, 2001) that open source isn't an easy option for libraries as it requires them to take more personal responsibility for their system and they have to carry the burden of development themselves, or to turn to a commercial vendor to mould the product to their needs. True, but one should not forget that FLOSS is not only a software development and delivery model, it is also a software solution model that helps users through discussion forums, FAQ (Frequently Asked Questions), online chats, manuals and developer's guides. In this context we may quote Andy Powell (2002), assistant director of the U.K. Office for Library and Information Networking (UKOLN) - "You might well need a higher level of technical understanding, but with good open source solutions help is often just an e-mail message away".

3. FLOSS BASED LMSS: AVAILABILITY AND APPLICATIONS

There are many open source software in the domain of library automation now but Koha appeared first in the year 1999. Mukhopadhyay (2008) identified a set of sixteen FLOSS based LMSs in his book on Koha. These are listed as below (along with the required companion software).

i. Avanti (FLOSS based Dependencies : Java Run Time Environment (JRE), Any Web server, PicoDB); URL: http://home.earthlink.net/~schlumpf/avanti/index.html

ii. Emilda (FLOSS based Dependencies : Apache , PERL, MySQL, PHP, Zebra server, YAZ toolkit); URL: http://www.emilda.org/

iii. Evergeen (FLOSS based Dependencies : Apache , PERL, MySQL, PHP, Zebra server, YAZ toolkit); URL: http://www.emilda.org/

iv. FireFly (FLOSS based Dependencies : Any Web server, Any SQL, Python & PHP); URL: http://savannah.nongnu.org/projects/firefly/

v. GNU Library Management System (GLIBMS) (FLOSS based Dependencies : Any Web server, PostGreSQL, PHP, PERL); URL: http://sourceforge.net/projects/glibs/

vi. GNUTeca (FLOSS based Dependencies : Apache, PostGreSQL PHP); URL: http://gnuteca.codigolivre.org.br/

vii. Karuna (FLOSS based Dependencies : Apache, PHP, PostGreSQL); URL: http://sarovar.org/projects/karuna/

viii. Koha (FLOSS based Dependencies : Apache, MySQL, PERL); URL: http://www.koha.org/

ix. LearningAccess ILS (FLOSS based Dependencies : Apache, MySQL, PHP, YAZ); URL: http://www.learningaccess.org/website/techdev/ils.php

x. NewGenLib (FLOSS based Dependencies : Java Servlet Engine (JBOSS Tomcat), Java SDK, PostGreSQL); URL: http://www.newgenlib.com/

xi. OpenBiblio (FLOSS based Dependencies : Apache/ Any Web server, MySQL, PHP); URL: http://obiblio.sourceforge.net/

xii. OpenBook (FLOSS based Dependencies : Apache, PERL, MySQL); URL: http://www.trfoundation.org/projects/faq.html

xii. PHPMyBibli (FLOSS based Dependencies : Any Web server, MySQL, PHP); URL: http://phpmybibli.sourceforge.net/

xiv. PHPMyLibrary (FLOSS based Dependencie) : Apache, MySQL, PHP); URL: http://phpmylibrary.sourceforge.net/

xv. PYTHEAS (FLOSS based Dependencies) : JDK version 1.4 and above, MySQL, Apache-Tomcat Web server); URL: http://zeus.uwindsor.ca/library/leddy/people/art/pytheas/index.html

xvi. WEBLIS (FLOSS based Dependencies) : CDS/ISIS, Any Web server, ISIS.DLL); URL: http://www.unesco.org/isis/files/weblis.zip

Most of these LMSs are in their infancy. The mature LMS block includes Emilda, Evergreen, Koha, NewGenLib, PHPMyLibrary and WEBLIS. Evergreen is software for managing union catalogue of group of libraries. Three LMSs of the mature FLOSS based LMS group namely Emilda, Koha and NewGenLib support MARC 21 bibliographic format. In this paper we are considering management of Leader and Control tags/fields (the so called complex tags of MARC 21 bibliographic format) in Koha and NewGenLib. These FLOSS based LMSs are selected on the basis of their maturity and user base.

4. USE OF MARC 21 BIBLIOGRAPHIC FORMAT IN KOHA AND NEWGENLIB

The rapid development in computer communication engineering, availability of Internet and WWW in public domain and growth in cross-border data flow during the first half of 1990s made national boundaries irrelevant in exchanging bibliographic information. As a result, the Library of Congress (LoC) and the National Library of Canada harmonized the USMARC and CANMARC formats in a single edition in early 1999 under a new name MARC 21. The British Library in 2001decided to adopt MARC 21 (Bowman, 2002) and this way MARC 21 bibliographic format achieved the status of **de facto** international bibliographic format. MARC 21 format is a family of five coordinated formats:

MARC 21 format for bibliographic data: This format contains specification for encoding data elements required to describe, retrieve and control different forms of bibliographic items such as books, serials, computer files, maps, music, visual materials etc.;

MARC 21 format for holdings data: This format specifies encoding of data elements related to holdings and location information for all forms of materials;

MARC 21 format for classification data: This format prescribes encoding of data elements pertinent to classification numbers and associated captions;

MARC 21 format for authority data: It contains format specifications for encoding data elements relating to bibliographic records that may be subject to authority control; and

MARC 21 format for community information: This format provides specifications for encoding data elements related to non-bibliographic resources that fulfill the information needs of a community.

MARC 21 bibliographic format is composed of three elements – record structure, content designation, and the data content of the record. The record structure of MARC 21 family of formats is completely compatible with ISO-2709 or ANSI/NISO Z39.2. The record structure of MARC 21 bibliographic format consists of three main components – leader, directory

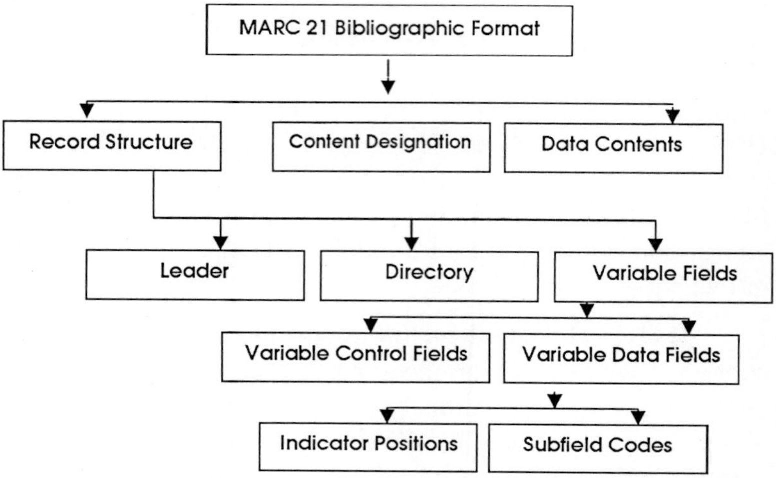

and variable fields (Library of Congress, 2004). The variable fields of MARC 21 bibliographic format are divided into two basic types – variable control fields and variable data fields. Variable data fields may again be divided into two kinds of content designations – indicator positions and subfield codes. A schematic presentation may be helpful to understand the complex MARC 21 record structure as given below.

The Bibliographic format blocks of MARC 21 include a few areas or groups of fields. These are –

- Leader and Control Fields (00X);
- 0XX = Control information, numbers, codes
- 1XX = Main entry
- 2XX = Titles, edition, imprint
- 3XX = Physical description, etc.
- 4XX = Series statements
- 5XX = Notes
- 6XX = Subject access fields
- 7XX = Name, etc. added entries or series; linking
- 8XX = Series added entries; holdings and locations

- 9XX = Reserved for local implementation

Both Koha and NewGenLib come with a default data entry framework containing a set of MARC 21 tags/subfields. NewGenLib provides three different templates for entering bibliographic data – Simple, General and MARC 21 based framework. In case of first two templates of NewGenLib, cataloguers can see only the labels for bibliographic data designed on the basis of ISDB (Monograph). The last option provides a data entry framework where cataloguers are free to use a full-fledged MARC 21 based data entry worksheet. In Koha, there is only one data entry template which is based on MARC 21 framework. This default framework can be utilized to design and develop number of frameworks as required by the concerned library (e.g. one for monograph, taking tags and subfields required for monograph; one for serials, taking tags and subfields required for monograph etc.). The concept is quite similar to the CDS/ISIS database utility of creating any number of worksheets from a single FDT. Here, all the tags and subfields of MARC 21 bibliographic format are preloaded in Koha, and the librarian needs to create the required bibliographic data entry frameworks by selecting appropriate tags and subfields.

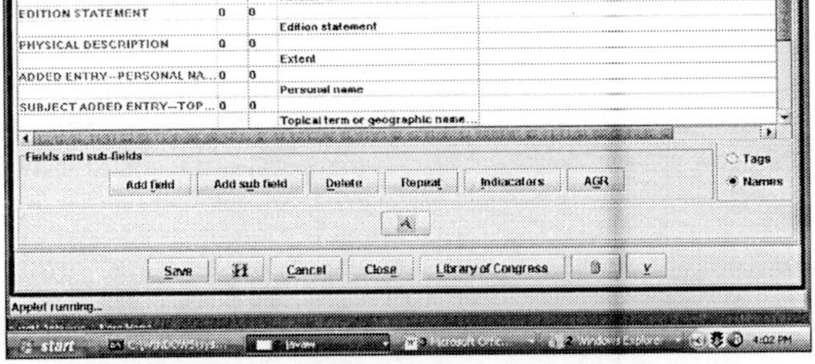

Fig. 1: MARC 21 based framework of NewGenLib

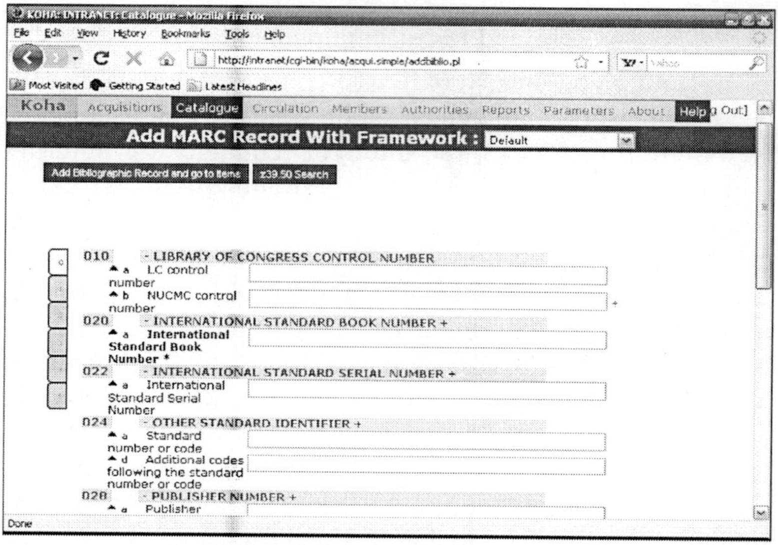

Fig. 2: MARC 21 based framework of Koha

5. LEADER AND CONTROL FIELDS OF MARC 21 BIBLIOGRAPHIC FORMAT

Leader and Control fields of MARC 21 bibliographic format are important areas for managing data entry activities in standardized manner.

5.1 Leader

There are 24 positions in the Leader, numbered from 00 to 23. The character positions for MARC 21 bibliographic format are as follows -

MARC 21 Bibliographic Fields (Leader)

00-04	Logical record length
05	Record status (c- Corrected, d- Deleted, n- New, a- Increase in encoding level, p- Increase in encoding level for prepublication)
06	Type of record (Codes: a-g, i-k, m,o,r)

07	Bibliographic data (Codes: a-d, m,s)
08	Type of record
09	Character coding scheme (#- MARC-8, a- UCS/ Unicode)
10	Indicator count
11	Subfield code length
12-16	Base address of data
17	Encoding level (Codes: #, 1-8, u,z)
18	Descriptive cataloguing form
19	Linked record requirement
20-23	Entry map

Leader of MARC 21 bibliographic format is a fixed field that comprises the first 24 character positions [00-23] of each record and provides necessary information for processing of the record. In the leader tag -

- Some character positions are computer-generated numeric string or number (e.g. Record length [00-04], Indicator count [10], Subfield code length [11], Base address [12-16], Entry map [20-23]);
- Some character positions are predefined (e.g. Length of the length-of-field [20] contains a 4, Length of the starting-character-position [21] contains a 5, Length of the implementation-defined portion [22] contains 0 and 23rd or the last character position contains a 0; and
- Some character positions require to be filled with coded data elements as prescribed by the MARC 21 community information format. These character positions may be termed as **user-defined positions** and are as follows –

05 – Record status (a – Increase in encoding level; c – Corrected or revised, d – Deleted, n – New, p - Increase in encoding level from prepublication);

06 – Type of record	(a- Language material (monography), c- Notated music, d- Manuscript notated music, e- Cartographic material, f - Manuscript cartographic material, g - Projected medium, i - Nonmusical sound recording, j - Musical sound recording, k - Two-dimensional nonprojectable graphic, m - Computer file, o – Kit, r - Three-dimensional artifact or naturally occurring object, t - Manuscript language material);
07- Bibliographic level	(a- Monographic component part, b- Serial component part, c- Collection, d- Subunit, i- Integrating resource, m- Monograph/item, s- Serial);
08- Hierarchic level	(# - No specific type, a- Archival);
09- Encoding	(# - MARC-8, a- UCS/Unicode);
17- Encoding	(# - Full level, 1- Full level, material not examined, 2 - Less-than-full level, material not examined, 3- Abbreviated level, 4- Core level, 5- Partial (preliminary) level, 7- Minimal level, 8- Prepublication level, u – Unknown, z- Not applicable);
18 - Descriptive	(# - Non-ISBD, a- AACR 2, i- ISBD, u- Unknown);
cataloging form	
19 - Linked record	(# - Related record not required, r- Related record required0;
requirement	

5.2 Control Fields

Fields 001-008 of MARC 21 bibliographic format contain control and coded information that are used for processing of bibliographic records. In this group, control fields 005, 006, 007 and 008 may be attached with pick up lists that include coded values for various character positions.

MARC 21 Bibliographic Fields(Variable Control Fields)

001 Control number

003 Control number identifier

004 Undefined

005 Date and time of last transaction

006 Fixed-length data elements — additional material characteristics

007 Physical description fixed field

008 Fixed-length data elements

The control fields 001 and 003 are library specific, and the field 004 is undefined. Therefore, we are concentrating here on four control fields namely 005, 006, 007 and 006.

1. **Control field 005:** This control field is meant for Date and time of last transaction (NR). This field must be filled in specific format like YYYYMMDDHHMMSS.MS e.g. 20090106233756.0 for 11 HR 37 Min. 57 Sec. of 6th January, 2009. Obviously, a small plugin, which can automatically collect the time-date information from the system and represent in the required way, is of immense help in data entry activities for the control field 005.

2. Control field 006: This control field is applicable for Fixed-length data elements — Additional material characteristics – General information (R). It has 18 fixed length character positions (00-17). It is applicable to different document types such as Books, Computer files, Maps, Music, Serials, Visual materials and Mixed materials. Each of these document types has different values for different character positions e.g. character positions 01-04 are meant for illustration in books, undefined for Computer files, relief for Maps, form and format for Music, frequency, regularity, ISSN and type for Serials, running time for Visual materials, and undefined for Mixed materials. Obviously, it is a difficult field for a cataloguer who deals with different document types. This field needs to be supported with utility program to ease the job of a cataloguer.

3. Control field 007: The field 007 is used to code for the physical characteristics of an item. We can also use 007 to code for the physical characteristics of the parts of an item such as accompanying material (Library of Congress, 2004). This field is applicable for different document types such as Electronic Resource, Motion Picture, Remote-sensing Image, Globe, Nonprojected Graphic, Sound Recording, Map, Projected Graphic, Tactile Material, Microform, Videorecording. Each of these document types has their own set of values for different character positions. This field also needs to be supported with utility program to ease the job of a cataloguer.

4. Control field 008: Field 008 is used for Fixed Length Data Elements ("Fixed Field Codes"). There are 40 character positions in field 008 (for books), numbered from 00-39. There are undefined positions that must contain either a blank (#) or a fill character (|). Positions 00-17 and 35-39 are equal/common for all media. The character positions 18-34 are meant for different types of documents e.g. Books, Computer files, Maps etc. Obviously, this field is impossible to manage without the help of a suitable support to pick and choose different values for different character positions for different document types.

6. TREATMENT OF LEADER AND CONTROL FIELDS IN KOHA AND NEWGENLIB

As discussed in the previous section, the support for managing Leader and Control fields in the MARC 21 formatted bibliographic framework is essential for two reasons – standardization of bibliographic data elements and ease of data entry operation. These facilities should be considered as value-added features of cataloguing Module of any LMS – be it commercial or open source. Unfortunately most of the commercial LMSs in India do not provide these very essential features of MARC 21 based online cataloguing. Let us check the availability of these very important facilities in Koha and NewGenLib.

6.1 Treatment of Leader field in Koha and NewGenLib

Koha is the only LMS in the open source domain that provides a mechanism to manage all the user defined character positions of the Leader field through user-friendly interface. In Koha, a plugin (small utility script, code or programme) facilitates selection of coded values, entering of predefined and undefined values, and generation of computer-produced number string. This plugin can be attached with the bibliographic framework to achieve consistency in data entry process for the leader field (the plugin can be attached with the Leader field easily).

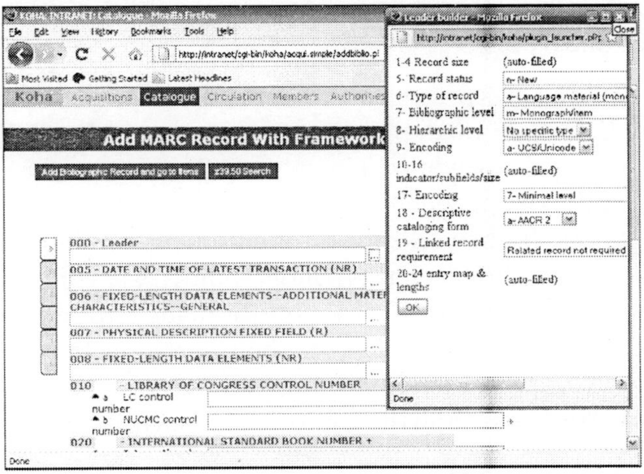

Fig. 3: Treatment of Leader field in Koha

Here (Fig. 3), cataloguer has to click the blue dotted line to display data entry utility for the Leader field. All the user-defined character positions are supported by pickup lists containing different values as prescribed by the MARC 21 bibliographic format.

In NewGenLib, there is no provision to control user-defined character positions of the Leader field. It produces a generic Leader field for all types of documents during exporting of bibliographic records in ISO-2709 compatible format.

6.2 Treatment of Control fields in Koha and NewGenLib

It is quite difficult to prescribe a set of tags and subfields which can satisfy libraries of any type or size. Obviously the bibliographic requirements of a college library can not be the same with a research library. Both Koha and NewGenLib provide libraries freedom to select and display the required tags and subfields for different document types from MARC 21 bibliographic format. As far as control fields are concerned, the cataloging module of LMSs should provide support to ease the job of a cataloguer. Fortunately, both Koha and NewGenLib provide comprehensive support in managing most of the control fields of MARC 21 bibliographic format. Let us check the utilities one by one.

In Koha, it is possible to attach support for each required control fields (although the support is not available readily) in bibliographic frameworks. The added advantage of Koha lies in its modular approach. It is possible to design different bibliographic frameworks for different document types and it is also quite easy to link each bibliographic framework with the support programs for different control fields required for the related document types. Let's see the snapshot given in Fig. 4. The bibliographic framework for monograph here includes support programs for all the control fields such as 005, 006, 007 and 008.

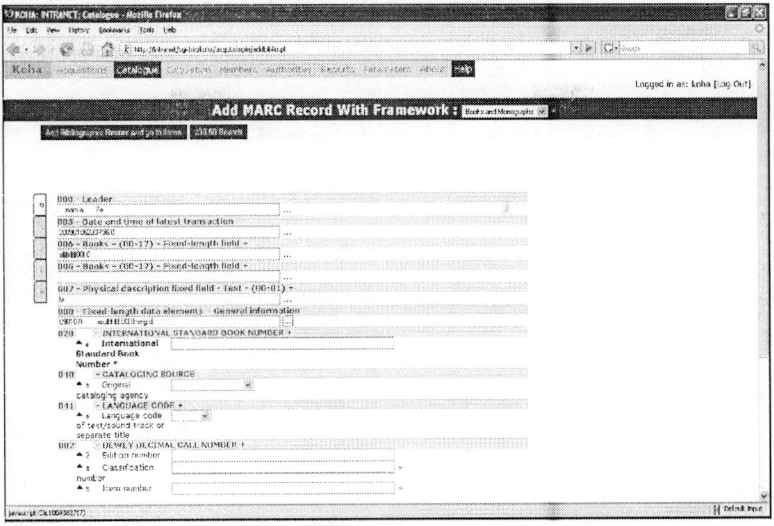

Fig. 4: Managing control fields in Koha

NewGenLib has comprehensive inbuilt support for managing two control fields (mostly used for different document types) namely field 007 and 008 (Fig. 5 and fig. 6).

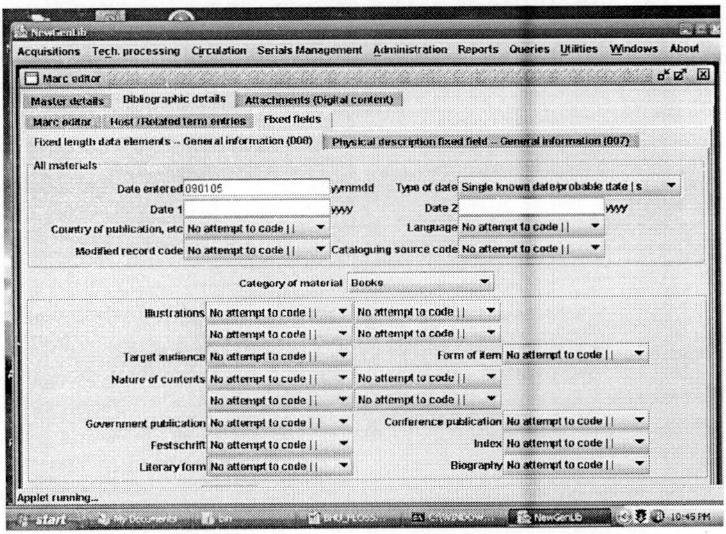

Fig. 5: Support for control field 008 in NewGenLib

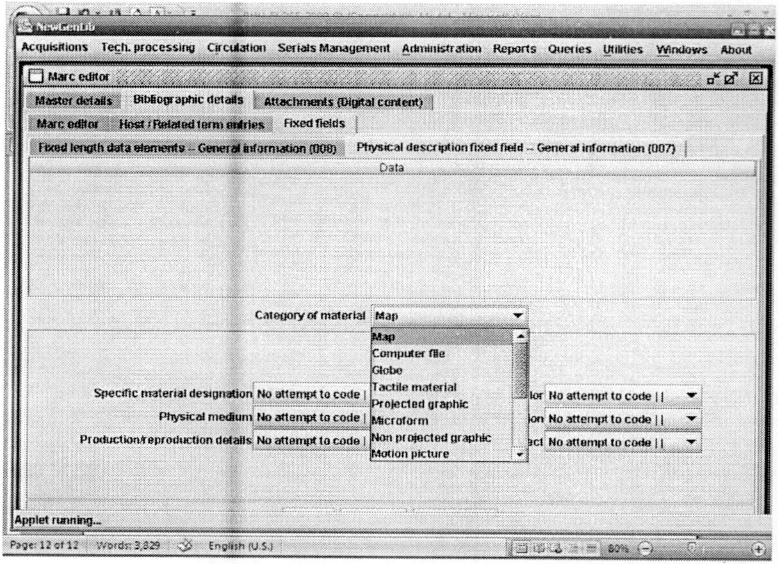

Fig. 6: Support for control field 008 in NewGenLib

7. CONCLUSION

In concluding part, this paper is going for a straightforward comparison of Koha and NewGenLib as far as treatment of Leader and Control fields of MARC 21 bibliographic format are concerned.

Fields under consideration	*Treatment in Koha*	*Treatment in NewGenLib*
Leader	Koha provides an easy to use and comprehensive support program for all the user-defined character positions of the Leader field of MARC 21 bibliographic format.	NewGenLib produces a generic Leader field during the time of exporting bibliographic data but provides no scope to manage user-defined character positions for the Leader field of MARC 21 bibliographic format during data entry activities.

Fields under consideration	*Treatment in Koha*	*Treatment in NewGenLib*
Control field 005	Koha supports this control field through a program to generate date and time of transaction in required format from the system data automatically.	No such support is available in NEWGenLib for the control field 005.
Control field 006	Koha helps cataloguer to manage this control field through a program that allows selecting values for different character positions (through a pickup list) for different document types.	No such support is available in NEWGenLib for the control field 006.
Control field 007	Koha helps cataloguer to manage this control field through a program that allows selecting values for different character positions (through a pickup list) for different document types. But in Koha a single program for this control field do not cover support for different document types. Cataloguer has to use different PERL scripts for different document types. This limitation is possibly originated from the modularapproach of Koha in managing different framework for different document types.	NewGenLib provides a comprehensive support for this control field through which cataloguer can manage different document types with the help of a single window utility program.
Control field 008	Koha helps cataloguer to manage this control field through a program that allows selecting values for different character	Like the control field 007, here also NewGenLib provides a comprehensive support through which cataloguer can manage

Fields under consideration	*Treatment in Koha*	*Treatment in NewGenLib*
	positions (through a pickup list) for different document types. But like the control field 007 here also we need to use different scripting programs for different document types.	different document types with the help of a single window utility program.

REFERENCES

1. Association of Research Libraries. (2004). *Keystone principles for research libraries*. Retrieved January 13, 2005, from http://www.arl.org/training/ keystone.html
2. Bowman, J. H. (2002). *Essential cataloguing*. London: Facet Publishing.
3. Chudnov, Daniel (1999). *Open source library systems: getting started*. Retrieved June 22, 2004, from www.oss4lib.org/readings/oss4lib-gettingstarted.php
4. Dasgupta, I. (2005). Setting up a digital library using Koha and open source technology. In Biswajit Banerjee (Ed.), *Automation and networking of the college libraries* (pp. 151-159). Kolkata: Moulana Azad College.
5. Digital Library Federation. (2004). *The future is open: digital libraries through open source software*. Retrieved January 13, 2007, from http://www.dlf.org/Dlinitiatives/archiv/open.htm
6. Haravu, L. (2004). *Library automation: design, principles and practice*. New delhi: Allied.
7. Library of Congress, Network Development and MARC Standard Office. (2004). *MARC 21 concise format for bibliographic data*. Washington: Library of Congress.
8. Moody, T. (2001). *Open source and libraries: A natural fit*. Retrieved June 22, 2007, from http://www.oss4lib.org/readings/moody.htm
9. Morgan, E. L. (2002). *Open source software in libraries*. Retrieved June 12, 2007, from http://dewey.library.nd.edu/morgan/musings/ossnlibraries.php
10. Mukhopadhyay, P.S. (2005). Comparative study of library management software. In Biswajit Banerjee (Ed.), *Automation and networking of the college libraries* (pp. 23-42). Kolkata: Moulana Azad College.

11. Mukhopadhyay, P.S. (2006). Five laws and ten commandments: the open road of library automation in India. *Proceedings of the National Seminar on Open Source Movement – Asian Perspective*, XXII, Roorkee, 2006. IASLIC, Kolkata. 2006. p. 27-36.
12. Mukhopadhyay, P.S. (2008). *Library automation through Koha*. Kolkata: Prova publications.
13. NUA. (2006). *NUA Internet statistics*. Retrieved January 13, 2007, from http://www.nua.org/stat.html
14. Open Source Initiative. (2003a). *Open source software certification process*. Retrieved January 23, 2004, from http://www.opensource.org/osslicense.htm
15. Open Source Initiative. (2003b). *OSI certified license: the ten basic criteria*. Retrieved January 23, 2004, from http://www.opensource.org/tencom.htm
16. Open Source Initiative. (2007). *Open source software certification process*. Retrieved January 23, 2007, from http://www.opensource.org/osslicense.htm
17. Powell, A. (2002). *Open source movement: news and views*. http://www.ukoln. ac.uk/powell.htm
18. Poynder, R. (2001). The open source movement: does this software provide a viable, user-friendly alternative to proprietary solutions? *Information Today*, 10 (9), 45-56 Retrieved January 13, 2005, from http://www. infotoday.com/it/oct01/it-cont.htm
19. Raymond, E. S. (1996). *The new hacker's dictionary*. Cambridge: MIT press.
20. Raymond, E. S. (2001). *The cathedral and the bazaar: Musings on Linux and open source by an accidental revolutionary* (Rev. ed). Cambridge: O'reilly and Associates Inc.

14

PIXELS OF KNOWLEDGE: AN OPEN SOURCE ENTERPRISE KNOWLEDGE MANAGEMENT SYSTEM

Anand Kumar Pandey
Senior Research Fellow, Documentation Research and Training Centre, Bangalore-560059
anand@drtc.isibang.ac.in

Anila S.
Librarian, Knowledge Centre, IBM India Pvt. Ltd., gurgaonanila@drtc.isibang.ac.in

Aditya Kumar Rai
Director, Vinayaka Solutions, Varanasi
adityarai.bhu@gmail.com

ABSTRACT

Knowledge management is proved to be pivotal for organizational development. The present paper proposes an enterprise knowledge management system using open source software. Technical architecture and the modules of the system are presented and the work flow of the system is demonstrated.

Keywords : Knowledge Management System, Content Management System (CMS), Wikis, E-learning.

Knowledge is a part of intellectual capital of an organization. In this challenging environment identification and use of organizational knowledge is an inevitable thing. The organization should have a proper infrastructure for knowledge management. A proper functioning knowledge management system should be supported by a well-defined architecture. KM is a fruitful combination of people and technology. Here knowledge of the individual is used for the benefit of the organization by using technology. Information and communication technologies (ICTs) offer valuable support for knowledge management activities. Indeed, many tasks in knowledge management are possible only through the use of appropriate technologies. The key challenges for effective knowledge management lies in the transfer of tacit to explicit knowledge and the storage and access of explicit knowledge. Information and Communication Technologies (ICTs) can play an important part in the aforementioned processes. But ICTs only serve as a catalyst to knowledge management and cannot deliver knowledge management.

1. ARCHITECTURE OF AN ENTERPRISE KNOWLEDGE MANAGEMENT SYSTEM

The proposed model (figure 1) contains four layers each in both server side and peer side. Each layer is connected to other layers according to their functional dependency. The user can access the system services through different channel interfaces. One of the main advantages of the peer to peer system is that the user can directly interact with different layers.

I. Server side

Layer I - Authentication layer

This layer is handling the administrative part of the system. It handles the transformation of contents and communication to and from the knowledge management system. The infrastructure services handle the personal data and knowledge sources. It includes the P2P infrastructure for locating peers, exchanging data with other peers, resource management etc. The authentication services include assigning authentication to collections as well as users. This layer also deals with security services such as user name password etc.

Layer II - user specific layer

This layer is deals personal knowledge services such as user profile management, push services etc.

Layer III – Knowledge organization layer

This layer handles the organization of knowledge using a variety of tools such as taxonomy, ontology etc. This layer also handles different kinds of metadata formats and templates for knowledge records according to their content.

Layer IV- Knowledge resources management system

All the backend technologies behind the system are collected in this layer. Relational database management system (RDBMS) supports to store data. Transaction Processing System (TPS), stores the daily routine transaction of the organization. Data warehouse is the main repository of an organization's historical data, its corporate memory. E- learning platform supports the distributed learning. Content management system (CMS) helps to handle the content from the users. CMS can provide a common gateway to all the knowledge management related activities. The document management system (DMS) helps to archive the documents. Internet and intranet makes the basic facility for the well functioning of the knowledge management system. Virtual Private Network (VPN) and extranet supports the access of the system from outside of the intranet.

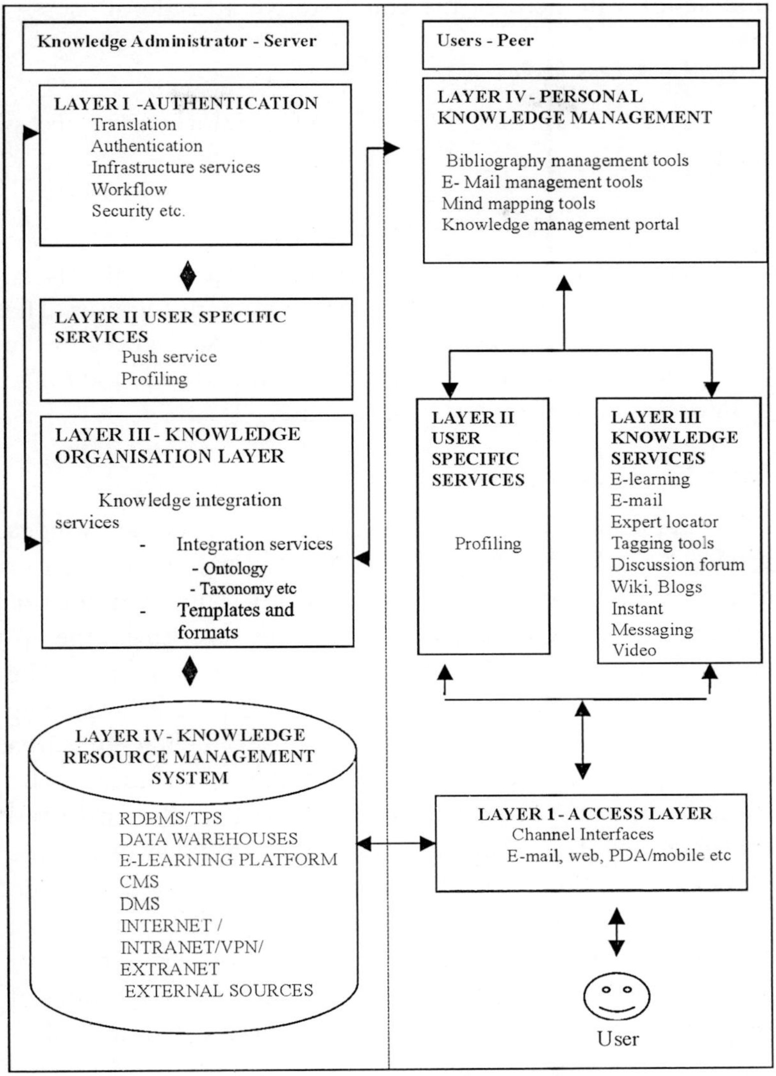

Fig. 1: Technical architecture of a KM System

II. The peer side

It is the user's side of the system, where the entire user related activities and services are located. The peer to peer interaction will increase the collaborative attitude of users.

Layer I - Access layer

This layer includes various channel interfaces to access the system.

Layer II - User specific services layer

This layer deals with the personal services for the users. User profile will contain the information about the user. The user profiles will express the interests and experiences of the users. The user has the complete freedom to decide the range of information which they want to share.

Layer III - Knowledge services

Publication of knowledge records is a part of knowledge service. Knowledge awareness services to users. The knowledge discovery is supported by the search facility. The expert locator is a directory of experts. RSS feeds help the user to get the updates concerned with the system or their area of interest. The tagging facility helps the user to tag relevant items according their need and it is also helpful to other users having same area of interest. The collaborative service enhances the transformation of tacit knowledge trough the informal conversations. The discussion forums provide a platform to the users to clear their doubts, reveal their opinions etc. Video conferencing or Webinar helps to interact with the experts from remote locations. Wikies and Blogs support the collaborative publishing environment. Blogs helps to create communities of special interests, which can enhance the sharing of knowledge.

Layer IV - Personal knowledge management

The personal knowledge management services support the user to handle the personal knowledge. The PKM tools include bibliography management tools, mind mapping tools, e-mail client software etc.

Open source software and knowledge management : The expensiveness and limitations of the proprietary software are forcing the users towards an open source solution. The process of knowledge management varies from organization to organization, so there is no single software package for knowledge management. And the main advantage of open source software is its ease of customization. The users have the full freedom to customize the software according to their requirement. Most of these tools are general, but can be used in different stages of knowledge management.

Relational Database Management Systems (RDBMS)

- **PostgreSQL** (*http://www.postgresql.org/*)
  - Object-relational database management system (ORDBMS)
  - built-in language called pgSQL
  - Supporting scripting languages such as PHP, Python, Ruby, Perl etc.
  - Index methods include user defined,B-tree, hash table, GiST etc.
  - Multi-Version Concurrency Control
  - Referential integrity constraints
- MySQL (*http://mysql.com/*)
  - Multithreaded, multi-user SQL database management system
  - MySQL databases are available in all major programming languages with language-specific APIs
  - Supporting scripting languages such as PHP Ruby etc
- Apache Derby
  - Java relational database management system
  - Embedded JDBC driver

E- Learning Packages

- **ATutor** (http://www.atutor.ca)
  - — Apache, PHP, MySQL
  - — Sharable Content Object Reference Model (SCORM)
  - — Use of XHTML and CSS ensures the uniformity in display among different browsers
- Moodle (Modular Object Oriented Dynamic Learning Environment) (*http://moodle.org*)
  - — Apache,PHP, MySQL
  - — SCORM
  - — Supports LDAP authentication
- DrupalED (*www.funnymonkey.com/come-and-get-it*)
  - — Apache, PHP, MySQL

Content Management Systems (CMS)

- Drupal (www.drupal.org)
  - — Apache, MySQL,PHP
  - — Unlimited categorization
  - — In built blog facility
- Joomla (www.joomla.org)
  - — Apache, MySQL and PHP
  - — Good WYSWYG editor
- PHP-Fusion (*www.php-fusion.co.uk*)
  - — Apache, MySQL and PHP
  - — Around fifteen types of content categorization
  - — Administrator can edit file formats

Document management systems

- Knowledge tree *(http://www.knowledgetree.com)*
  - — Apache , MySQL and PHP

— Lucene search engine

— XPDF and PDF conversion of files are possible

• Dspace (*http://www.dspace.org*)

— Written in Java and JSP using Java servlet frame work

— PostgreSQL

— METS and OAI/PMH

• Contineo (*http://contineo.sourceforge.net*)

— Organize documents as file folders or by keyword list

— Developed in Java

Ø Greenstone (*http://www.greenstone.org*)

— OAI-PMH.

— Dublin Core metadata

Wikies

• MediaWiki (*http://www.mediawiki.org*)

— PHP ,MySQL

— Supporting multiple languages

• DokuWiki (*http://www, wiki.splitbrain.org*)

— PHP

— Multilingual support

— Apache web server

• coWiki (*http://www.cowiki.org/*)

— PHP and MySQL

— Unix-style access control

— Pseudo-hierarchical file system

• MindTouch (*http://www.mindtouch.com/)*

— Developed in C# on Mono and PHP

— Supports UTF8

- MoinMoin (*http://moinmo.in/*)
  - — Developed in Python
  - — Supports flat files and folders
  - — Support for Access Control Lists
  - — Cross-platform

Bibliography management tools

- Aigaion (http://www.aigaion.nl)
  - — PHP and MySQL
  - — Format can export to TXT, HTML or RTF in common citation styles such as IEEE, Harvard etc.
  - — Support Bibtext and RIS formats
- RefDB (*http://refdb.sourceforge.net/*)
  - — A client/server reference database and bibliography tool
  - — It supports a variety of bibliographic formats, such as BibTeX, Endnote, RIS, MODS XML, MARC etc.
  - — Out put can be take in the formats of TEI, DocBook, HTML, or XHTML documents
- Pybliographer (www.pybliographer.org)
  - — Written in Python
  - — It supports bibliographic formats such as BibTeX, ISI, Medline, Ovid etc.
- Refbase (*http://refbase.sourceforge.net/*)
  - — PHP and MySQL
  - — It can import and export a variety of standard bibliographic formats, including BibTeX, Endnote, RIS, ISI, MODS XML etc.
  - — It can generate formatted bibliographies and citations in LaTeX, RTF, HTML, and PDF
  - — It's advanced search features help to generate RSS feeds from searches

E- Mail Client Software

- Mozilla Thunderbird (http://www.mozilla.org)
  - Adaptive junk mail controls
  - Integrate RSS news and blog reader
  - Saved search folders and search bar
  - Tools to efficiently manage email such as global inbox, message filters, grouping, message views, labels etc.
  - Extensible with themes and Add-ons - Extensions like Palm Synchronization with address book.
  - Easy migration - easy to switch from other email clients such as Outlook Express and Eudora and Netscape Communicator
- Eudora (*http://www.eudora.com*)
  - Recent mailboxes
  - Expanded Media for Alert Sounds
  - Saved Searches
  - Minimize to Windows System Tray
  - Insert Downloadable Picture - Include references to graphics stored on web servers

2. A PROTOTYPE TO PROPOSED ARCHITECTURE (KM PORTAL)

Four different kinds of software have been used to create this prototype. It includes a Content Management System, an E-learning software, a document management system and wiki software. The users of the system are students of DRTC. Inputs to the system include class presentation, colloquiums, theses and articles by the students. Content management system 'Drupal' is used to create the knowledge management portal. 'Moodle' is used to support the e-learning system. 'Dspace' is supporting the document management system. 'Mediawiki' is used to enhance the collaborative environment. The prototype was completely built on the Linux platform, (Fedora Core 5).

2.1. The prototype

The main users of the system are DRTC students, both first year and second year. The inputs of the system includes the class presentations, seminars, project works etc done by the students. The main part of the system is the portal named as "Pixels of Knowledge", which is the gate way to other related services. The portal provides access to other service like knowledge collection, e-learning etc. The users can create account, can visible the profiles of others to know about others. The main parts of the system include, 'Pixels of knowledge' the portal, 'Lessons to try' the e-learning platform, 'Acknowledgement' the wiki, and the 'knowledge collection', where the knowledge assets are stored. This system provides a common platform to the students to share knowledge and to interact with each other. The e-mail facility of the institution itself used to provide e-mail facility.

2.2. Pixels of Knowledge: - the portal

The name of the portal is 'Pixels of knowledge' (figure1). It is the portal which is a gateway to other services. As the name mention it contains pixels of knowledge from its users.

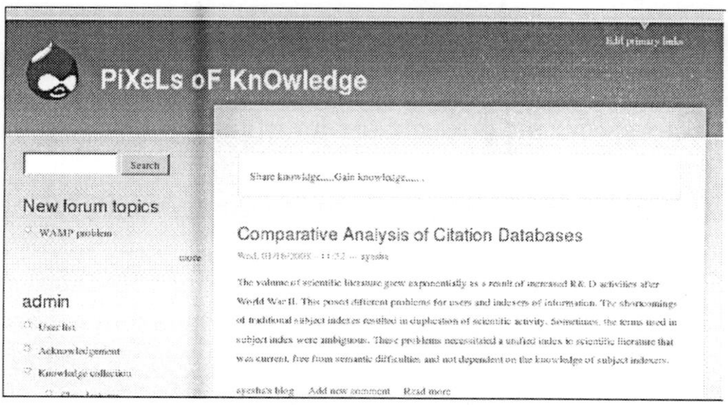

Fig. 1: Pixels of Knowledge

2.3. Services through the portal

2.3.1. User specific services : Here user can create their account. The user can create own profile and can keep it either private or public. The user roles are assigned by the administrator. The registered users can access all the items of the portal. The user profile (figure3) will give a brief description about the user. The user will have full right to personalize their account. The registered users can visit the blogs of other users, and can give comment to the articles.

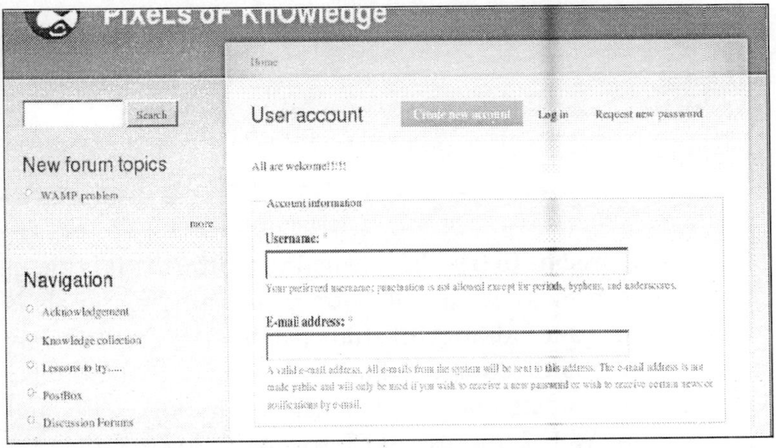

Fig. 2 : Create user account

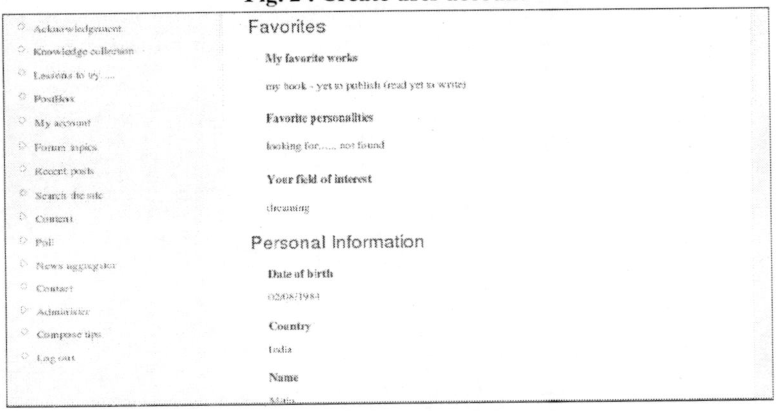

Fig. 3: User profile

2.3.2. Acknowledgement: the wiki : The basic aim of a wiki is to enhance the collaborative environment. Here all the students can share their knowledge in the form of articles .The registered users will have the permission to edit the articles, thus to make it more comprehensive.

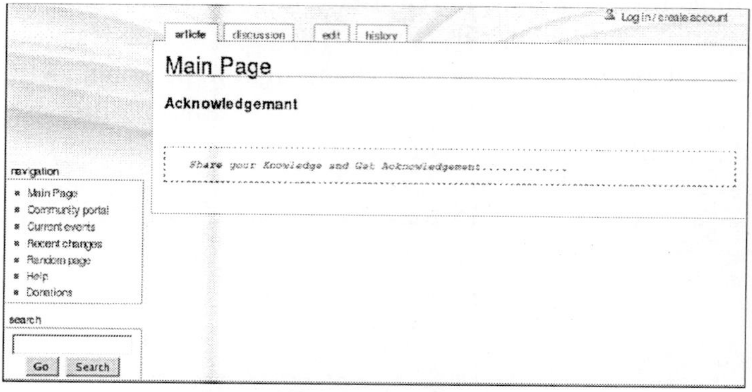

Fig. 4: The main page of Acknowledgement

2.3.3. Lessons to try- the e-learning platform : It is the e-learning platform where a collection of learning materials is collected related to our area of study (figure 5). It contains six main categories of courses. The categories are Database Management Systems, Scripting languages, Ontologies, Faceted classification, Web 2.0 tools, and Information processing and retrieval.

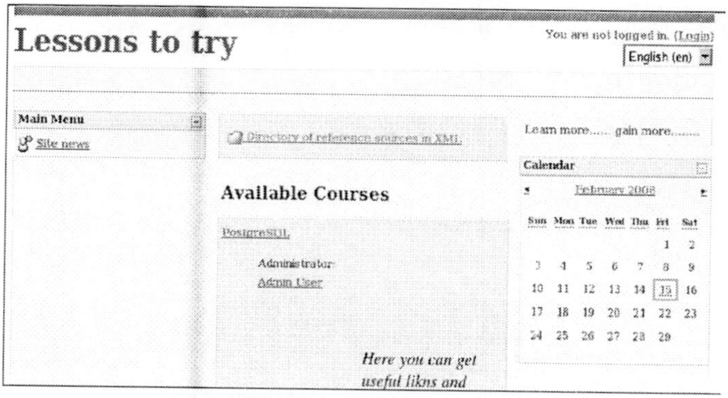

Fig. 5: lessons to try- the e-learning platform

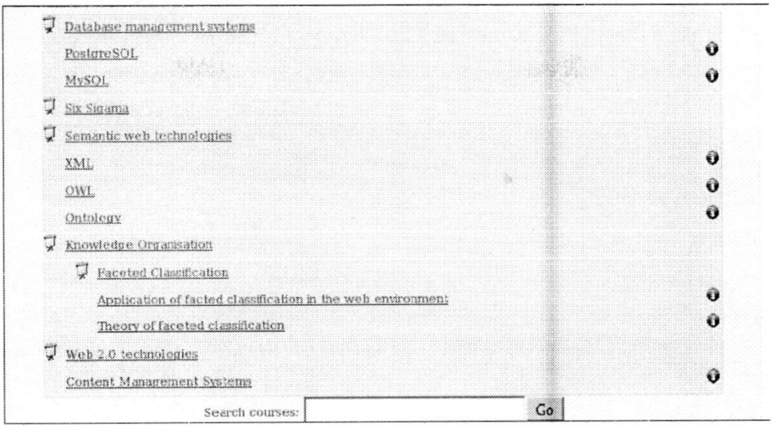

Fig. 6: Available Courses

2.3.4. Knowledge Collection : The knowledge collection (figure 7) is the repository where all the collections of knowledge assets are stored. The collections include class presentation by students, class lectures by teaching faculties, theses and dissertations etc. The collection is arranged according to subject (figure 8 and 9) and within the subject resource type. The main subject categories (figure8) include digital libraries, information processing and retrieval, information society, information technology and knowledge organization.

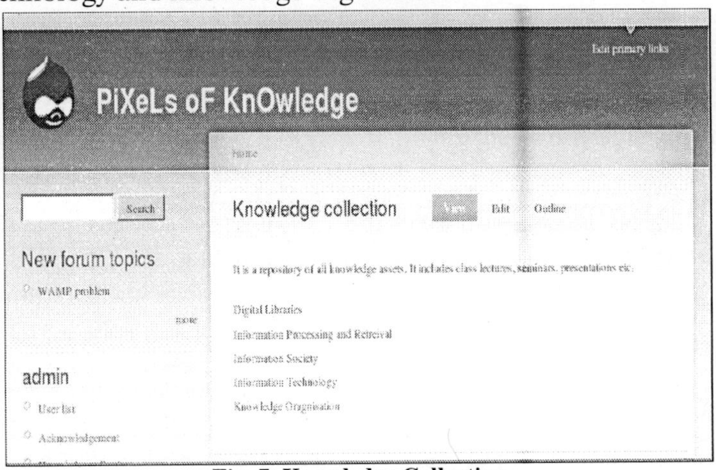

Fig. 7: Knowledge Collection

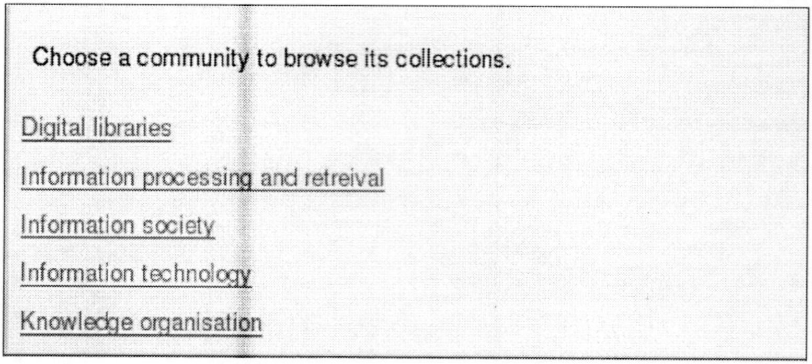

Fig. 8: Knowledge Collection - Organization

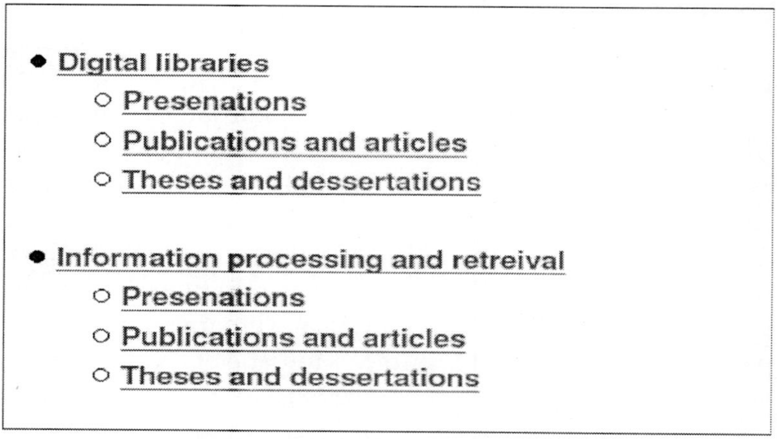

Fig. 9: Knowledge Collection - Organization

2.3.5. Post Box – The e-mail : E-mail is used as the main communication medium in the system. The existing e-mail facility of the institution (figure 10) is used for this purpose.

2.3.6. Discussion forums : The registered users have the right to create discussion forums (figure11). The discussion forum provides a platform to discuss the various problems, doubts etc.

Fig. 10: Post – Box - e-mail

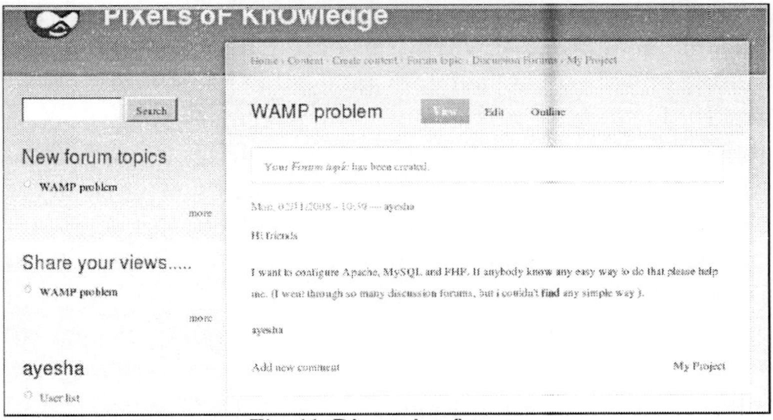

Fig. 11: Discussion forums

7. Polls : The polls is (figure 12) a platform where users can share their views about current topics. Only registered users can participate in polling. The user will have the permission to create topics to the polls.

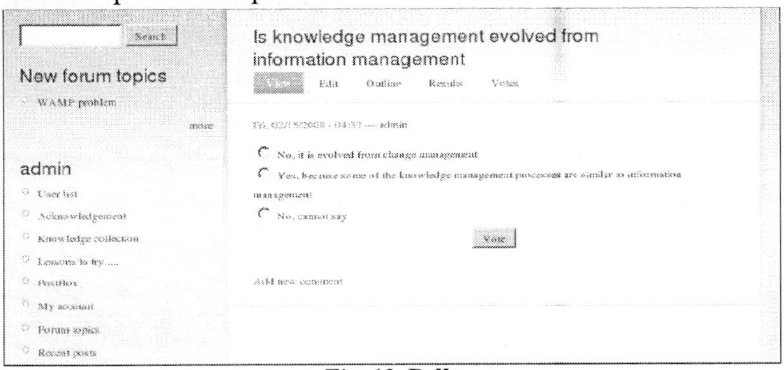

Fig. 12: Polls

2.3.8. News Forums : The news forum is a place to discuss current events going on the related fields. This is a place to announce special news etc.

2.3.9. Blogs : The users are free to write anything in blogs, personal blogs are also possible. The other users of the system can write comments on the blogs.

3. CONCLUSION

Over the past few years, open source software (OSS) has become an alternative when considering new software. Open source software offers many advantages but it has its downsides as well. In the case of knowledge management systems, each and every system is different. The knowledge management system of an organization is completely depends on the structure of the organization. There is no single software to support a knowledge management system. The solutions to this problem can be either a built in software package or customization of other software packages. Open source software can play an important role in this situation, as the source code of the software is free customization of the software is possible. And another important thing is that it will help to reduce the cost to create and maintain the system.

The Advantages of OSS can be

- Reduced costs and less dependency on imported technology and skills
- Affordable software for individuals, enterprise and Government
- Universal access through mass software rollout without costly licensing implications
- Ability to customize software based on unique requirements
- Lowered barrier to entry for software businesses
- Lower security risks because of custom made packages

The above factors make OSS a complex phenomenon. Ample of open source software is available in the market, but selecting a suitable one is the most difficult part. The software which has more active community of developers and users will be suitable one for the future maintenance of the software. If you are looking the technical side of knowledge management, not a single tool but different tools are required to develop a knowledge management system. And almost all tools are available in the open source world, with equal more quality than the proprietary counterpart. OSS can play a big part in effective knowledge management in organizations, as an increasing number of tools are being designed and developed for this purpose.

REFERENCES

1. Al-Hawamdeh, Suliman (2003). *Knowledge Management: Cultivating knowledge professionals*, Oxford: Chandos.
2. Bahra, Nicholas (2001). *Competitive Knowledge Management*. New York: Palgrave.
3. Batley, Sue (2007). The I in information architecture: The challenge of content Management. *Aslib proceedings.* 59.2.
4. Becerra-Fernandez, Irma and Sabherwal, Rajiv (2006). *ICT and Knowledge Management Systems.* Encyclopedia of Knowledge Management . Hershey:Idea Group.
5. Coakes, Elayne and Clarke, Steve (2006). *Encyclopedia of Communities of Practice in Information and Knowledge Management.* Hershey and London: Idea Group Reference.
6. J.K.Suresh and Kavi Mahesh (2006). *Ten Steps to Maturity in Knowledge Management: Lessons in Economy*. Oxford, UK: Chandos Publishing Oxford Ltd.
7. Keyes, Jessica (2006). *Knowledge Management, Business Intelligence and Content Management: The IT practitioner's guide*. New York: Auerbach Publications.
8. Maier, Ronald and Hadrich, Thomas (2006). *Knowledge management systems*. Encyclopaedia of Knowledge Management. Hershey: Idea Group.
9. Tiwana, Amrit (2000). *The Knowledge Management Toolkit: practicle techniques for building a Knowledge Management system*. 2nd Edition.USA: Prentice- Hall.

15

Open Source Software (OSS) In Knowledge Management

Shyam Sunder Pandey
Research Scholar, DLIS, University of Lucknow, Lucknow
e-mail: shyamrsdlislu@gmail.com
Garima Verma
DLIS, University of Lucknow, Lucknow
e-mail: ms.garima_verma@rediffmail.com

ABSTRACT

Knowledge management can be defined as the management of corporate knowledge that can improve a range of organizational performance. It is a process that helps an organization to identify, create, codify, store and transfer important information and expertise necessary for activities such as problem solving, dynamic learning and decision making. OSS plays an important role in each and every step.

The article discusses the application of OSS in different process of knowledge management.

Keywords: Open Source Software, Knowledge Management, Knowledge Management Software, Explicit Knowledge, Tacit Knowledge.

In this world the only thing which is permanent, is the change. Changes are taking place in products, services, industry, organization and society. The main challenges faced by the managers are it to manage the change. Managing change requires competence and capability to identify and foresee the future trends, challenges and responds appropriately. In high-tech sectors especially where knowledge is changing very fast building distinctive competence becomes critical to respond to changes. The high-tech and research-focused organizations are seeking the fundamental insights to help them nurture, harvest and manage the immense potential of their knowledge assets to provide the capability to excel at the leading hedge of innovation.

The role of the libraries in knowledge management has become more and more important. As bases for acquiring, processing, storing and describing knowledge and information, libraries represent an important link in the scientific knowledge system. Libraries take part in scientific research process directly. The library work is a component of knowledge innovation. Libraries have also to play attention to diffusion and conversion of knowledge. They act as bridges for turning the results of knowledge innovation into realistic productive forces. Knowledge management in libraries is to promote relationship in and between libraries, between library and user, to strengthen knowledge internetworking, and to quicken knowledge flow. In this knowledge era, libraries are carrying out researches on development and application of information resources, construction of virtual libraries, protection of intellectual property rights in the electronic era, etc, and thus founding the base for knowledge innovation. OSS is one of the product of research and development

1. OPEN SOURCE SOFTWARE (OSS)

The Open Source Initiative ("OSI") defines Open Source

as software providing the following rights and obligations:

- No royalty or other fee imposed upon redistribution.
- Availability of the source code.
- Right to create modifications and derivative works.
- May require modified versions to be distributed as the original version plus patches.
- No discrimination against persons or groups.
- No discrimination against fields of endeavor.
- Software together. All rights granted must flow through to/with redistributed versions.
- The license applies to the program as a whole and each of its components.
- The license must not restrict other software, thus permitting the distribution of open source and closed source

The terms Free Software and Open Source software are used interchangeably. While they are similar, there are some differences worth appreciating.

According to the Free Software Foundation (FSF) definition:

"Free software is a matter of the users' freedom to run, copy, distributes, study, change and improves the software. More precisely, it refers to four kinds of freedom, for the users of the software:

- The freedom to run the program, for any purpose (freedom 0).
- The freedom to study how the program works, and adapt it to your needs (freedom 1). Access to the source code is a precondition for this.
- The freedom to redistribute copies so you can help your neighbour (freedom 2).

- The freedom to improve the program, and release your improvements to the public, so that the whole community benefits (freedom 3). Access to the source code is a precondition for this.

OSS is software whose source code may be freely modified and redistributed to third parties with few restrictions. The software is developed and released under some sort of "open source" licenses, with a range of different features, but all allow inspection of the software's code. The term "open source" is now generally used to refer to free or open source software.OSS has been receiving a lot of attention over the last few years as the movement gains momentum and people are beginning to finally believe that the potential that open source software always presented can now be translated into results. But, despite the hype surrounding open software and its potential benefits to organizations and governments, the situation at present would suggest that there is a long way to go before it can be widely used and network externalities comes into force.

The benefits of OSS are obvious and organizations and governments would be tempted to adopt but the practicality of OSS remains an issue. But, as more and more people start using OSS and the programs become compatible with existing software, and more software developers are trained in OSS, the popularity of OSS will begin to grow.The OSS brings with it a host of other issues like the digital divide, knowledge economy, knowledge management, and network society. It might be interesting to note that all these issues are connected in more than one way and open source software has a large role to play in each of these issues. Hence, it becomes imperative for organizations and governments to understand these role and shape policies accordingly.

One very interesting aspect of OSS is the nature of the movement. Plenty of research has been done to understand the development process, the knowledge management issues in the development, the players involved and the benefits for the players. With the issue of digital divide gaining importance, a lot of researchers have also focused on the role of OSS in bridging the divide.

2. BRIEF HISTORY OF OPEN SOURCE SOFTWARE

Period	*History*
1969	Creation of Unix in AT&T Bell Labs
1969	Development of ARPANET, first transcontinental high speed computer network.
1973	Growth in popularity of UNIX. AT&T was prohibited by law to start any other business than telephone or telegraph services. Hence, AT&T started licensing UNIX without support
1974-1975	User groups were starting to grow wherever UNIX introduced to share ideas, information, programs, bug fixes and hardware fixes
1983	Development of the ARPANET into what is today known as the Internet.
1985	Richard Stallman, a programmer at the MIT AI Lab, starts the Free Software Foundation in response to trends in software world towards proprietary software packages and non-access to source code. Starts the design on new operating system called GNU. New license called General Public License (GPL) developed to allow individuals to incorporate their own rights in "free software".
1990	Most components of GNU complete except for Kernel.
1991	Linus Torvalds, then a student in Finland, developed the UNIX-compatible kernel called

	Linux under the GPL, releasing the source code freely and later combined with GNU with Linux to create the operating system Linux. User communities helped modify the source code to make the operating system function better.
1994	Launch of the first Linux distribution by Torvalds led to an explosion of new Linux based Open Source operating systems and application software to run on the Linux platform.
1998	The "free software" idea did not immediately become mainstream and hackers Bruce Perens and Eric Raymond agreed that the problem lay in the term "free". Together with other prominent hackers, they founded the "open source" software movement and called it the Open Source Initiative.

3. OPEN SOURCE TOOLS

Linux: This is the most well known open-source project today. Its popularity is heightened by the fact that it is philosophically free, and it runs a on a multitude of hardware platforms and many software applications have been designed to run on it. Most of the software applications that run on it are provided for free, philosophically, under several free licenses. But, though Linux is widely used on various hardware and for several task-intensive purposes, it has not really garnered much popularity in the desktop market or average home user market.Linux, the Unix-like kernel, is as flexible, versatile and powerful as any other kernel on earth, proprietary or otherwise. It is not only used on desktops, it is used on wrist watches, cellular phones, mainframes, servers and other embedded appliances to mention a few. Linux has a thorough support for Internet-based developers compared to most other open source projects. In addition there is extensive documentation and online books to aid users.

Apache Web Server: A web server is a computer that stores Web documents and makes them available to the rest of the world. A server may be dedicated, meaning its sole purpose is to be a Web server, or non-dedicated, meaning it can be used for basic computing in addition to acting as a server. Apache is the most popular Web server, open source or otherwise. Its is believed to have more than 60% of the market today, to be the most popular server since mid-1995, and as being more popular than all other servers combined since the beginning of 1999. To put it simply, Apache powers most of the Web. Apache is written with robustness, performance, security, and standards-conformance in mind. Apache is also extensible - its capabilities can be augmented through the inclusion of other modules that are not part of the core server. Apache's behavior can be tailored to the requirements of individual sites, allowing it to serve the needs of sites small and large.

Mozilla Web Browser: Mozilla is a free, cross-platform Internet software suite, whose components include a web browser, an email client, an HTML editor, and an IRC client. It was started by Netscape Communications Corporation and is now developed by the Mozilla Foundation.The main technical thrust of Mozilla has been to implement and extend public standards that are supportive of major Internet communication systems such as the World Wide Web and email. By seeking to do so freely and portably, Mozilla technology takes a leadership position in the evolution of those technologies as well as providing public infrastructure that is mostly free of commercial motives.

4. KNOWLEDGE MANAGEMENT

Knowledge Management (KM) can be defined as the collection of processes of creation, dissemination, and utilisation of knowledge. Knowledge Management is the explicit and systematic management of vital knowledge and its associated processes of creating, gathering, organizing, diffusion, use and exploitation. Knowledge Management comprises a range of practices used in an organisation to identify, create, represent, distribute and enable adoption of insights and experiences. Such insights and experiences comprise knowledge, either embodied in individuals or embedded in organisational processes or practice. Knowledge Management focuses on two types of Knowledge i.e. Tacit and Explicit.Its aim is to ensure transformation of knowledge from tacit to explicit knowledge and from individual to collective or social knowledge.

Tacit to Tacit

- Transfer of knowledge between the people
- Through meetings and social interactions
- Use of technologies like web conferencing and electronic meetings

Tacit to Explicit

- Transfer of knowledge from people to physical form
- Through development of reports and manuals or answering queries
- Use of technologies like word processing documents, presentation tools and email.

Explicit to Tacit

- Transfer of knowledge from physical form to actionable knowledge in people.
- Through video, audio or text presentations. Browsing through documents.
- Use of technologies like multimedia technologies, word processing and presentation tools.

Explicit to Explicit

- Transfer of knowledge from one physical form to another.

- Through text search, queries and document categorization.
- Use of technologies like search tools, query languages and databases.

5. KNOWLEDGE MANAGEMENT PROCESS PERSPECTIVES ON OPEN SOURCE SOFTWARE (OSS)

OSS is a prominent tool which has had an enormous influence on knowledge management process. The purpose of the tools is to facilitate problem solving.Some of the tools are especially for identifying knowledge in any organization, whereas others are for creation, codification, storage etc. It is evident that OSS tools supports the KM process.

Knowledge Identification : This is the first step in the knowledge management process. A knowledge intensive task is selected and the main knowledge types are identified. After identifying the knowledge types a list of possible information sources is to be compiled. The information sources could be both explicit sources and people. Mbone developed by The Networked Multimedia Research Group at University College, London is a popular open source application used for knowledge identification process. Mbone is currently of practical use for shared communication such as videoconferences or shared collaborative workspaces. It is not generally connected to Internet service providers, but often to universities and research institutions.

Knowledge Creation : Once the knowledge requirements and sources are identified, the knowledge has to be created and a process has to be setup to enable this. Knowledge may already exist in people but knowledge that may not be available through people in the organization must be created through meetings and interviews. Knowledge may also be created through training sessions for employees and from reading journals and books.The central theme of this process is to transform an individual's tacit knowledge into explicit knowledge and make it available to the organisation as a whole. The Internet is a very useful resource to search for resources and information. Various online free search tools are available. The Intranet is probably a better tool to sue for knowledge creation as it has literature and information more focused based on the needs of the organization. Convea and Digger internet open source are the two OSS tools for the creation of knowledge in organizations and institutions. Convea is an open source intranet solution with many web-based applications including email, calendar, knowledge base, and instant messaging. Digger Intranet Open Source (IOS) includes a time management system, a communications forum, a client database manager and a lot more.

Knowledge Codification : The third step is called knowledge codification . In this step the created knowledge has to be codified on the basis of variety of reuse-situations and frequency of appearance and whether to integrate the package to a repository or not. Scattered information is converted into explicit knowledge that can be accessed, stored and transferred by validating content, codification, classification, organization and integration. Content Management System is a system that supports effective collection, management and presentation of conglomerates of information formed as a cohesive whole through targeted publications. The system is also beneficial when the design and content of the document need to be manipulated separately or when more than one publication needs to be derived from a single base of content. Content Management Systems are easily one of the most popular open source software available. There are plenty of options for the buyer. A lot of companies offer to design customized solutions for an organization's unique requirements. Some common system names are MySource, OpenCMS, Midgard, eZ Publish, etc.

Knowledge Storage : This step of the knowledge management process deals with the storage of data sets, article abstract databases and body of own work. Depending on the type of knowledge that is to be integrated, a medium for its storage has to be decided upon. While explicit knowledge can be kept in documents tacit knowledge might have be stored in a suitable medium like audios or videos. MySQL is the most popular open source database and the fastest growing database in the industry. It has the capabilities to handle most corporate database application requirements with an architecture that is extremely fast and easy to use.

Knowledge Diffusion and Use : Knowledge Diffusion is a cross-functional and collaborative information distribution and learning activity. Knowledge residing in databases will have to be accessed and used to effectively meet organizational goals. Systems and search technologies to locate necessary information are necessary when faced with key decision-making. Decision Support Systems are sets of tools which help managers or teams make better decisions when faced with unstructured or semi structured problems. These systems make use of stored explicit and tacit knowledge as well as new contributions from individuals. Dicodess is an open source software framework for developing distributed cooperative decision support systems. It helps build DSS for mission-critical decision-making situations happening in dynamic, rapidly changing and often, unpredictable distributed environments.

6. CONCLUSION

Over the past few years, open source software has matured into a serious alternative when considering new software. Organizations in developed and developing countries are increasingly considering replacing proprietary software packages with open source packages.

Open source software offers many advantages but it has its downsides as well. We have a look at both the pros and cons of OSS.

Pros

- Reduced costs and less dependency on imported technology and skills
- Affordable software for individuals, enterprise and Government
- Universal access through mass software rollout without costly licensing implications
- Ability to customize software based on unique requirements
- Lowered barrier to entry for software businesses
- Lower security risks because of custom made packages

Cons

- Lack of technical support
- Most open source software is not very user friendly
- Difficulty in finding the right package, as open source software is not marketed well
- Lack of critical mass as few users exist and not many applications are designed to be compatible with other open source software

Apart from its weakness the OSS can play a big part in effective knowledge management in organizations, as an increasing number of tools are being designed and developed for the purpose. But, for the popularity of OSS to grow, especially in developing countries, governments must formulate ICT policy accordingly to improve awareness and integrate an OSS policy with its education, administration and e-governance policies. But before governments are entirely convinced to move forward several issues, such as those illustrated above, need to be addressed. Nevertheless, OSS is set to play a major part in taking the benefits of digital age to organizations and economies in developing countries.

REFERENCES

1. Bhojaraju, G. Knowledge management: Why do we need it for corporate? Malaysian J,Lib, Inform. Sc., 2005, 10(2) 37-50
2. Broadbent, M. The emerging phenomenon of knowledge management. The Australian Lib. J., 1997, 6-24.
3. Goldin, Ian & Reinert, Kenneth, Globalization for development. Washington, World Bank, 2007.
4. Marr, Bernard. Consider the culture when benchmarking KM process. KM Review, 2003, 6(5), 6-7.
5. Menknoff, Thomas, (Ed) Governing and managing knowledge in Asia, Singapore, World Scientific.
6. Moorthy, A. L.; Rao, N. Laxman and Goud, K. Sudhakar, (Eds) Technology management in libraries. New Delhi: Allied Publisher, 2006.
7. Das, Bhagwan. Knowledge management in corporate culture: Emerging challenges of tacit knowledge and its integration, edited by K.S. Raghavan, IKONE 2007. 2007, pp. 365-82.
8. Kumar, D. S. G... Information and Communication, New Delhi: B.R. Publishing Corporation, p. 419.
9. Rangnathan, S. R. Prolegomena to library classification. Vol.1.Ed.3.Banglore, Sarda Rangnathan Endowment for library Science, 1990, 81.
10. Sangam, S.L. Pattern of development of knowledge. In 44th FID Conference and Congress, Finland, 1998. http://www.gartner.com.
11. http://www.kmresource.com
12. http://www.systemo-thinking.org

16

USE OF PROTÉGÉ IN BUILDING ONTOLOGY FOR VISUAL ARTS : A FACETED APPROACH

Amrita Majumdar
Assistant Librarian, MGKV, Varanasi
amritaarty@gmail.com

ABSTRACT

Information in a web is often difficult to get (with or without tool) ,the information available on web is disorganized ,chaotic and unsystematic ,non semantic structure .Due to which the user often end up with irrelevant results for their queries . Faceted classification system (FCS) is a method of multidimensional description and arrangement of resources that can significantly improve the information architecture on web and used in developing ontology for semantic retrieval of information from web. Tools like protégé help to express the ontology in OWL and carry out the validation. This paper tries to explain the application of colon classification for building ontology for the Visual Arts Discipline with the help of Protégé software. The present study is a demo presentation of few classes of Visual Arts.

Keywords: Ontology, Faceted Approach, OWL, Faceted Classification System.

1. INTRODUCTION

Disciplinary is a key feature of Knowledge Organization Systems (KOS) as most of them are structured primarily according to discipline like classification scheme, ontology and thesaurus. However the Growth of research and development tend to create a Integrated multidisciplinary relationship between the various KOSs .These integrated level KOS are basically structured according two principals i.e. One is the classical hierarchal relationship holding between a class and its subclass, the other is the relationship holding between two integrated level of KOS. These two principal are incorporated up with two concept first is faceted classification scheme and second ontology. Faceted classification scheme are based on hierarchal relation, other kind of relationship can expressed by common isolate, facet, phase. User can browse a classification scheme by moving from a class to a more general or more specific class. On other side as is now recognized ontology is a formal explicit description of concepts in a domain of discourse. Ontology is constituted by classes (sometime called concept) class can have subclass representing concepts more specific than their superclass. [3]According to Noy &Mc Guiness 2001 all class have- 1).slots (sometimes called roles or properties) that is the properties of each concept describing various features and attributes of it, all subclass of class inherit its slots. A slot should be attached at most general class that can have the property.2) Facet (sometime called role restrictions): slots can have different facets describing the value type and features of class. Ontologies allow to express any kind of relationship provided, they have been defined usually in the form of slot. Thus we can see that the faceted classification scheme and ontology has sharing some common features, can used to develop discipline based domain structure in more specific way.

For developing domain web ontology language is used which allow user to write explicit, formal conceptualization of domains of model .Their are many OWL are available to develop a n ontology like DMAIL+OIL, ONTODAMIL ,Protégé etc . Protégé OWL is an open source tool created to super ontology development for the semantic web. The present paper explored the significance of Colon Classification of 7th edition which is freely faceted scheme into designing the ontology using protégé owl editor for development of knowledge structure for Visual Arts discipline.

2. OBJECTIVE

- To show how the traditional classification (Colon Classification of 7th edition) system can be use for organizing the information on web interface.
- To test the significance of protégé in developing ontology for visual arts discipline with help of Colon Classification 7th edition.
- To examine how the knowledge of domain can be organized and retrieve meaningfully to serve our various purpose.

3. TOOL USED

- Protégé 4.0 beta- a free open source ontology editor
- Colon classification (7th ed.) scheme.

4. ABOUT PROTÉGÉ 4.0

Protégé is an extensible, platform independent environment for creating and editing ontologies and knowledge base structure originates from Standford University. It is an open source tool created to support ontology development for semantic web .It has a plug in extension which allows user to exploit protégé's core features and services such as graphical user interface, availability of storage formats and data acquisition and visualization tool. Protégé OWL provides access to emerging knowledge representation standard such as OWL and high performance classifiers. It facilitates the use to edit ontologies in the web Ontology language and to use description logic classifiers to maintain of their ontology.

5. SPECIAL FEATURE OF PROTÉGÉ

There are several features which made protégé different from other knowledge base tools which are as follows-:

- It has Intuitive and easy to use graphical user interface
- Protégé's database has back end loads frame only on demand and uses catching to free up memory when needed. There is virtually no deterioration in performance as one can go for from several hundred frames to several thousand.
- Extensible plug in architecture can easily extend protégé to-
- Use smaller user interface components that are well suited to displaying and acquiring values in domain
- Custom back end plug- ins that use their own storage mechanisms
- New application intricately linked with knowledge base as a protégé tab.

6. COMPONENT OF PROTÉGÉ [4]

Protégé has some major components which are depicted in form of table are as follows:

Name of component	*Features*
I. Individuals	Also known as instances can be referred to as being "instance of classes". It may belong to more

	than one class. It has Unique Name Assumption (UNA).This means that different names could actually refer to the same individual. Individual represents object in the domain that we are interested.
II. Properties	Properties are binary relations on individuals i.e. properties link two individuals together. Proprieties are roughly equivalent to slots in Protégé.It reperesents the relationship between individuals

Kinds of Properties

6.1. Object Type Properties : They are relationship between two individuals

OWL Object Property characteristics : OWL allows the meaning of properties to be enriched through the use of property characteristics which are as follows:

Name	*Feature*
a. Functional Property	If a property is functional for a given individual, there can be at most one individual that is related to the individual via the property. It is also known as single valued properties and also features.
b. Inverse functional properties	If a property is inverse functional then it means inverse property functional
c. Transitive properties	If the property relates individual a to individual b and also b to c

	then we can refer that individual a is related with individual c via property P.
d. Symmetric properties	If a property P is symmetric and the properties relates individual a to individual b then individual b is also related to individual a via property P.
e. Antisymmetric properties	If a property P is antisymmetric and the property relates individual a to individual b then individual b cannot be related to a via property P.
f. Reflexive properties	A property P is said to be reflexive when the property must be related with individual a to itself.
g. Irreflexive properties	If a property P is irreflexive, it can be described as a property that relates an individual a to individual b where both are not same.
h. Properties may have a domain and range specified .	Properties link individuals from the domain to individuals from the range.

6.2. Data type properties : Data type properties describe the relationship between individuals and data values.

6.3. Annotation Properties : It can be used to add information (metadata) to class individuals and object and data type properties. Object type/Data type Properties may be marked as Annotation properties.

III. Classes : OWL classes are interpreted as sets that contain individuals. they are described using formal descriptions that stae precisely he requirements for membership of the class.

Methodology for building ontology

We are going to built an ontology for the classes of visual arts namely Numismatic Arts Drawing , Painting.

Step1. Determine the domain and scope of ontology.

- Starting with development of ontology we will defining its domain and scope which will able to answer the following questions:
- What is the domain that ontology will cover?
- What is the use of ontology?

Considering this points we will define the ontology as domain of knowledge which will further categorized into Visual Arts and Value Partitions. The domain of visual arts further defines subclasses visual class whereas value partition define the other aspects of visual Arts viz. application, cultural heritage and techniques. Which play the role of entities in the ontology as shown in fig 1.

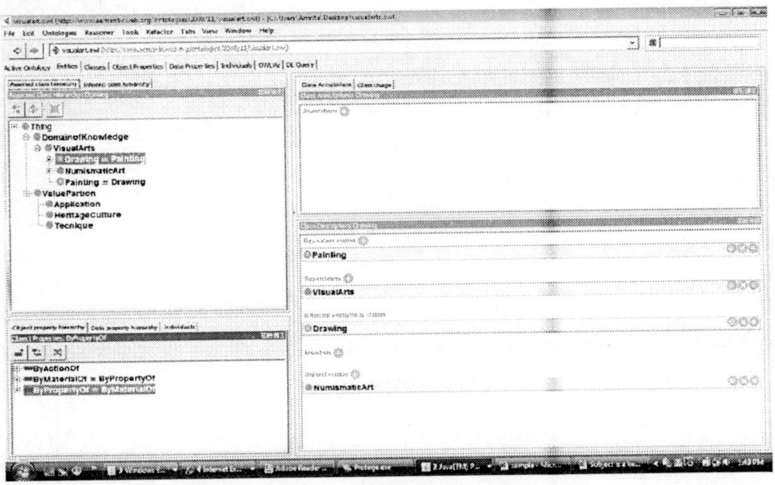

Fig 1.

Step 2. Enumerate important terms in the ontology

It is useful to write down a list of all terms we would like either to make statement about or to explain to a user .This will include what are the terms we would like to talk about? what properties do those term have ?Initially it is important to get a comprehensive list of terms without worrying about overlap between concepts they represent relationship among the term or any properties that the concept may have or whether the concepts are classes or properties. The next two steps developing the class hierarchy and defining properties are closely intertwined. [5]

Step 3. Define the class and the class hierarchy

We will define the class hierarchy of visual arts with their properties by implementing the schedule of colon classification 7th edition. Which are as follows:

- There are three level of classes top level class , middle level class, bottom level subclass

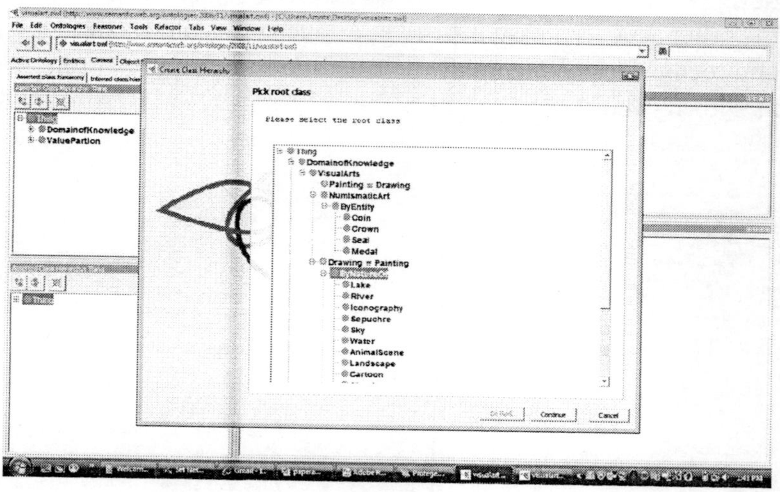

Fig 2

- As shown in fig2. top level class is Visual art under which the middle level class

- Painting, Drawing and Numismatic Arts is incorporated and similarly bottom level of class is implanted under middle level of class.
- Now all middle level of classes are disjoint to each other
- Now we will define the classes and subclasses as per given schedule of CC7 shown in fig2 for example we will choose numismatic art as middle level and under which all subclasses of it will incorporated.
- Here the important point is that middle level class Painting and Drawing has common bottom level class "figure" so, they will considered as an equivalent class and represent by symbol "a""class shown as fig 2 .

Step 4. After defining the class and its hierarchy we will continue with describing properties of the classes with their specific characteristics as defined in schedule of cc7 which are shown in following figures.3

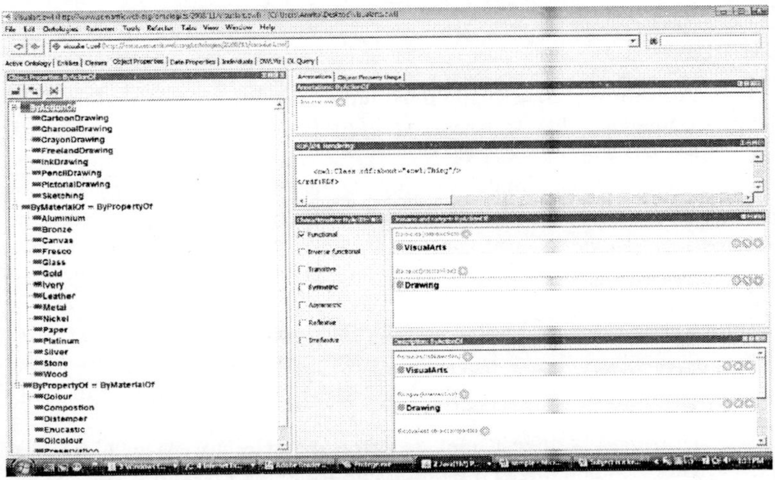

Fig. 3

- Fig 3. shows that the class drawing has an action property as per schedule of CC7 under which sub property are defend to describe the concept of drawing which has functional characteristics. Similarly we will defined the properties for the class of Numismatic Arts and Painting

- Similarly the "By material Of" property of Numismatic Art is equivalent to "By material of" property of painting because they contain some similar sub property as given in schedule which will explained in fig3

7. CONCLUSTION

The implementation of the Colon Classification scheme on the ontology has give the hospitality for new concepts and subjects terminologies and multiplied the effect in opening up the accommodative facility under defined "subject facet". It is more annotative to the user need ,giving him freedom to search documents using any combination of facets. Tool like protégé help to express ontologies in owl and carry out validation. However these tools are to be modified to make them handle faceted ontologies. The objective is to develop a computational model to trans form traditional classification schemes to schemes based on web ontology.

REFERENCES

1. Antoniou , Grigoris and Hamelin, Frank Van .Web Ontology Language : OWL. *www.cs.vu.nl/frank/postscript/ontoHandbook03/owl.pdf* .
2. Cregan ,Anne ; Mocol, Malgorzata and Vrandecic , Denny. Pushing the limits of OWL Rules and Protégé : a simple example. *www.ftp.infomatik.rwth.aachen.de/publication/CEUR-WS/vol-188/sub-22.pdf*
3. Gnoli, Claudio ; Bosch ,Mela and Mazzocchi , Fulvio .2007. A New Relationship for Multidisciplinary Knowledge Organization System : dependencies . In Interdisciplinary and transdisciplinartiy in the organization of Scientific Knowledge, proceedings of the eith ISKO Spain Conference 18-20 April 2007.
4. Horridge , Mattew ;Kunblauch, Holger and Rector ,Alan . A practical Guide to building OWL ontologies using the Protégé –OWL plugin and CO-ODE tools ed.2.0 http:// *www.protegestandford.edu*.
5. Noy .F, Natalya and Guninness, Deborah L Mc . Ontology Development 101: a guide to creating your first ontology.
6. Rubin, Daniel; Fergerson and Ray W . Protégé –OWL: creating ontology –driven reasoning application with web ontology language.

17

From Tacit to Explicit Knowledge Management in Context of Digital Environment

Bhaw Nath Pandey
Assistant Librarian Amity University,
Lucknow Campus, Lucknow.
bpandey@amity.edu

ABSTRACT

In the knowledge economy era, as a sub-discipline of the knowledge economy, knowledge management is absolutely new idea, concept & method of management. It also works for converting tacit knowledge of professionals & staff members in the organizations into explicit knowledge & higher motivation forces; competition power and value added commitment. In the "E- Revolution "age through growth of the global networks, knowledge management is increasingly becoming a crucial tool in providing a multidimensional dynamic and effective service with maximum exploitation of resources and with maximum efficiency rate to Library patrons. The paper focuses one aspect of knowledge management in the global

Library digital environment & its context attempts to outline the need, & benefits to include knowledge management in Library services development to retain 'know –How' for the benefits of its professionals & users.

Keywords : Knowledge Management System, Tacit Knowledge, Explicit Knowledge.

1. KNOWLEDGE

Knowledge is actionable information, actionable refers to the notion of relevant and being available in the right place at the right time, in the right context and in the right way so that anyone can bring it to bear an decision being made every minute on. It perceives as the interpretation and action that follow the understanding of stored texts, notes or information. It is also used to refer to qualified, captured and accumulated facts, techniques, principles, such as books, documents, papers, formulas, procedure manuals & computers code. It also is perceived as composed of truths, beliefs, perspectives, concepts, judgments, expectations and methodologies. Moreover, knowledge is the product of action, that lead to creating or recreating new products and services using mental ingenuity in conjunction with recorded information. In any organizations, knowledge manifests itself in opinions, actions, process comments, minutes of meetings, presentations, websites of portals, databases, e-mails, records management systems, integrated financial management systems, human resource management systems, communication systems E-commerce, E-governance, E-library, E-journals, E-books. According to Davenport & Prusak's, "knowledge is a fluid mix of formed experience, value, contextual information expert, insight & grounded intuition that provides an environment and framework for evaluating and incorporating new experience and information. It originates and is applied in the minds of knower. In organizations it often becomes embedded not only in documents or repositories but also in organizational routines, processes, practices and norms".

It is the key resource in intelligent decision making, forecasting, design, planning, diagnosis, analyses, evaluation and intuitive judgment. It is formed in and shared between individual and collective minds. It does not grow out of databases but evolves with experiences, successes, failures and learning overtime.

2. KNOWLEDGE MANAGEMENT

It refers to any process or practice of creating, acquiring, capturing, sharing and using knowledge, wherever it resides, to enhance learning and performance in organization. According to Jain & Nfila (2006), "Knowledge management as a purposeful management process to capture, explicit, share & apply both implicit & explicit knowledge for the benefit of the employees, organization and its customers. According to White (2004), "Knowledge management as a process of creating, storing, sharing & reusing organizational knowledge or know-how to enable an organization to achieve its goals and objectives.

Knowledge Management is a newly emerging interdisciplinary business-model that has knowledge within the framework of an organization as its focus. It is rooted in many disciplines including business, economics, psychology, cognitive science, behavioral science, information management, expert systems, artificial intelligence, data mining, web technology, simulation, semantic web etc.

Its comprises technical organizational and interpersonal skills and is based on personal experience, learning and expertise. The focus of knowledge management is on creating new knowledge, sharing enhancing and utilizing knowledge to achieve organizational goals.

Main Focus of knowledge management

- Intellectual capital
- Individual experience
- People centric issue- beliefs, perspectives, judgments, expectations, intentions
- Know how/ skills/ competencies
- Learning/ critical thinking/ innovation
- Knowledge application
- Creation, recreation, sharing & enhancements of information.
- Tacit and explicit representations
- Knowledge management recognizes

Value in originality, innovation, agility, adaptability, intelligence and learning. It is people focused and concerned with critical thinking innovation, relationships, exposures to ideas, patterns and competencies and encourages learning and sharing of experiences. It is dynamic, active resource residing in people's heads.

Knowledge management is the process of capturing and making use of a organizations collective expertise any where in the process in paper, in documents, in databases i.e. called explicit knowledge or in people's head i.e. called tacit knowledge. According to survey up to 95 percent of information is presence as tacit knowledge.

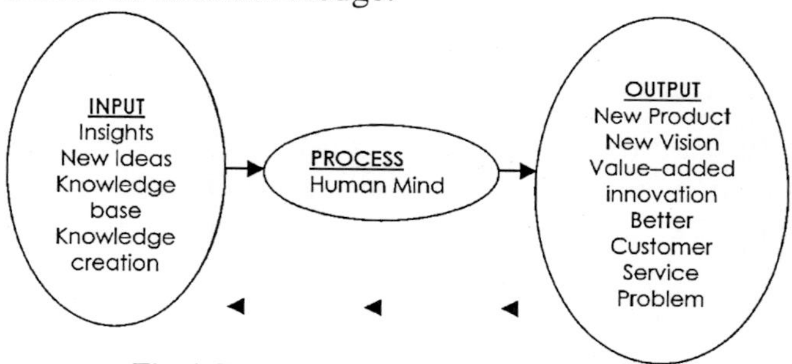

Fig. 1. Process of Knowledge Management

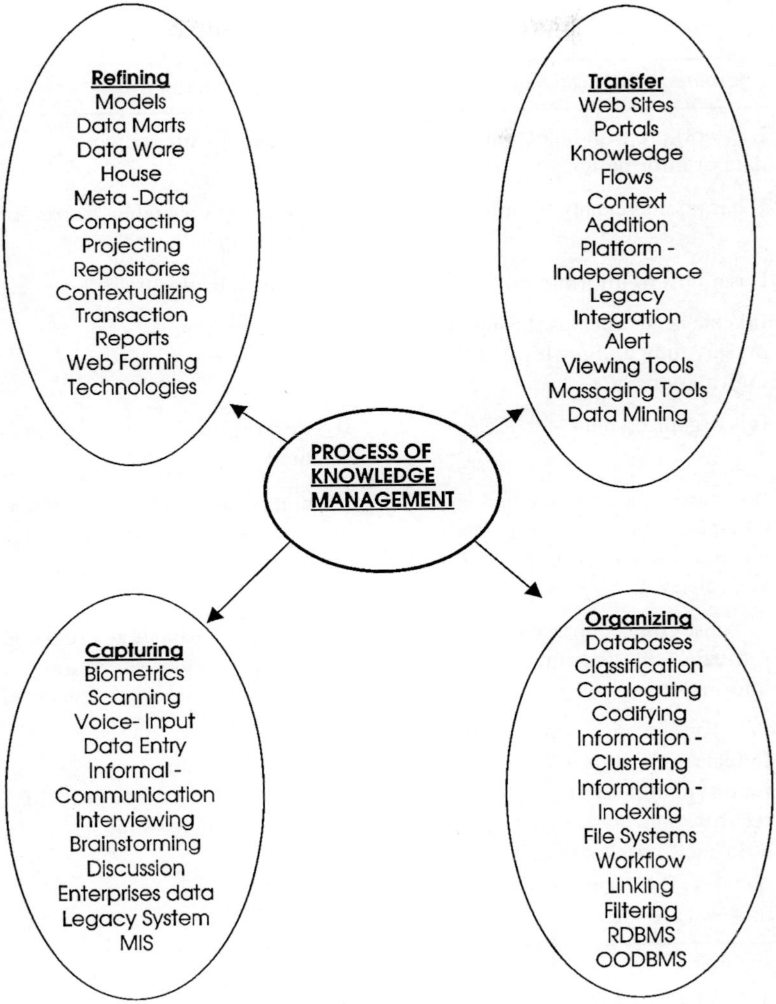

Fig. 2: Process of Knowledge Management

***Table 1.** Differences between Information and Knowledge Management*

Information Management	*Knowledge Management*
It is working with objects such as data or information.	It is working with people.
It has no universally accepted meaning	It depends on a higher degree of certainty and validity.
It is a flow of information.	It is formed by this flow.
It achieves its success through the preservation and retrieval of information.	It uses knowledge.
It is organized data.	It is extrapolative and future – oriented.
It behaves as a resource and lays emphasis on human involvement in terms of information audit, storage and retrieval.	It emphasizes people management in order to harness the knowledge stored in people's heads.
It focuses on acquiring, storing, retrieving and disseminating information.	It focuses on sharing, creating, learning, and enhancing information for organizational development.
It deals exclusively with explicit representations and ensures access, security, delivery and storage where efficiency, timeliness accuracy, veracity, speed, cost storage space and retrieval are the main concerns.	It recognizes value in originality, innovation, adaptability, intelligence and learning.

3. IMPORTANCE OF KNOWLEDGE MANAGEMENT

- It enhances productivity, competitiveness and lower costs in organizations.
- It enables knowledge- intensive organizations to manage knowledge resources effectively.
- It enables the harnessing of aging civil servants and

departing staff knowledge in order to preserve institutional memory.

- It facilitates adaptation to and technology transfer within organizations.
- It improves working relations and trust in organizations.
- It promotes lifelong learning.
- It enhances innovations and teamwork in public organizations.
- It puts pressure on an organization to demonstrate accountability in managing public resources.
- It provides tools, procedures and environment for knowledge management policy formulation.
- Knowledge mapping or information architecture.
- Adoption and use of standards-metadata and best practices.
- Performance evaluation and Management tools.
- Developing communication systems.
- Methodologies for content management and content quality management.
- Technologies for managing knowledge such as intranet/ extranet, search engines, portal building software, language tools.
- Addressing security issues.
- Integration, interoperability and scalability.
- Interface design.

4. KNOWLEDGE MANAGEMENT TECHNOLOGY

- Web browsers
- Web pages
- Groupware
- Search and retrieval tools

- Data – mining technologies
- Expert systems
- Simulation
- Artificial Intelligence
- Web Mapping Tools
- Database Management System
- Document Management System
- Knowledge Base Management System
- Help Desk Technology
- Push Technology
- Data mining
- Messaging systems
- Intelligent agents
- Intranet
- Information Retrieval
- Electronic Publishing Technology
- Internet:
  - — E- Mail
  - — Listservs
  - — Newsgroups
  - — Web-Conferencing
  - — Internet Relay Chat
  - — I Phone and Internet Radio
  - — Desktop Videos Conferencing
  - — VRMAL Chat system

***Table2:** Knowledge management tools and it's vendor's name*

Sr. No.	*K M Tool Name*	*Vendor's Name*
1	ALISE	Pacific software publishing
2	ALTA VISTA	Alta Vista, Inc.
3	DB/TEXT	In Magic, Inc.
4	EXCITE	Excite, Inc
5	GLIMPSE	University of Arizona
6	LIVE LINK SEARCH	Open Text
7	LYCOS INTRANET SPIDER	Lycos and In Magic, Inc.
8	MICROSOFT INDEX SERVER	Microsoft
9	NET RESULTS	Innotech
10	PL WEB	PLS
11	RETRIEVAL WARE	Excabibur Technologies
12	TECUMSEH SCOUT	Tippecanoe systems, Inc
13	SEARCH'97	Verity
14	WEB WORKS SEARCH	Quadralay
15	ACTIVE ANSWERS	Compaq
16	ACTIVE KNOWLEDGE	Autonomy
17	ALEXA for NETSCAPE & INTERNET EXPLORER	Alexa
18	BACK WEB FOUNDATION	Backweb
19	CENTERBURY	Chrystal Software Inc.
20	FULCRUM	Fulcrum
21	DOCUEDIT	Datacap
22	DOCUSHARE	Xerox
23	DOCU-X WEBSERVER	Minolta
24	DOMINO.DOC	Lotus
25	ECLIPSE	Haley
26	EDMS	Documentum
27	EMAIL SPECIALIST	Yy Software
28	FIRSTCLASS INTRANET SERVER	SoftArc Inc.
29	FREEDOM	Zero- Knowledge Systems
30	GRAPEVINE FOR NOTES	GRAPEVINE

31	INSIGHT	Information IN Inc.
32	KNOWLEDGE BUILDER	Autonomy
33	KNOWLEDGE INNOVATION	Knowledge Associates
34	KNOWLEDGE RETRIEVAL PRODUCT SUITE	Verity
35	KNOWLEDGE SERVER 2.0	Intraspect
36	KNOWLEDGE X	Ibm
37	NETOCTOPUS	Netopia
38	PORTAL-IN-A-BOX	Autonomy
39	SAGEWAVE	Sagemaker
40	WORK SAVER	Cuadra
41	TRACKER	Engfish
42	UNISEARCH	ComSquared
43	VIADOR-E-PORTAL	VIADOR
44	WEBFORIA ORGANISER	Webforia
45	WEBPROJECT	Webproject
46	WISDOM WARE SALES	Wisdom Ware
47	2 SHARE	2 Bridge Software
48	BEEHIVE	Abuzz
49	BROAD QUEST	Broad Quest
50	VENTRIX BRIDGE	Ventrix
51	PANAGON	Filenet

5. CHALLENGES OF IMPLEMENTING KNOWLEDGE MANAGEMENT SYSTEMS

- Inadequate of human resources
- Inadequate of infrastructure, Finance, illiteracy, relevant content & technologies
- Critical ICT skills
- Knowledge management strategies
- General understanding of knowledge & ICT potentials
- Integrating & managing the knowledge & information needed to perform effectively

- The difficulty associated with learning to mange oneself, formal & informal exchanges & interaction with others
- The difficulty of understanding individual's disposition including goals, capabilities, knowledge strengths & weakness.
- The difficulty of appreciating social, technical & business environment.
- The difficulty of managing knowledge & information residing in people's heads without roadmaps of a filtering function.
- The difficulty of handling knowledge in different formats such as websites, personnel files, accounts, order books, customers history & procurement records
- Issues relating to protection of intellectual property, patent processing & confidentiality protection.
- The difficulty of dealing with intangible products & auditing intellectual capital, namely knowledge that involves establishing its existence, its ownership & its value.
- The difficulty associated with the transfer with innovations from one staff member to the another staff member.
- Research and development to prepare, staff in knowledge organizations incurs high costs for products and services such as computer chips, CD-ROMs disks, DVD & tape publishing, advertising & public relation & consultancy
- Problems of gaining access to the form of knowledge that knowledge workers have and use.
- Winning trust, motivation and commitment
- Managing non- conventional employees, such as contract workers and consultants, Visiting faculties.
- Reliance on knowledge workers who may leave the organization without the organization the having

captured their knowledge capital.

- Web-based systems and other technology infrastructure used in knowledge management are vulnerable as they can be easily replicated and pirated, making them less valuable for strategic purposes

6. TACIT & EXPLICIT KNOWLEDGE

Tacit Knowledge

Nonaka (1995) coined the terms tacit & explicit knowledge. It is knowledge embedded in the human mind & through experience & jobs. It includes intuitions, values & beliefs that stem form years of experience. It is the knowledge used to create explicit knowledge & is best communicated personally through dialogue & scenarios with use of metaphors.

Explicit Knowledge

It is knowledge codified and digitized in books, documents, reports, white papers, spreadsheets, memos; training courses etc. it can be retrieved and transmitted more easily then tacit knowledge.

Table 3: *Diffrences between tacit and explicit knowledge*

Tacit Knowledge	*Explicit Knowledge*
Embodied Knowledge	Theoretical Knowledge
Personal, hard to formalize	It is Knowledge codified and digitized in books
Hard to Communicate	Physical entity
It is not measurable	Can be measurable
Mind-sets of individuals	Distributable
Cumulative store of the experiences, mental maps, insights, accumulated expertise, know-how, trade secrets, skills and learning	Deals with more objective, rational, and technical knowledge

Involving personal belief, perspective & values	Transmitting among individuals
It is knowing-how	It is knowing –what
Sticky knowledge	Leaky knowledge
Personal Knowledge rooted in individual experience	Documented Knowledge
Intangible, insights, intuitions, hunches, gut feelings, values, images, metaphors	Which can be articulated in language
Informal Knowledge	Formal Knowledge

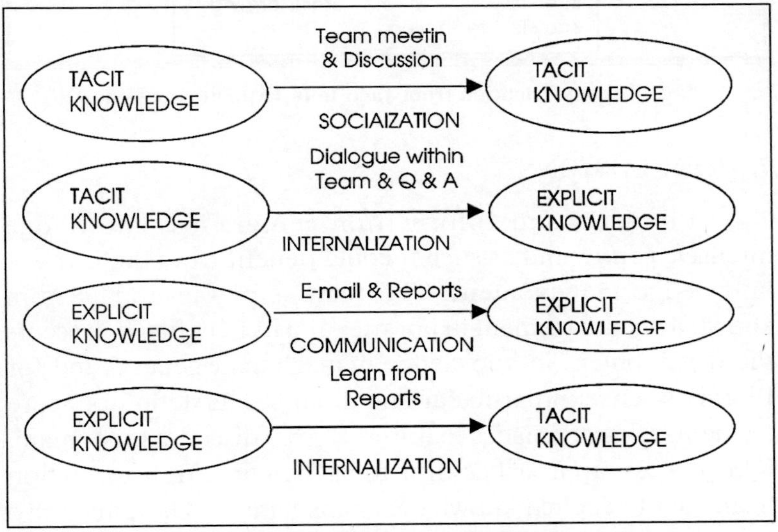

Fig. 3. Conversion from Tacit to in Explicit Knowledge

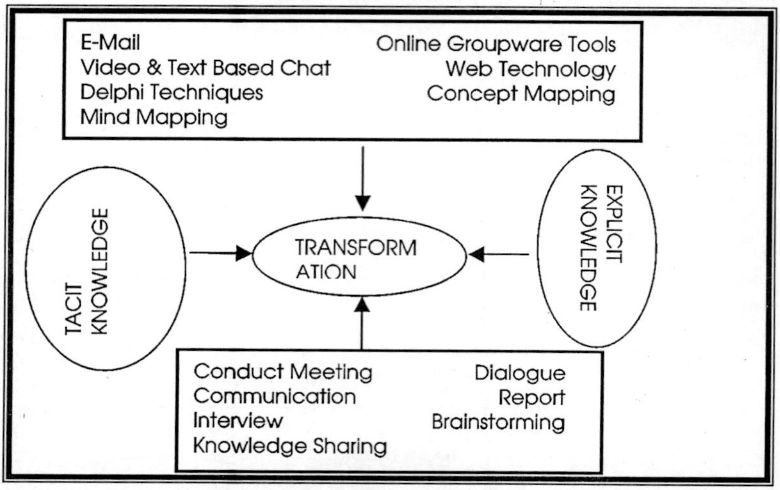

Fig. 4: Transformation from Tacit to in Explicit Knowledge

7. CONCLUSIONS

Libraries and Information centers are knowledge intensive centre and as such it could benefit from the ideas of knowledge management. The focuses of these articles in knowledge management in libraries and its benefits. It presents the development in knowledge management general and for Library science in particular and discusses its definition, core elements, characteristics features, a cross disciplinary domain, KM process, approaches of it tools, benefits, transformation from tacit to explicit knowledge management. This paper also presents resources that can provide help, inspiration and information to organization that want to better manage their knowledge. For any library to succeed in implementing knowledge management will require strong leadership and vision from the top level management which can influence the organizations and knowledge sharing efforts in a positive way. The best knowledge creators are scientists, research scholars, academics. Knowledge creation is best performed by research and development centers like R&D Department & its laboratories, Universities, Intellectual organizations.

As a learning and knowledge organization those should empowered their libraries to developed campus-wide knowledge management systems. It is now time for libraries to repositories them self central stage and pivotal role in knowledge management.

REFERENCES

1. Award, Elias, M, & Ghaziri, Hassan. M. Knowledge Management. Delhi, Pearson Education, 2003.
2. Dikshit, Pramod, E-track: Business of future, knowledge Management in software enginerring,32(2), vol.iv,2008
3. Nonaka, Ikujiro. The knowledge Creating Company," Harvard Business Review (Nov.-Dec.1991); 96-99.1991.
4. Drucker, Peter. Post-Capitalism Society. Oxford, Great Britain: Butterworth-Heinemann.1993.
5. Agresti, W., Knowledge Management. Advance in Computers.
6. Marwick, A.D., Knowledge Management Technology," IBM Systems Journal,40(4),2001
7. Raman, A. Thothathri. Knowledge Management: A Resource book. New Delhi, Excell Books,2004.
8. Baired and Lloyd et.al. The Knowledge Engine. New Delhi, Viva books, 2002.
9. Warrier, E. Sudhir, Knowledge Management. Delhi, Vikas Pub. House Pvt. Ltd. 2003.
10. Tiwana, Amrit, The Knowledge Management Toolkit: Orchestrating IT, Strategy & Knowledge Platforms, Delhi, Pearson Education,2005.
11. Pandey, Bhaw Nath, et.al. Knowledge Management Software and Tools for Global Libraries. In National Conference on Digitization & Digital Preservation,11-12 Dec,2008 DESIDOC.pp.430-437.
12. Natarajan, Ganesh et.al. Knowledge Management. New Delhi
13. *http://www.kmresource.com*
14. *http://www.systemo-thinking.org*
15. *http://www.expertexchange.com*
16. *http://www.capterra.com*

18

E-RESOURCES IN KNOWLEDGE MANAGEMENT IN HEALTH SCIENCE LIBRARIES IN INDIA

Rakesh Kumar Srivastava
Librarian, Christian Medical College, Ludhiana
rakeshlko51@gmail.com
rakeshsrivastava1@in.com

ABSTRACT

Knowledge Management in health science institutions is a major issue today. Health Science professionals are routinely dealing with evidence based medicine and problem based learning. Health Science Libraries has a significant role in the making of clinical practice.

Keywords : Knowledge Management System, Electronic Resource, India, Health Science Libraries.

1. INTRODUCTION

Knowledge Management caters to the critical issues of organizations adaptation survived and competence in taking increasingly discontinues environment charge, essentially it, embodies organizational processes that seek synergistic combination of data and information processing capacity of information technology and the creative and innovative capacity of human beings.

2. KNOWLEDGE MANAGEMENT IN THE OLD INFORMATION ERA

In the information era characterized relatively predictable change technology gurus, as Well as hardware and software providers, have been offering out of box solutions that are expected to offer means for storing best practices devised by human experts in Information databases which may be later used for eructing out the per determined solutions based on per defined parameters.

Knowledge management caters to the critical issues of organizational adoption, survival and competence in dace of increasingly discontinuous , environmental change , Essentially it embodies organizational process that seek synergistic combination of data and information processing capacity of information technology and creative and innovative capacity of human beings.

The traditional paradigm of information systems is based on seeking a consensual intermediation of information abased on socially dictated norms or the mandate of the comparing bosses. This has resulted in the confession between knowledge and information how ever knowledge and information are destined entitles while information generated by the computer systems is not a very rich carrier of human interpretation for potential action. Knowledge resides in the user's subjective context of action based on that information hence it may not be incorrect so state that knowledge resides in the user and not in the collection of information a point made two decades of by west churchman that leading thinker of information systems.

"New organization wealth: Management and measuring knowledge based assets, contends that the confusion between knowledge and information has caused managers to sink billions of doe tares in technology ventures that have yielded marginal results.

3. WHAT IS THE KNOWLEDGE MANAGEMENT

"Rudy Ruggles" a leading KM thinker has identified the following items as integral component of KM:

1. Generating New Knowledge.
2. Accessing valuable knowledge from and out side sources.
3. using accessible knowledge in decision making
4. Representing knowledge in documents, databases and software.
5. Transferring existing knowledge in to other parts of the organization.
6. Measuring the value of knowledge assets and / or impact of knowledge management.

4. WHY IT IS IMPORTANT

A Variety of factors have contributed to the growth of and interested in Knowledge Management.:

1. Accelerating pace of change
2. Staff Attrition
3. Growth in organizational Scope
4. Global integration
5. Increases in networked organization.
6. Growing Knowledge – Intensity of goods & services
7. Revoluation in information technology.

5. PURPOSE OF KNOWLEDGE MANAGEMENT

The Purpose of Knowledge Management to:

i. Train every user's in accessing information and guide the user's to the appropriate resources.

ii. Develop Collection on important subject.

iii. Develop links with resources both physical such as institutions and individuals and electronic search as electronic resources available through the internet

iv. Give as much information to the users as the user's need to complete assignments.

v. Collect new materials select materials for inclusion in database in put data, Index data search and retrieve data and deliver the output to the end user's Perform data cleaning or delectation of redundant records from the. Data base Check for the systems security from this knowledge librarian's can build a web front and can allow the user's to access the information in a quick and easy way.

vi. Gain significant returns out of the data and information we produce and the way in which we produce it.

6. HEALTH SCIENCE RESOURCE MANAGEMENT

Health Science Librarians must know the theory of as well as have skills needed for identifying collecting, evaluating and organizing resources and developing and providing access to data base including identification and selection of material and sources , acquisition of materials bibliometric technique. The cataloguing and classification theory, national & international standards and conventions including cataloguing and filling rules, indexing, abstracting and classification systems, inventory control systems, serial publications resource, conservation and preservation, publishing industry, trends in information formatting, production packing dissemination and copy right issues.

7. SEARCH IN KNOWLEDGE MANAGEMENT IN MEDICAL HEALTH SCIENCE

a. Artificial database A to Z

b. Pub med

c. Full text database Catalogue

d. 1. Library Catalogue as Title ,Authors, Subject

   2. NLM(National Medical Library of Medicine)

e. Digital Collection and Multimedia

   1. HEAL (Health Education Assets Library)

   2. NOVEL (Nero Ophthalmology, Video Education Library)

   3. Web Path (As Internet & Search engine as Google, yahoo. msn, etc)

f. Electronic Journals as e. journals a to z.

g. Electronic Books as e. books all subject

h. Orders and Requests.

i. Order Articles, Books etc

j. Order Literature Search

k. Suggest & Purchase

l. Scholarly Communication and Publishing

m. Subject Links.

Medical education especially in the advanced stages of training has many unique problems such as the temporal and geographic distribution of students, residents and the physician instructors. Further complications that are present in most areas of medicine leading to poorly attended or cancelled lectures. Medical Progress demands the reconciling of old and new information with in the local context of the clinical and this presupposes individual's critical appraisal of evidence and integrations with clinical experience.

The challenges faced by medical educators accompanied

by the tremendous amount of information explosions and the advancement of information technology have initiated the necessity of knowledge management.

Knowledge Management is not managing or organizing books or journals, searching the internet for clients of arranging the circulation of materials, how ever, each of the activities can in some enchaining the use of organizational knowledge through sound practices of knowledge management and organizational learning. Thus knowledge management is a combination of information management, communication and human resources. Good knowledge centers will put as much emphasis on connecting people with people –"

Know-who"-as they do on connecting people with "Active" not archive knowledge, so need to be fully up to speed with what is happening in the organization including current priorities and works in progress. "**Who is doing what know.**"

REFERENCES

1. Dynamic Knowledge Systems- accessed on Augest,29 ,2007
2. Electronic Journals of Academic and Special Librarianship-Vol-8, No.2,2007
3. www.infolibrarian.com - accessed on Augest,29 ,2007
4. www.bhojarajug.freeservers.com - accessed on Augest,29 ,2007
5. www.e.zest.net/knowledgemgmt.html - accessed on Augest,29 ,2007

19

Dimensions of Knowledge Management and It's Application in Libraries in 21st Century

Rabinarayan Mishra
LecturerDept. of Lib. & Inf. ScienceMizoram University, Aizawl
rabinarayan_mishra@rediffmail.com
Sanjeev
Assistant Librarian, Mizoram University, Aizawl

ABSTRACT

The dawn of Information Technology in manifold directions altered the horizons of library services. There is a tremendous impact of internet and computer technologies not only in the field of library services but also in the field of document management which practically gave way to the birth of information management. With the proliferation of ocean of information through World Wide Web, the term information management was altered to a new and recent expression known as knowledge management. Knowledge in true sense of the term is categorized into three types such as, Explicit Knowledge, Embedded Knowledge and Tacit Knowledge.

Knowledge Management has become a new research area in comparison to other research areas such as data processing, information management, and network management. The innermost assignment of a library is to accumulate, systematize, preserve, and endow with access to knowledge and information. To arrive to this gigantic mission the libraries requires preserving valuable records of culture that can be passed down to succeeding generations. Libraries through out the ages have proved to be essential link in this communication among past, present, and future. Libraries ensure for preservation of recorded knowledge whether through print form or electronic form so as to disseminate and retrieval of records as and when required.

Keywords : Knowledge Management.

1. GENESIS OF INFORMATION

Information is the upshot of the human excavation which is recorded both in print and electronic form. Information acts as a communication that can be transmitted by a transmitter to a receiver. Information basically triggers on a human being to take action for a piece of assigned plan and it may be very well compared with kinetic and potential energy where, the former moves things and the latter is recorded and acts as the reservoir. Lack of proper, coordinated, complete and authentic information seldom leads to disillusion and improper decision that bring serious threat to the various developmental plans. Hence, the importance of information as a resource has been recognized for centuries. The Oxford English Dictionary defines 'Information' as the action of informing; formation or component of the mind or character, training, instruction, teaching; communication of edifying knowledge. The concept of information has been visualized by different authors in different angles.

Information can be considered as, (i) Knowledge communicated or received concerning a particular fact or circumstances; (ii) Communication or reception of knowledge or intelligence, (iii) Knowledge communicated by others or obtained through investigation, study or instruction; (iv) a concept, statement, and idea or an association of concepts, statement, and the ideas; (v) Knowledge derived from observation, study, experience, or instruction and (vi) Message conveyed or intended to be conveyed by a systematized body of ideas.

The genuine, pinpointed, extensive, and judicious information is one of the crucial factors accountable for the augmentation and expansion of a society. Information happens to be one of the indispensable and effectual tools to resolve the current problems faced by an individual, a community, and an organization as well.

Electronics encompasses an exceptionally broad range of technology. Electronics is essential, for example, in telecommunications, an ever-increasing volume of information is transmitted in digital form. Digital techniques, in which signals are converted into groups of pulses, allow the intermingling of voice, television, and computer signals into one very rapid series of pulses on a single channel that can be separated at the receiving end and reconstituted into the signals originally sent. Because the digital pulses can be regenerated perfectly after they become attenuated with distance, no noise or other degradation is apparent at the receiving end (Encyclopedia Britannica CD: 2001). Further, the unstinted growth of information irrespective of the fields in the midst of Information Technology (IT) era shaped mayhem for the availability of pinpointed, authentic and timely information in a structured form that paved the way to establish the multidimensional, multidisciplinary, and versatile information in an organized form. The management of the increased complexities of prolix information due to technological revolution, causing technological advancement - thereby, intensive research and development, varied tastes of information of the user communities, and more pertinently the information explosion in the 21st century created much impact upon the information managers and the decision making authorities to obtain, store, process, retrieve, and dissemination of the same in an organized form. Thus, knowledge may be defined as an organized body of information or understanding of facts that by thorough assimilation, one can acquire which in turn, helps in the generation of new knowledge or information.

The information is one of the most effective tools that ameliorate to solve the day-to-day problems of the society. Lumberton, however, discloses that, the term information and knowledge revolution has far reaching economic, social and political consequences. In the present state, both information and knowledge have primacy over the building, land and machinery. Information is thus delineated as the knowledge, intelligence of news irrespective of the subjects on which it has been taught. Bertrand Russell, in connection with his celebrated theory of descriptions has categorized information in two ways i.e, (a) Knowledge by acquaintances and (b) Knowledge by description. He, however, has argued that information that is based on direct experience is basic and needs no justification, which is otherwise known as "Knowledge by acquaintance." The information that is not based on direct experience is known as "Knowledge by description." One is justified in calling such information knowledge, if one can show that it can be traced back to and thus ultimately rests upon knowledge by acquaintance (Encyclopedia Britannica CD 2001).

2. KNOWLEDGE GENERATION

Knowledge is the totality of ideas that are generated out of human mind at different points of times that also emanates from the very interaction of human beings with nature and its surroundings that infect, has no definite shape in its structure. It is the human intellect that organizes itself into different modules for assimilation and use. Dewey has identified the following five main functional stages through which knowledge can effectively be acquired which include:

i. Identification and definition of the problems faced by an individual;

ii. Observation, Collection, Organization, and Classification of relevant data that may solve the problem;

iii. Formulation of tentative hypotheses, which provide guidelines while solving problems;

iv. Testing of hypotheses through collected data; and

v. Analysis of data and formulation of conclusions.

Knowledge is generated through various organizations in manifold ways and means which include Industrial and Commercial Organizations, Research institutions, Universities, and such other Academic institutions. It is preserved for dissemination and retrieval as and when required. It is applied for action after testing by a researcher who creates a new knowledge over the existing one. Thus, the effective utilization of the existing knowledge in a field of research leads to new inventions, discoveries, and innovations.

Preoccupation with information and knowledge as an individual, organizational, and societal resource is stronger today than at any other time in history. At present, however, there are several new dimensions relative to the information resource which includes modern information systems. New information systems capitulate, generate and organize information i.e, knowledge automatically which provides rapid and high-resolution access to the corporation of information. Further, they manipulate information or knowledge with previously unattainable versatility and efficiency.

Modern information systems also bring new efficiency

to the organization, retrieval, and dissemination of recorded information. The control of the world's information store has been truly revolutionized, revealing its diversity in hitherto unattainable detail. Information services provide mechanisms to locate documents nearly instantaneously and to copy and move many of them electronically. New digital storage technologies make it economical for some to obtain for personal possession those collections equivalent to the holdings of entire libraries and archives. Alternately, access to information resources on electronic networks permits the accumulation of highly individualized personal or corporate collections in analog or digital form or a combination of both.

Digital information is stored in complex patterns that make it feasible to address and operate on even the smallest element of symbolic expression, as well as on larger strings such as words or sentences and on images and sound. From the viewpoint of digital information storage, it is useful to distinguish between "structured" data, such as inventories of objects that can be represented by short symbol strings and numbers, and "unstructured" data, such as the natural-language text of documents or pictorial images. The principal objective of all storage structures is to facilitate the processing of data elements based on their relationships; the structures thus vary with the type of relationship they represent. The choice of a particular storage structure is governed by the relevance of the relationships it allows to be represented to the information-processing requirements of the task or system at hand. Further, the rapid developments in computers, telecommunications, and other technologies have made it possible to store and retrieve information in many different forms and from any place with a computer and a telephone connection. The terms digital library and virtual library have begun to be used to refer to the vast collections of information to which people gain access over the Internet, cable television, or some other type of remote electronic connection.

3. INFORMATION MANAGEMENT

The propagation of information, telecommunication technology, computer technology added with skills and development of new technologies in manifold dimensions have resulted impact acquisition, storage, organization, coordination and proper diffusion of information. The Libraries and Information Centers in the midst of the information technology scenario no longer reckoned on the traditional contour of meeting the versatile requirements of the users. They rather adopted new technological devices to satisfy the wide-ranging tastes of information requirements of the users in the libraries and service oriented organizations.

Information Revolution in the rudder of present technological scenario has resulted to generate the term Information Management. The unprecedented explosion of information through Internet, Intranet and other electronic sources has also resulted for creation of Information overload almost in every service organizations in general and Library and Information Center in particular. The overwhelming growth of information from all quarters became a serious concern to propagate the right information to the right reader in right time in such an electronic environment. The Librarians and Information Officers necessitated the change in management system of information and adopted new budding techniques in relation to the process involved in information generation, collection, storage, processing and dissemination, utilization and above all feedback. The ontogenesis of a system to grip information is the most complex and it involves considerable investment. Social activities of such dimensions have to be planned and guided to give maximal benefit to all sections of the society. This is in general the objective of the Information Management (Rao, 2002).

Efforts to explore an identity for Information Science almost continue unremittingly. Despite the fact that, there exists a unanimous opinion by the scientists regarding prominent role of information to human society, both the concept of 'Information' and the 'Science' remain tangled in loosely defined terminological controversies and multifaceted opinion. It may not be out of place to mention that, the term 'Science' has some greater connotations. The extent of its nature and scope is away from a common viewpoint. Broadly, electronics and knowledge contribute to the origin of Information Science.

There is no universal accepted definition of information management though the concept was generated during 1980s. (Ravichandra Rao, 2002). But, information management has been defined in various ways. While, Keary (1997,pp.35-7) has defined it as a methodology for identifying all available information in an organizing, Taylor and Farrell (1992, pp.319-22) has highlighted it as Management of Information System in the angles of IT application in libraries for organizing of information resources, acquiring, management, and retrieval; System Analysis and Design and more specifically as Data Management. These are primarily required for effectual means of information use and for decision making. In the words of Ravichandra Rao (2002) Information Management is not only about managing the processes of selection, collection, processing, controlling and dissemination of information but also enabling the effective use of information. Information Management is thus, can be broadly defined as a methodology for proper acquiring of information in any form whether traditional or electronic such as, On-line Databases, CD-ROM Databases, Web Sources etc, and organization of information resources in libraries, for the purpose of retrieval and dissemination of the same in the right manner.

4. KNOWLEDGE MANAGEMENT

Knowledge has been widely recognized as a primarily commodity in the current knowledge-based economy. The optimum use of the products and resources as well, from the Computer Technology Systems in an edifice and consolidated form including accumulated pool of information generated from the brains of the scientists in their fields and more specifically the Personal Knowledge precipitated to the establishment of Knowledge Management. It is the end result to contrive the irresistible growth of information in an effectual way with the help of the modern technological devices and has thus, became an indispensable path in the highly competitive service oriented including business environment which require more responsive, innovative, and competitive including efficiency. Knowledge Management is a revolutionary method by which, the dispersed knowledge available from diversified sources are captured, assimilated and converted into a powerful competitive intelligence through various electronic segments such as CD-ROM, DVD-ROM, Web, Pen drive, Floppy, Hard disks, Software etc. Moreover, Knowledge Management can be defined as a study of strategy, process and application of technologies to acquire, select, organize, share and influence critical information and apply expertise to improve the qualities of information services in the libraries. It embodies synergistic integration of information processing capacity and creative capacity of human beings in order to maximize the responsiveness and flexibility of organization (Siau, 2005, 117-23.).

It may not be out of place to mention that, INSPEC (http://www.iee.org/publish/inspec), which is a bibliographic database, provides access to the world wide literature on Physics, Electrical Engineering and Electronics, Control Theory and Technology and Computers. INSPEC which accumulates more than 7,503,985 citations, covers 4000 journals including the fields in Communications, Computer Applications, Computer Hardware and Software, Information Technology and Office Automation. From 1980 to 2005, it has indexed 1789 articles on Knowledge Management (Zhuang; 2006). The data pertaining to articles available on Knowledge Management in INSPEC from 1980 to 2005 are reflected in Table-1 as under supplemented with graph for crystal clear.

***Table-1:** Knowledge Management articles in INSPEC*

Sl.No.	*Years*	*No. of articles*
1	1980-1985	6
2	1986-1990	52
3	1991-1995	54
4	1996-2000	503
5	2001-2005	1174

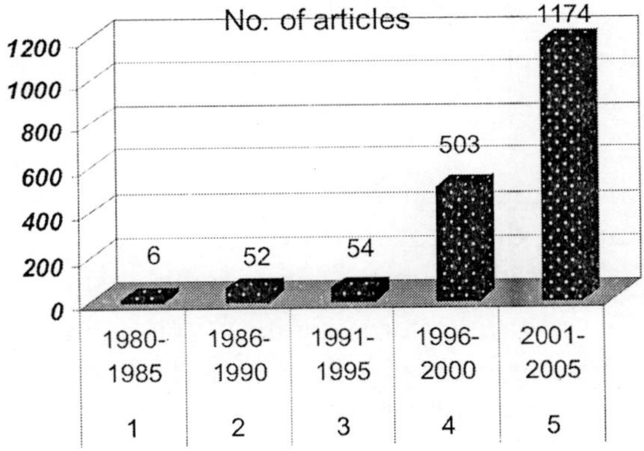

5. IMPETUS OF KNOWLEDGE MANAGEMENT

Knowledge Management, as a strategic lever came into existence especially during 1970s and 1980s where the potentiality of knowledge solved many important issues and problems in business organizations through Knowledge based Computer System i.e, 'Expert System'. Subsequently, however it emerged an indispensable tool in the field of Libraries, Information Service and in other service oriented sectors.

Mention may be made that, extensive knowledge in business and service activities are evolved from a number of management authorities including practitioners as visualized by Amidon in 1997 (Skhrrme, 2004). This throws light upon the evolution and convergence of accepted wisdom and scripts about knowledge as a strategic parameter along with other initiatives such as responsive manufacturing, innovations and the learning organization.

The types of knowledge can be broadly categorized into (i) Explicit Knowledge and (ii) Tacit Knowledge. The conversion processes of knowledge can be categorized into following four types,

- Tacit-to-tacit (socialization) – Here, the individuals irrespective of the tpes acquire new knowledge directly from others;
- Tacit-to-explicit (externalization) – It concerns with the articulation of knowledge into tangible form through dialogue;
- Explicit-to-explicit (combination) – It resembles to combining different forms of explicit knowledge found in the printed documents or in databases;
- Explicit-to-tacit (internalization) – It is related to learning by capturing internalize knowledge from documents into their own body of experience.

5.1. State of Knowledge Practice

Knowledge adds substantial value to a Library and Information Services apart from other areas of its applications especially through its products, processes, dissemination and knowledge workers. The product contribution of knowledge as described by Davis and Botkin (1994) is associated with the most common activities in the Knowledge Management initiatives which can be well initiated, developed, organized and disseminated by Libraries and Information Centers to satisfy the wide-ranging needs of the user communities including commercialization of knowledge as a part of marketing of knowledge products and services. He further has also visualized knowledge in different angles such as,

- Creation of knowledge teams – Here, people from all disciplines are required to develop the methods of knowledge management
- Sharing of Best Practices – Experts, Innovators from one part of the organization to another need to share their knowledge gained through experiences either through databases or through personal interaction including sharing events, memories.
- Development of Knowledge Databases – Databases can be developed out of the best practices, experiences. Creation of expert directories, market intelligence databases etc. add substantial value in the field of Libraries and Information Science for addition of knowledge and decision support system.
- Creation of Knowledge Centres – Knowledge Centers can be created in Libraries and Information Centers to develop knowledge skills, and this will facilitate for managing and enhancing knowledge databases for knowledge flow.
- Collaborative Technologies – This is primarily concerned with the use of Intranets (internal Internet) or groupware for rapid knowledge access and dissemination.
- Intellectual Capital Teams – They happen to be core identified groups for intangible assets of knowledge.

The Working Group of Libraries of National Knowledge Commission meant for challenging mandate to transform India of 21st Century into a knowledge society also equally emphasized for promotion of Knowledge Management in public as well as academic and special libraries. In the emerging knowledge society era, special libraries must be reshaped as knowledge management centers that will require linking people, knowledge, and technology that would facilitate knowledge flow and transfer to foster knowledge assimilation and knowledge creation.

More over, to improve the management of institutions engaged in intellectual property rights, the National Knowledge Commission apart from other primary issues focused to,

- Promote innovation and entrepreneurship, and knowledge applications in agriculture, industry and healthcare.
- Promote the use of knowledge capabilities in making government an effective, transparent and accountable service provider to the citizen and
- Promote widespread sharing of knowledge to maximize public benefit.
- Promote the utilization of traditional knowledge.

6. KNOWLEDGE MANAGEMENT IN LIBRARIES

According to Shanhong, the contents of Knowledge Management broadly can be grouped as follows which can be applied for innovative outputs in the Library and Information Centres (*www.ifla.org*)

6.1. Knowledge Innovation Management

Knowledge Innovation Management in Libraries and Information Centres is associated with the management of the production, diffusion and repositioning of knowledge both inside and outside the libraries through network systems developed by the concerned institutions and organizations.

This includes three primary aspects, such as, (i) Theoretical Innovation Management of Knowledge, (ii) Technical Innovation Management and (iii) Organizational Innovation Management.

The Theoretical Innovation Management is concerned

with to augment and broaden the theoretical and practical research fields in library and information science by way of implementing the most recent development trends in the field whereas, Technical Innovation Management manages the network systems of technical innovations. In the changing scenario of library and information services including technology alterations, the Libraries and Information Centers need to espouse the Knowledge Management through technical expertise. The Organizational Innovation Management opens a set of windows for effective organizational management systems adaptable to the requirements in a digital library era for supporting and strengthening different activities of knowledge management by optimizing the functional departments and operation procedures of libraries and information centers. Formulation of management plans, Coordination of Knowledge Management activities, Establishment of leading groups of Knowledge Flow, Evaluation of information to shape knowledge, Creation of knowledge through electronic resources are some of the important accomplishing tasks for application of Knowledge Management activities in Libraries and Information Centers (Sheng;1999; 29-32).

6.2. Knowledge Sharing Management

One more important segment of Knowledge Management and Knowledge Dissemination Management is Knowledge Sharing Management. The strategy for utilizing a Knowledge Management System involves the procedure to capture, accumulate, organize and share out the knowledge where, the subject experts, scientists etc. contribute their knowledge to a system for the use by unknown persons, instead of restricting the knowledge within them or close group sharing. It is evident from various instances that, even some of high dignitaries and experts brains reserve their knowledge within themselves and do not disseminate or share knowledge as they consider knowledge is a power dictum. As there are a massive amount of knowledge users, it is very difficult to acquire knowledge that already exists in the minds of knowledge creators restricted by them due to various constraints. Therefore, Libraries and Information Centres play a very crucial role with the knowledge creator by using diversified medias and channels and techniques to get hold of innovative knowledge in varied areas. The Internet, flooded with un-paralleled and unevaluated information add considerable knowledge for a wide range of user communities irrespective of the areas and subjects. Library and Information Centers at this moment act as positive bodies to explore information on a wide range of subjects, consolidate, organize and disseminate the information with the help of new technological devices to the user communities. Here, the Libraries and Information Centers act as a filtering body and scale the information to suit to the need of the users and as well as manage the information for effective dissemination. In such cases, it becomes vital to reinforce Knowledge Dissemination management in libraries which can be carried out in the following ways.

Library requires to create document resources in multifarious areas with addition of new knowledge in the concerned field from internet and disseminate the information in house and aboard through network.

- Imparting continuous new technology skills to the library staffs to acquire the information, consolidate and repackaging information.
- Creating an environment of expert system in proper dissemination of knowledge.
- Use of all medias to ensure security of operation of networks, and prevent online criminal activities and online dissemination of inappropriate information (Sheng; 1999; 29-32).
- Proliferation of knowledge through all available channels.

6.3. Knowledge Application Management

Library and Information Centers in the domain of Internet era during 21st century essentially requires to keep abreast with the latest services opportunities for its clienteles so as to built a need-based collection by way of collecting, amalgamating exhaustive information with due filtration irrespective of the areas. The information thus collected by the libraries requires to be transmitted to the users with high bandwidth networks which are the demand of the day.

With the present trend of the demands of the user communities in Libraries and other service organizations, it has practically complicated to organize knowledge coherently which involves the practice of through knowledge in the area and it also involves huge financial burden. However, Libraries can take an effort to create virtual libraries system or information centers for and disseminates knowledge to the users' communities according to their respective information requirements by using abundant information resources through high-speed information networks.

Setting up digitized knowledge services is actually a development trend of libraries in the 21st century which presupposes creating step by step the users-oriented information service systems such as information dissemination, information search and special supply of information; quickening the creation of digitized libraries; studying the methods, means and techniques of information distribution and search with the Internet as the base and WEB technique as the core entity including digitizing libraries' resources. The electronic libraries or digitized libraries are the technical modes and development trends of libraries in the knowledge economy era. The knowledge services of libraries in the future will start with creation of databases comprising electronic journals and books in different languages that have discipline features and can operate on high-speed information networks. Great efforts should be made to transform all existing large non-electronic information resources into electronic information and integrate them into electronic libraries.

6.4. Human Resources Management

Human resources management is another important component of the knowledge management which basically begins with quality training in consonance with new information technology. It further requires a specialized training so as to produce a spell bound information resources for the academic world. In practice, attention is required to be agreed to diversity and variation of library staffs' requirements, strengthening management of different library staffs by applying contingency management approach.

7. TECHNOLOGIES FOR REALIZING KNOWLEDGE MANAGEMENT IN LIBRARIES

The primary focal point of knowledge management in libraries and information centers concerns to the generation, accumulation, organization and proper dissemination of knowledge. To built a proper knowledge center it is required to strengthen innovation consciousness and abilities among the library staffs with proper technological training and to make knowledge applicable most effectively in the libraries so as make library a viable knowledge center. Hence, the foremost train of thought in realizing knowledge management of libraries is a rational design of the organizational structure and procedures of libraries, and cultural fostering, as well as modernized information support, thus creating an environment and incentive mechanism for innovation, exchange, study and application of the knowledge. Though it is tough job to apply all technological applications and compile, regrouping, organize and disseminate the right information to the right users at right time still, it is necessary for the Library and Information Centers to adapt to the changing environment and make knowledge processing value chain. The data mining, text summarizing, intelligent agents, information retrieval etc. are some of the basic components of input processes and are viable tools for creation of knowledge database which can be disseminated through intranets, groupware, decision support, and collaborative as output process. This has been depicted in Figure- 2 for better clarification and understanding.

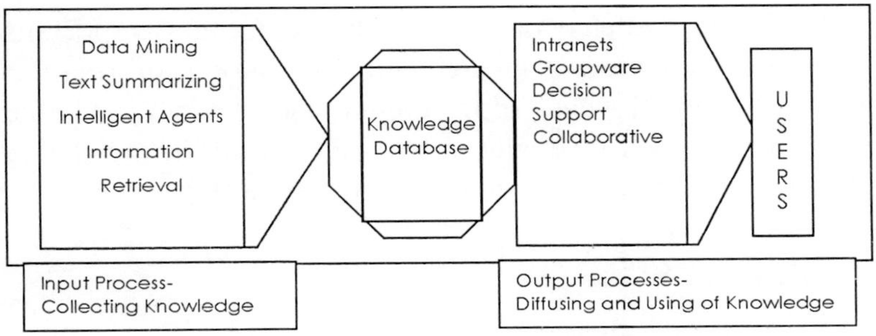

Fig. 2 : Computer support for knowledge processes

8. CONCLUSION

The Libraries and Information Centers act as bridge for turning the results of knowledge innovation into realistic productive forces for extensive use of knowledge by the users' communities. New innovations in the technologies scenarios become an indispensable in the present era as a tool in all-organizational growth in regards to accumulating, organizing and disseminating knowledge in the preferred structure to accomplish the multifarious objectives. Information Technology provides a defined and well guided structure through various in-built softwares where explicit knowledge could be generated and exploited and organized through databases. Information Technology has contributed significantly in Knowledge Management scenario and it has three primary advantages such as, (i) Efficiency; (ii) Effectiveness; and (iii) Velocity. Knowledge Management though a complex and multifaceted term by nature practically acts as the foremost information in the systems and processes with the application of incentives to motivate employees and forging alliances to infuse business with knowledge. Effective Knowledge Management requires a culmination of many organizational elements such as, technology, human resources practices, organizational structure and culture in order to ensure that the right knowledge is brought to bear at the right time.

Knowledge sharing happens to be another important segment in knowledge management for sharing information among the employees, departments, users etc. Knowledge implementation also equally adds immense value in knowledge management for effective library and information services.

REFERENCES

1. Encyclopedia Britannica CD (2001).
2. KEARY (Mal). (1997). Information Management as an instrument of change. Managing Information. 4(3), 35-7.
3. RAVICHANDRA RAO (I K). (2002). Issues and Challenges in Information Management in the context of fast emerging electronic sources. In. Proceedings of Information Management in e-libraries. IIT, Kharagpur.
4. SHENG Xiaoping. (19990. Knowledge Management of Libraries in the 21st Century, *Library Magazine*, 8, 29-32.
5. SIAU (N F) & TIAN (Y). Knowledge Management mechanisms of financial service sites. *Communications of the ACM.* 48(6), 117-23.
6. SKHRME (D J). (204). From Information Management to Knowledge Management: Are you prepared? *On line Information.*
7. TAYLOR (Allan) and (FARRELL). (1992). Stephen. Information Management in context. *Aslib Proceedings.* 44(9), 319-22. www.ifla.org (Accessed on 10.12.2007)
8. ZHAUNG (Dongsong). Knowledge Management in Organization. *Journal of Database Management.* January-March, 2006.

20

DIGITAL PRESERVATION : AN OVERVIEW

Rajkumar Singh
Librarian, Deptt. of Library & Information Science
K.P.Mishra Govt. Mahila Degree College, Aurai,
Sant Ravidas Nagar, Bhadohi, U.P.
Devendra Kumar
Chaudhary Charan Singh University, Meerut, U.P.

ABSTRACT

Digital preservation is an ongoing operation, requiring considerable recurring expense. It is a potential impediment to digital library development and a key issue for digital archiving. Collection and preservation are the important core areas which are steadily, improving to attain the goals/objectives of the parent organizations. Preservation of traditional materials became more successful and systematic after libraries and archives integrated preservation into overall planning and resource allocation. Digital preservation is the processes in which one cannot attain success until one adopt certain strategy. These strategies are shaped by the needs and constraints of repositories with little consideration for the requirements of current and future users of digital scholarly resources. One thing to recognize that procedures must be taken to secure the long-term persistence of digital materials and another to articulate precisely what the outcome of preservation should be. This article is discusses the basic concept of preservation, processes, strategies, system architectures, requirements for users as well as custodians, technical challenges and opportunities.

Keywords : Digital Preservation.

1. INTRODUCTION

Museums, archives, Libraries and information centers, are playing vital role in the selection, collection, organizing storing, preserving and archiving of educational, research, cultural and heritage information resources or materials since hundred decades for realize the needs of information of present and future generation. Information technology has made tremendous changes in the library and information centers and its activities, services and development and preservation of collections. Due to information technology the Library can enhance the long-term preservation of its materials (books and periodicals, maps, printed, music, manuscripts, microforms, sound recordings and other non-print media, etc.) through conservation and reformatting solutions, such as microfilming and digitization. Digital collection reflect their importance to academic education and research, it is increasingly common to refer collectively to these sources as "assets" of education and research institutes, Industrial or social or cultural or in general. The digital Preservation has significant impact on our future.

2. DIGITAL PRESERVATION

Maggie Jones and Neil Beagrie [1] has discuss about the Digital Preservation and said that Digital preservation refer to the series of managed activities necessary to ensure continued access to digital materials for as long as necessary. Digital preservation is defined very broadly for the purposes of this study and refers to all of the actions required to maintain access to digital materials beyond the limits of media failure or technological change. Those materials may be records created during the day-to-day business of an organisation;"born-digital" materials created for a specific purpose (e.g. teaching resources); or the products of digitisation projects. This handbook specifically excludes the potential use of digital technology to preserve the original artefacts through digitisation. See also Digitisation definition below.

Long-term preservation : Continued access to digital materials, or at least to the information contained in them, indefinitely.

Medium-term preservation : Continued access to digital materials beyond changes in technology for a defined period of time but not indefinitely.

Short-term preservation : Access to digital materials either for a defined period of time while use is predicted but which does not extend beyond the foreseeable future and/or until it becomes inaccessible because of changes in technology.

3. DEFINITIONS

According to glossary of **LIFE**[2] "Digital preservation is a process of ensuring that a digital object is accessible over the long term".

Accoring to **Wikipedia**[3] "Digital preservation is defined as: long-term, error-free storage of digital information, with means for retrieval and interpretation, for all the time span that the information is required for".

According to Trusted Digital Repositories (**TDR**)[4] "Digital Preservation encompasses a broad range of activities designed to extend the usable life of machine-readable computer files and protect them from media failure, physical loss, and obsolescence".

4. NEEDS DIGITAL PRESERVATION

1. Digital resources are playing vital role in the fulfill the need of users working towards higher education and research.
2. The education and research institutions are heavily inventing in digitization of pront resources or in subscription and licensing on Digital content,
3. Much of the knowledge base and intellectual assets of institutions and staff are now in digital form.
4. Developing e-learning materials, corporate records and publications, and in arts and scientific data.
5. Users of and heavily dependent on, digital resources created or curated by other sectors including publishers, government and the national libraries and archives.
6. The needs of researchers, students, staff and institutions will often require ongoing availability and confidence in the future accessibility of these materials.
7. Continued access to digital materials, or at least to the information contained in them, indefinitely.
8. To promote, support and develop the management of institutional and community digital materials for the benefit of education and research
9. Attempt to predict data sets which are endangered
10. Identification of strategically important data sets
11. Fill gaps
12. Build specialist collection
13. Widen holdings

5. DIGITAL PRESERVATION STRATEGIES

The following digital preservation strategies have been adopted for the preservation of digital objects for long time access.

Selection of Materials : Preservation Collection should be based on the condition of the materials, value, utility, rarity, Photocopying and reprographics services as well as the handling and use of books, etc. so that priority will be decided for the preservation of the library collections..

Digitization : Digitisation process is highly cost consuming process in the preservation process which can be done in house or outside of the organisation / institutions. It includes Assessment and Selection of Source Material, Digitization assessment, Full Digitization ,Quality Assessment , Post-Editing, Application of Metadata etc.

Canonicalization : Canonicalization is the process of converting data that has more than one possible representation into a "standard" canonical representation. This can be done to compare different representations for equivalence, to count the number of distinct data structures (e.g., in combinatorics), to improve the efficiency of various algorithms by eliminating repeated calculations, or to make it possible to impose a meaningful sorting order.

Replication : Creating duplicate copies of data from one format to another is known as replication, it is necessary to save the data from natural, social and technological disaster for life-long usage and perpetual access of digital objects.

Refreshing : Refreshing allows us to store the digital information from one long-term storage medium to another of same type of newer media or system. It is always very important due to the deterioration of physical media; it is a process to overcome the decay and obsolescence issues related to storage media.

Migration : Migration is period-based process that holds the core-concept of a digital data during conversion from one hardware or software to another newer form and preserving its ambiguity and integrity. One can say it is an enhanced form of refreshing but differs in sense that exact copy of any database or any digital object is not possible due to hardware or software change.

Emulation : It is a process of replacement of functionality of an obsolete system by a newer one. It is a popular strategy for retaining of the functionality of the older system. It requires the formation of emulators that translate code and instructions from one computing environment to newer one so that it can be properly executed in the later one.

Encapsulation : Encapsulation is a technique of grouping digital objects and metadata which is necessary to provide access of digital object. Digital objects include reference, representation, provenance, fixity, context information with appropriate types of metadata for the encapsulation, which is considered as a necessary component of emulation.

6. PRECAUTION FOR DIGITAL PRESERVATION ACTION[5]

i. Maintain consistent temperature -20 deg C (68 deg F)
ii. Maintain relative humidity around 40%.
iii. Avoid large and rapid fluctuations in temperature/ humidity.
iv. Control dust (maintain a slight positive pressure environment).
v. Avoid exposure to magnetic fields (for magnetic media).
vi. Avoid exposure to fumes.
vii. Establish a no food, drink, or smoking policy in media storage areas.
viii. Store media in closed metal cabinets, electrically grounded.
ix. Shelve media vertically (not stacked).
x. Store media in their original cases.
xi. Minimize exposure to sunlight and UV from light fixtures.

xii. Allow media to acclimate to new temperature and humidity before using.

xii. Return to controlled storage immediately after use.

7. LIMITATIONS

Digital preservation represents a complex set of limitations, which are exceptionally difficult for institutions to address individually they are as mentioned below:-

7.1. Technological Limitations

Digital media is fragile and have limited shelf life even under the best storage conditions. Efforts to preserve physical media thus provide only a short-term, partial solution to the general problem of preserving digital information. Technological obsolescence shows a far greater threat to information in digital form than the inherent physical fragility of many digital media.

7.2. Legal and organizational

Many of the institutions and organisation have legal and organisation problems for the preservation of copyright contents available on the particular organizations. Because migrating of intellectual property in digital form necessarily involves a complex set of interested parties, including the creators and owners of intellectual property, managers of digital archives, representatives of the public interest, and actual and potential users of intellectual property.

7.3. Integrity of digital objects

The purpose of migration is to preserve the integrity of digital objects and to retain the ability for clients to retrieve, display, and otherwise use them in the face of constantly changing technology. Migration includes refreshing as a means of digital preservation but differs from it in the sense that it is not always possible to make an exact digital copy or replica of a database or other information object as hardware and software change and still maintain the compatibility of the object with the new generation of technology.

7.4. Keeping Current

Digital preservation is a fast-growing area in research for information science and technologies underscoring the complexity of those issues. Additional resources can be found in the Further Reading section of this chapter and the Resources section at the end of these Guidelines.

7.5. Trained Manpower

Digital preservation requires new workflows, scarce skills, and close co-operation across different professions from traditional preservation management to computing science. New organizational structures and skills to support this are not yet in place.

7.6. Cost involvement

Digital preservation involved right clearance of digital materials as well as printed materials for Digitization or creation of replica of it, which may be time-consuming, costly, or in some cases impossible.

8. ADVANTAGES

8.1. Research and Development

Digital information is a core component in research and development. Without information is very difficult to pursue any research work in the world. Information is required not only for the pursuing research but its often needed for the validation of research. Digital information observed as necessary things for ongoing and future research. Such information we need to preserve for present and future use. Digital information is now enabling new method of research dissemination and scholarly communication among the scientist community. It is a power of accelerating the research and development work in the world.

8.2. Knowledge Management

Many private and government institutions or organizations have being involved in the knowledge management. They are capturing and preserving of knowledge or ideas or intellectual contents of a group of professionals or individuals involved in various activities (creation of policies, plans, guidelines, and decision making process, etc.) for present and future use. If a employ or a group of employees have leaved the organisation, but knowledge will remain with organisation. Such knowledge can be use in future to, create plans, policies, guidelines, procedures, decision-making process and solution for any problems occurs in future.

8.3. Teaching and learning

Digital resources are playing vital role in the fulfill need of the users (students, researchers, teachers, etc.) of academic institutions. Simultaneously the teaching communities have keen interests on the digital resources for preparation of lecture, research publications, Guidelines, policies and delivery of teaching materials. Many e-learning education programs are offered by the various organizations in the country as well as abroad since a decade. Digital resources are facilitating to delivery of teaching and education materials on the electronic form which offers e-learning and self assessment method for the students and learners. Such type of sources will need to be retain, access and re-packaged in over time for future use. Digital resources are offering opportunities to promote education and learning through distance education or life-long learning education systems.

8.4. Corporate Information assets

Many business and industrial organizations are involved in the Digital preservation of corporate information. It includes prospectuses, course guides and corporate policies and research papers. Such information is published on their websites on digital form only. Many Decisions are often taken with the help of such type of information. Therefore the corporate has taken vital steps in the preserve of this content as evidence of the decision-making process.

8.5. Transmission of moral and cultural values

It facilitates to store digital content on cultural and heritage which create the moral values of the societies and its available is rarely. There for Digital preservation are communication moral and cultural values in present and future generations. It helps in generation of replica of the Digital contents in over period of time. Such information has very important impact on the societies to develop its moral values.

8.6. Securing of the investment

Digital content needs to be preserved in perpetuity. Investment in digital resources over the longer term to secure the intellectual and cultural record that increasingly exists only in digital form. Digital preservation is securing the investment made on the subscription or/and Digitization of Digital contents/print resources. It provides perpetual access of digital content in long term. In such manner it's saving the money which was invested in the Digitalization and subscription of Digital content for the information users.

8.7. Greater access & Replication

Digital preservation facilitates wider access. Digital materials provide both greater access opportunities and remove the risk that increased use traditionally poses for preservation.

And relocation of digital materials can be done cheaply so multiple preservation copies are distributed in different geographical locations.

8.8. Digital Storage

Decreasing costs of digital storage invited long term preservation. Digital preservation not required physical space and do not have to be reshelved or located by staff. it is significantly less than that for paper. The removal of the link between physical location of the material and points of access opens up new opportunities for collaboration and services and for moderating the mounting national cost of physical storage.

8.9. Reduce Risk

Digital preservation reduce the risk of the destroyed, stolen and misplace of print materials when is has been converted in digital form, it's become the bits or bites form so that these resources are not handled frequently which reduces wear and tear.

9. CONCLUSION

Much of the knowledge base and intellectual assets, e-learning materials, corporate records and publications of institutions and staff are now in digital form and users are heavily dependent on, digital resources created or curated by other sectors including publishers, government and the libraries and archives. Such resources need to preserve for ongoing availability and confidence in the future accessibility of these materials. Preservation is the important core areas which are steadily, improving to attain the goals/objectives of the parent organizations. It allows long-time storage and perpetual access of digital information for the benefit of education and research.

REFERENCES

1. Definitions and Concepts from Preservation Management of Digital Materials: A Handbook by Maggie Jones and Neil Beagrie. http://www.dpconline.org/text/intro/definitions.html
2. IFE: Glossary and reference http://www.ucl.ac.uk/ls/lifeproject/glossary.shtml
3. wikipedia http://en.wikipedia.org/wiki/Digital_preservation
4. Digital Preservation management http://www.library.cornell.edu/iris/tutorial/dpm/terminology/preservation.html
5. Digital preservation management http://www.library.cornell.edu/iris/tutorial/dpm/oldmedia/threats.html
6. A Digital Retention and Preservation Policy for JISC www.jisc.ac.uk/uploaded_documents/dpstrategy2002b.rtf
7. Beagrie, Neil (2002), A Continuing Access and Digital Preservation Strategy for the Joint Information Systems Committee (JISC) 2002-2005, JISC, London. Available at: http://www.jisc.ac.uk/uploaded_documents/dpstrategy2002b.rtf
8. Gavrel, Sue (1986) "Preserving Machine-Readable Archival Records: A Reply to John Mallinson." Archivaria 22(Summer): 153-55.
9. Michelson, Avra and Jeff Rothenberg (1992) "Scholarly Communication and Information Technology: Exploring the Impact of Changes in the Research Process on Archives." American Archivist 55 (Spring): 236-315.
10. Garrett, J.(etal.) (1996). "Preserving digital information: Report of the task force on archiving of digital information". Commission on Preservation and Access and the Research Libraries Group. http://www.rlg.org/legacy/ftpd/pub/archtf/final-report.pdf
11. MIT Technology Review, "Data Extinction," by Claire Tristram, October 2002, p.42
12. Granger, Stewart (2000). "Emulation as a Digital Preservation Strategy". D-Lib Magazine 6 (10). http://www.dlib.org:80/dlib/october00/granger/10granger.html
13. Guidelines for Digitization. Edited by Katherine M. Wisser, 2005 Edition http://www.ncecho.org/Guide/preservation.htm

21

FUTURE OF OPEN SOURCE LIBRARY SOLUTIONS

Akhandanand Shukla

Senior Research Fellow

Dept. of Lib. & Inf. Science

Banaras Hindu University, Varanasi

Email: akhandanandshukla@gmail.com

ABSTRACT

The paper describes concepts and definition of open source with the very historical beginning of open source. Describes the need of open source software in library arena and how many are most prevalent in use with categorization into integrated library software and digital library / institutional repository software. General features and release versions of most prevalent open source library software's are discussed which provides development and use of open source library software's in future. Distinguishing features of free and open source software's is discussed. Concluding remarks are made at end of the paper with the suggestion that librarians should frankly use open source library software.

Keywords : Open Source, Open Source Initiative, Open Source Library Software, Free Software.

1. CONCEPT OF OPEN SOURCE

Wikipedia defines "Open source is an approach to design, development, and distribution offering practical accessibility to a product's source (goods and knowledge)." Some consider open source as one of various possible design approaches, while others consider it a critical strategic element of their operations.[1] The basic idea behind open source is very simple given by Open Source Initiative (OSI) is "When programmers can read, redistribute, and modify the source code for a piece of software, the software evolves. People improve it, people adapt it, people fix bugs. And this can happen at a speed that, if one is used to the slow pace of conventional software development, seems astonishing."

Open Source Initiative (OSI) says it is a method of developing software that harnesses the power of distributed peer review and transparency of process. The aim of open source is to provide better quality, higher reliable, more flexible and lower cost software to the public without any licence.[2]

2. DEFINITION OF OPEN SOURCE

Open Source Initiative (OSI) has given definition of "Open Source" which is recognised as the original definition and it was derived from the **Debian Free Software Guidelines** by Bruce Perens.[1] The original draft of Open Source Definition is as under:

Open Source doesn't mean access to the source code. The distribution terms of open source software must comply with the following criteria:[3]

2.1. Free Redistribution: The license shall not restrict any party from selling or giving away the software as a component of an aggregate software distribution containing programs from several different sources. The license shall not require a royalty or other fee for such sale.

2.2. Source Code : The program must include source code, and must allow distribution in source code as well as compiled form. Where some form of a product is not distributed with source code, there must be a well-publicized means of obtaining the source code for no more than a reasonable reproduction cost preferably, downloading via the Internet without charge. The source code must be the preferred form in which a programmer would modify the program. Deliberately obfuscated source code is not allowed. Intermediate forms such as the output of a preprocessor or translator are not allowed.

2.3. Derived Works : The license must allow modifications and derived works, and must allow them to be distributed under the same terms as the license of the original software.

2.4. Integrity of The Author's Source Code : The license may restrict source-code from being distributed in modified form *only* if the license allows the distribution of "patch files" with the source code for the purpose of modifying the program at build time. The license must explicitly permit distribution of software built from modified source code. The license may require derived works to carry a different name or version number from the original software.

2.5. No Discrimination Against Persons or Groups : The license must not discriminate against any person or group of persons.

2.6. No Discrimination Against Fields of Endeavor : The license must not restrict anyone from making use of the program in a specific field of endeavor. For example, it may not restrict the program from being used in a business, or from being used for genetic research.

2.7. Distribution of License : The rights attached to the program must apply to all to whom the program is redistributed without the need for execution of an additional license by those parties.

2.8. License Must Not Be Specific to a Product : The rights attached to the program must not depend on the program's being part of a particular software distribution. If the program is extracted from that distribution and used or distributed within the terms of the program's license, all parties to whom the program is redistributed should have the same rights as those that are granted in conjunction with the original software distribution.

2.9. License Must Not Restrict Other Software : The license must not place restrictions on other software that is distributed along with the licensed software. For example, the license must not insist that all other programs distributed on the same medium must be open-source software.

2.10. License Must Be Technology-Neutral : No provision of the license may be predicated on any individual technology or style of interface.

3. HISTORY OF OPEN SOURCE

The history of Open Source Initiative (OSI) begins with the evolution of Unix, Internet free software and operating systems. But, major work has been done after the publication of Eric Raymond's paper "**The Cathedral and the Bazaar**" in 1997. This paper became the landmark in the history of "Open Source" and the formation of "Open Source Initiative (OSI)". Raymond has presented the paper in O'Reilly's Perl Conference at Palo Alto, California in September, 1997 which have given direction to Netscape. By the effect of this conference, Netscape releases source code of his favourite web browser "Navigator" as free software in January 22, 1998. A strategy session held at Palo Alto, California on February 3, 1998 where 'open source' label was given by Chris Peterson. The attendee of the strategy session were Todd Anderson, Jon Hall, Chris Peterson, Larry Augustin, Sam Ockman, Michael Tiemann, and Eric Raymond. The Open Source Initiative (OSI) was jointly founded by Eric

Raymond and Bruce Perens in late February 1998, with Raymond as its first president. On April 8, 1998, representatives of many most important free and open source projects including Linux, sendmail, Perl, Python, Apache etc. and allies of Interenet Engineering Task Force (IETF) and Internet Software Consortium brought together in the O'Reilly's "Free Software Summit" which was later called as "Open Source Summit." At the meeting, the participants voted to promote the use of the term "Open Source". [1,4]

4. NEED OF OPEN SOURCE LIBRARY SOFTWARE

There is abundant availability of library softwares. Library Authority has to choose one of them which serve their service needs, financial needs and users' needs in a better way. In this critical situation, open source library software fulfills the financial need of libraries. The different problems faced by libraries are:

4.1. Severe budget cuts : Libraries are facing funding problems which create problems in smooth running of library services and operations. Increasing cost of library materials, books, periodicals and services as well as limited budget allocation hindering the various developments of library.

4.2. Increased demand for services : Libraries are changing their pattern of services and collection by the use of information communication technology. The implementation of advanced technology needs heavy budget, for which libraries are suffering from a very long period.

4.3. Lack of adequate staffing : Libraries are facing problems of adequate staff. Severe budget cuts are a very important reason in recruitment of staff. There are other various reasons for lack of staff but library budget is also one of them. It is known fact that about 50% of the library budget is allocated for library staffs' salary. This reduces the fund for other library services and operations.

Thus, due to above said reasons, if libraries adopt open source library softwares, it reduces the operational cost of various library services and operations. Library automation and digitization requires heavy budget which can be minimize by using the open source softwares. These softwares are as similar in function and features as purchased software. Open source softwares are available free to all and can be modified according to need of the library. Regular updates and bug support helps in smooth functioning of open source softwares in libraries.

5. OPEN SOURCE SOFTWARE IN LIBRARY ARENA

Library is recognized as store house of books and known as "Saraswati Bhandar" in old days while "Resource Centre" in present scenario. It has very wide collection of information, sources, resources and services to the public in general. Collection of library includes books, periodicals, maps, atlases, manuscripts, pamphlets, reference sources, brail books and other digital materials. Libraries are divided into various kinds according to the purpose they served. The most common division is academic, public & special libraries. By the use of information and communication technology, libraries are now becoming networked, digital, electronic and virtual. Collections of libraries are used more than earlier due to the use of these new technologies. Now, it is became the need of libraries to make available their resources to the public via new emerging technologies and softwares. The new emerging technologies, softwares and their services available are very costly which cannot be afforded by any library due to cutting cost of libraries fund. Moreover, libraries are somehow trying to manage the technological advancement to improve their services. Library automation, digitization, digital preservation of documents & institutional repositories, etc. are various facets of technological advancement. There is need of various softwares to fulfill above said facets. The purchasing and running cost of different softwares are very high that makes library sources and services very difficult.

In this juncture, open source softwares have given new hopes to the libraries. By the use of open source softwares, any library can make their sources and services very useful and simple to use, read, search or print. There are various open source library softwares available for various purposes and services of libraries. The few of them are:

Integrated Library Softwares (Automation)	*Digital Library Softwares*
Evergreen	Greenstone
Koha	DSpace
NewGenLib	EPrints
PMB (PhpMyBibli)	Dienst
BiblioteQ	CDSware
PhpMyLibrary	
Open Biblio	
GNUTECA	

5. 1. Evergreen

Evergreen is an open-source, consortial-quality integrated library automation software which helps library users to find library materials and helps libraries to manage, catalog, and circulate library materials. It is licensed under GNUGeneral Public License. Equinox Software is the company that provides support, development, migration services, and other services for libraries using Evergreen.[5] It is initially created by the Georgia Public Library Service (GPLS) to support the Public Information Network for Electronic Services (PINES) Consortium which have the network of more than 275 public libraries and affiliated service outlets in nearly 140 counties. SITKA is a growing Evergreen consortium in British Columbia. Presently 12 libraries have live installations of Evergreen whereas at least 16 SITKA libraries will migrate to Evergreen in 2009. Michigan Library Consortium and Grand Rapids Public Library are developing Michigan Evergreen, a shared Evergreen library system. Evergreen Indiana, a shared Evergreen system is looking for 19 libraries to come online in Evergreen Indiana. So far 13 libraries are on board. Some single plantings of Evergreen are also running. In India, there is no such a known planting of Evergreen found till date.[6]

Versions and release dates : The very first release of Evergreen was came out in September, 2006 as Evergreen 1.0. Presently Evergreen 1.2.4.0 was released on November 6, 2008.[5]

Version		*Release Date*
Past		
	Release 1.0	September, 2006
	Release 1.0.1	October, 2006
	Release 1.2	October, 2007
	Release 1.2.1	December, 2007
	Release 1.2.2	April, 2008
	Release 1.2.3	August, 2008
	Release 1.2.4.0	November, 2008
Future		
	Release Candidate 1.4	October, 2008
	Release 2.0	Winter, 2008/2009
	Release 3.0 and higher	2009 and beyond

5.2. Koha

Koha is a full-featured open-source integrated library software. It is the first open source integrated library software in the world developed by New Zealand based Katipo Communications Ltd in 1999 for Horowhenua Library Trust and first implemented in January, 2000. It is web based platform independent multi featured integrated library software released under GNU General Public License.8 Paul Poulain (of Marseille, France) had began adding multiple languages support to Koha in 2001. Koha is available in English, French, Chinese, Arabic & other several languages. It supports the international bibliographic records and cataloguing standards MARC21, UNIMARC, Copy Cataloguing and Z39.50. An Ohio based company LibLime was established to support Koha in 2005. There are about 160 Koha users around the world in which 15 Koha users are in India. Public, academic and special libraries are using Koha for their Live Catalogue. Recently in India, Delhi Public Library has adopted Koha 3.0 for Live Catalogues on October 2, 2008. DPL is very proud to be the first public library in India to implement the latest version of Koha 3.0. Users from across the world and nearly 45000 Delhi Public Library members can now access the most current catalogue of Delhi Public Library system on its website at http://59.176.17.111 .7,21

Versions and release dates : The first release of Koha came out in 1999. The current Koha version 3.0 was released on August 11, 2008. Its new features include a new user interface design, more advanced search functions, better multi-branch capabilities, user tagging, and many generic enhancements.[7]

Koha Release Version	*Platform*	*Release Date*
Koha Version 3.0	Linux	August 11, 2008
Koha 3.0.0 RC1 released	Linux	June 24, 2008
Koha 3.0.0 Beta	Linux	March 23, 2008
Koha 3 Alpha	Linux	January 8, 2008
Koha Version 2.2.9	Linux	May 21, 2007
Koha Version 2.2.8	Linux	March 12, 2007
Koha Version 2.2.7	Linux	November 27, 2006
Koha Version 2.2.6	Linux	October 18, 2006
Koha Version 2.3.0 (development version)	Linux	July, 2006
Koha Version 2.2.5	Linux	January 10, 2006
Koha Version 2.2.4	Linux	October 11, 2005

Koha Version 1.2.3	Linux	January, 2003
Koha Version	Linux	———
Koha Version 2.2.9	Windows	———
Koha on Caudium	Caudium	———
Koha Version 2.2.5	Mac OS X	———

5.3. NewGenLib

NewGenLib is an integrated library management system developed by over a 4 year joint effort between a professional charitable trust, Kesavan Institute of Information and Knowledge Management (KIIKM) and a fledging software development company Verus Solutions Pvt Ltd (VSPL), both in Hyderabad, India. Its version 1.0 was released in March 2005. Previously it was totally proprietary library software but on 9th January 2008, it was declared as Open Source Library Software under the GNU GPL v3 Licence by both the organisations Verus Solutions Pvt. Ltd. & Kesavan Institute of Information and Knowledge Management (KIIKM). Before becoming an open source library software at the end of 2007, it was already installed in 122 libraries in India and abroad. Amongst 122 installtions, 12 are only in BHU campus. It is compliant with MARC 21 format, has a MARC editor, and allows seamless bibliographic and authority data import into cataloguing templates. Form letter templates are configurable using OpenOffice 2.0 as ODT and htm. NewGenLib can be installed on Linux and Windows operating systems. Institutional Repositories can be created by using this software.[9,10]

Versions and release dates[11]

VSPL is working on development of new version (3.0) for UN Food and Agriculture Organisation (FAO), Rome.

Package	*Release version*	*Release Date*
NewGenLib	3.0	Under development
NewGenLib	2.2 Beta 1	April 24, 2008
NewGenLib End of day process	1.0	July 30, 2008
NewGenLib Desktop	1.0	December 11, 2007

5.4. Greenstone

Greenstone is a suite of software for building and distributing digital library collections on Internet or CD-ROM, produced by the New Zealand Digital Library Project (NZDL) at the University of Waikato in 2000. It is an open source, multilingual (English, French, Spanish, Russian and Kazakh) software developed and distributed in cooperation with UNESCO and the Human Info NGO of Belgium under the GNU General Public License.[12] Greenstone is easy-to-use software for building large, searchable collections of digital documents. It has a Greenstone Librarians Interface (GLI) for librarians or information professionals to build collections without computer programming knowledge. It is capable of building up multi-media digital documents such as text, PDF, audio and video very easily. Greenstone can build collections of Unicode documents in any language. It is the only software that can build Malayalam language documents into digital library collections.[13] Greenstone runs on all versions of Windows, Unix/Linux, and Mac OS-X. For the default Windows installation absolutely no configuration is required. About 70 international digital libraries and archives containing various types of digital collections are presently running on the Greenstone. In India, Greenstone based three digital libraries / archives are functioning. The names of these three are: Archives of Indian Labour, Noida; Indian Institute of Management, Kozhikode and Indian Institute of Science Publications Database, Bangalore.[12]

Versions and release dates

Version	*Release Date*
Greenstone version 3 family	under development having all the features of Greenstone 2
Greenstone Nightly release (Snapshot of Greenstone 3)	16.04.2008
Greenstone 3.03	26.10.2007
Greenstone 3.02	19.02.2007
Greenstone 2.81	13.11.2008
Greenstone 2.80	11.12.2007
Greenstone 2.75	09.11.2007
Greenstone 2.74	01.08.2007
Greenstone 2.73	15.06.2007
Greenstone 2.72	13.12.2006
Greenstone 2.71	11.10.2006
Greenstone 2.70w	02.06.2006
Greenstone 2.70	04.04.2006
Greenstone 2.63 (interface pack)	03.02.2006
Greenstone 2.62 (language pack)	01.12.2005
Greenstone 2.40a	05.08.2003
gsdl 2.35 and WORD Plug	28.05.2001
gsdl 2.35	17.05.2001
Greenstone 2.31	28.02.2001
Greenstone 2.30	25.12.2000
Greenstone 2.27	06.11.2000
Greenstone Windows binary release 2.26a	12.10.2000
Greenstone 2.26	09.10.2000

5.5. DSpace

DSpace is an open source software package for academic, non-profit, and commercial organizations building open digital repositories. DSpace is the first digital repository to address the myriad issues inherent in a multi-disciplinary archive. DSpace preserves and enables easy and open access to all types of digital content including books, theses, 3D digital scans of objects, photographs, film, video, research data sets and other forms of content. DSpace is not only confined to Linux/Unix but also for Windows. It is a product of joint effort of HP Labs & MIT Libraries. The project started in the year 2000 and first release of Dspace was came out in 2002. Dspace is freely available under BSD licence, which enables users to customize or extend the software as needed. On July 17, 2007, HP Labs & MIT Libraries jointly made the DSpace Foundation which is a non-profit organization that will provide leadership and support for the DSpace community. DSpace identifies two levels of digital preservation: bit preservation, and functional preservation. Bit preservation ensures that a file remains exactly the same over time i.e. not a single bit is changed whereas in Functional preservation, the file does change over time and digital formats evolve over time. Since 2002 more than 518 universities / institutes / banks / governmental departments / research labs etc. around the world have successfully installed Dspace for institutional repositories / digital libraries / archives. There are 24 known DSpace installations in India.[14,15]

Versions and release dates

The first version of DSpace was released in November 2002. DSpace 1.3 was released in 2005 and in June 2008, the DSpace Community released DSpace 1.5.1.[16]

Version	*Release Date*
DSpace 1.5.2	(yet to come in future)
DSpace 1.5.1 released	10.09.2008
DSpace 1.5 Released	26.03.2008
Updated DSpace language packs released	12.07.2007
DSpace 1.4.2 released	10.05.2007
DSpace 1.4.2 beta released	20.04.2007
DSpace 1.4.1 released	08.12.2006
DSpace 1.4.1 beta 2 released	30.11.2006

DSpace 1.4.1 beta 1 released	08.11.2006
DSpace 1.4 Released	26.07.2006
Language packs released	27.03.2006
DSpace 1.4 alpha 1 released	17.03.2006
DSpace 1.3.2 Released	05.10.2005
DSpace 1.3.2 Beta 2 released	27.09.2005
DSpace 1.3.2 Beta 1 Released	19.09.2005
DSpace 1.3.1 Released	05.08.2005
DSpace 1.3 released	04.08.2005
DSpace 1.3 Beta 1 released	28.06.2005
DSpace 1.2.2 released	05.05.2005
DSpace 1.3 Alpha released	12.04.2005
DSpace 1.2.2 beta 2 released	01.04.2005
DSpace 1.2.2 beta 1 released	17.02.2005
DSpace version 1.2.1 released	04.02.2005
DSpace 1.2.1 beta3 released	16.12.2004
DSpace 1.2.1 beta2 released	12.11.2004
DSpace 1.2.1 beta 1 Released	21.09.2004
DSpace 1.2 Released	13.08.2004
DSpace 1.2 Beta 3 released	02.07.2004
DSpace 1.2 Beta 2 Released	07.05.2004
DSpace 1.2 Beta 1 Released	23.04.2004
DSpace 1.1.1 released	29.08.2003
DSpace 1.1 released	08.03.2003
Documentation version 1.0.1-1 released	05.03.2003
DSpace 1.0.1 released	23.12.2002
DSpace 1.0 Source Code Released	08.11.2002

5.6. EPrints

EPrints is an open source software which have the most flexible platform for building high quality, high value open access repositories that are compliant with OAI-PMH and recognized as the easiest and fastest way to set up repositories of research literature, scientific data, theses, project reports, multimedia artifacts, teaching materials, scholarly collections, digitized records, exhibitions and performances. EPrints is developed at the School of Electronics and Computer Science, University of Southampton, UK in 2000 and released under GNU GPL license. EPrints software was enthusiastically received and became the first and one of the most widely adopted free, open access institutional repository software. It is platform independent software which can be installed on Linux, Solaris, Mac OS X & Microsoft Windows. Since 2000, more than 269 known EPrints archives are running around the world which has more than 519952 records. About 9 known EPrints archives are running in India.[17,18]

Versions and release dates : EPrints version 3 was officially released on the 24th January 2007 at the **Open Repositories 2007 Conference** and was described by its developers as "a major leap forward in functionality, giving even more control and flexibility to repository managers, depositors, researchers and technical administrators."[19]

Volunteers / Developers	*Version*	*Release Date*
Gutteridge, Christopher et al.	EPrints 3.1.2	03.12.2008
Gutteridge, Christopher et al.	EPrints 3.1.2-beta-1	03.12.2008
Gutteridge, Christopher et al.	EPrints 3.1.1	20.10.2008
Gutteridge, Christopher et al.	EPrints 3.1.0	08.09.2008
Gutteridge, Christopher et al.	EPrints 3.1.0-rc-6	19.08.2008
Gutteridge, Christopher et al.	EPrints 3.1.0-rc-2	16.06.2008
Gutteridge, Christopher et al.	EPrints 3.1.0-rc-1	02.06.2008
Gutteridge, Christopher et al.	EPrints 3.0.5	21.04.2008
Gutteridge, Christopher et al.	EPrints 3.1-beta-2	03.04.2008
Gutteridge, Christopher et al.	EPrints 3.1-beta-1	03.04.2008
Gutteridge, Christopher et al.	EPrints 3.0.5RC1	13.03.2008
Mason, Harry	EPrints 3.0 Windows Installer (r3380)	12.03.2008
Gutteridge, Christopher et al.	EPrints 3.0.4 Release Candidate 1	14.12.2007

Gutteridge, Christopher et al.	EPrints 3.0.3	05.12.2007
Gutteridge, Christopher et al.	EPrints 3.0.3 Release Candidate 1	28.08.2007
Gutteridge, Christopher et al.	EPrints 3.0.2-beta-3	13.06.2007
Gutteridge, Christopher et al.	EPrints 3.0.2-beta-2	07.06.2007
Gutteridge, Christopher et al.	EPrints 3.0.2-beta-1	30.05.2007
Gutteridge, Christopher et al.	EPrints 3.0.1	25.05.2007
Gutteridge, Christopher et al.	EPrints 3.0.1-beta-2	13.04.2007
Gutteridge, Christopher et al.	EPrints 3.0	18.01.2007
Gutteridge, Christopher et al.	EPrints 3.0 RC 1	18.12.2006
Gutteridge, Christopher et al.	EPrints 3.0 Beta 3	05.12.2006
Gutteridge, Christopher et al.	EPrints 3.0 Beta 2	14.11.2006
Gutteridge, Christopher et al.	EPrints 3.0 Beta 1	26.10.2006
Gutteridge, Christopher	EPrints 3.0.0 Alpha 2	27.06.2006
Gutteridge, Christopher	EPrints 2.3.14.alpha.5	26.09.2005
Gutteridge, Christopher	EPrints 2.3.14.alpha.4	23.09.2005
Gutteridge, Christopher	EPrints 2.3.13.1	20.09.2005
Gutteridge, Christopher	EPrints 2.3.14.alpha.3	20.09.2005
Gutteridge, Christopher	EPrints 2.3.14.alpha.2	15.09.2005
Gutteridge, Christopher	EPrints 2.3.14.alpha.1	31.08.2005
Gutteridge, Christopher	EPrints 2.3.13	25.07.2005
Gutteridge, Christopher	EPrints 2.3.13.alpha.1	08.06.2005
Gutteridge, Christopher	EPrints 2.3.11.99.6-beta	24.05.2005
Gutteridge, Christopher	EPrints 2.3.12	24.05.2005
Gutteridge, Christopher	EPrints 2.3.11.99.5-beta	18.05.2005
Gutteridge, Christopher	EPrints 2.3.11.99.4-beta	07.04.2005
Gutteridge, Christopher	EPrints 2.3.11.99.3-beta	04.04.2005
Gutteridge, Christopher	EPrints 2.3.11-99-2-beta	21.03.2005
Gutteridge, Christopher	EPrints 2.3.11-99-1-beta	18.03.2005
Gutteridge, Christopher	EPrints 2.3.10.99.1-beta	08.03.2005
Gutteridge, Christopher	EPrints 2.3.11	08.03.2005
Gutteridge, Christopher	EPrints 2.3.10	02.03.2005
Gutteridge, Christopher	EPrints 2.3.9-99-1	02.03.2005
Gutteridge, Christopher	EPrints 2.3.9	17.02.2005
Gutteridge, Christopher	EPrints 2.3.7.99.3-beta	16.02.2005

Gutteridge, Christopher	EPrints 2.3.7.99.4-beta	16.02.2005
Gutteridge, Christopher	EPrints 2.3.8	16.02.2005
Gutteridge, Christopher	EPrints 2.3.7.99.2-beta	21.01.2005
Gutteridge, Christopher	EPrints 2.3.7.1	03.12.2004
Gutteridge, Christopher	EPrints 2.3.6.99.1-beta	01.12.2004
Gutteridge, Christopher	EPrints 2.3.7.99.1-beta	01.12.2004
Gutteridge, Christopher	EPrints 2.3.7	25.11.2004
Gutteridge, Christopher	EPrints 2.3.6.99.4-beta	24.11.2004
Gutteridge, Christopher	EPrints 2.3.6.99.3-beta	22.11.2004
Gutteridge, Christopher	EPrints 2.3.6.99.2-beta	29.09.2004
Gutteridge, Christopher	EPrints 2.3.6	09.08.2004
Gutteridge, Christopher	EPrints 2.3.5	06.08.2004
Gutteridge, Christopher	EPrints 2.3.4	06.07.2004
Gutteridge, Christopher	EPrints 2.3.3	04.03.2004
Gutteridge, Christopher	EPrints 2.3.2.99.1.alpha	03.03.2004
Gutteridge, Christopher	EPrints 2.3.2	25.02.2004
Gutteridge, Christopher	EPrints 2.3.1	05.02.2004
Gutteridge, Christopher	EPrints 2.3.0	12.01.2004
Gutteridge, Christopher	EPrints 2.2.1	14.11.2002
Gutteridge, Christopher	EPrints 2.2	31.10.2002
Gutteridge, Christopher	EPrints 2.1	04.07.2002
Gutteridge, Christopher	EPrints 2.1.1	04.07.2002
Gutteridge, Christopher	EPrints 2.0.1	16.04.2002
Gutteridge, Christopher	EPrints 2.0	14.02.2002

6. OPEN SOURCE SOFTWARE VERSUS FREE SOFTWARE

Term 'Open Source' creates an ambiguity with the term 'Free Software.' Open Source is also known as *Free / Open Source Software* (FOSS) or *Free / Libre / Open Source Software* (FLOSS). Open Source software is freely available to all and it may be used, copied, studied, modified and redistributed without any restriction whereas free software is free to download, install and use but you cannot modify it accordingly. Further development and assistance is fee based in free softwares. Majority of free softwares is for advertisement only. Open Source highlights the source code which is viewable and modifiable.[20]

7. WHY OPEN SOURCE SHOULD BE USED?

There are various common features available in open source library softwares which are commonly found in proprietary / purchased library softwares.

Table : *Comparison of features of purchased vs. open source software*

Features	*Purchased Software*	*Open Source Software* ←*Integrated Library Softwares*→ ←*Digital Library Softwares*→					
		Ever green	*Koha*	*New GenLib*	*Green stone*	*DSpace*	*E-Prints*
Integrated	Yes	Yes	Yes	Yes	No	No	No
Multiuser	Yes	Yes	Yes	Yes	Yes	Yes	Yes
OS independency	Yes / No	Yes	Yes	Yes	Yes	Yes	Yes
Modular	Yes	Yes	Yes	Yes	No	No	No
Stand-alone	Yes	Yes	Yes	Yes	Yes	Yes	Yes
Networked	Yes	Yes	Yes	Yes	Yes	Yes	Yes
Online help	Yes	Yes	Yes	Yes	Yes	Yes	Yes
Minimal data entry	Yes	Yes	Yes	Yes	No	No	Yes
Export / Import Format	Yes	Yes	Yes	Yes	No	No	Yes
Multilingual	Yes	Yes	Yes	Yes	Yes	Yes	Yes
Report Generation	Yes	Yes	Yes	Yes	No	No	No
Customised data entry	Yes	Yes	Yes	Yes	No	No	No
Barcode support	Yes	——	Yes	Yes	No	No	No
Multimedia Support	Yes	Yes	Yes	Yes	Yes	Yes	Yes
Web OPAC	Yes	Yes	Yes	Yes	Yes	Yes	Yes
Retrospective Conversion	Yes	——	——	Yes	No	No	No

Graphic User Interface	Yes	Yes	Yes	Yes	Yes	Yes	Yes
Upgradation	Yes	Yes	Yes	Yes	Yes	Yes	Yes
Cataloguing Standards	Yes	Yes	Yes	Yes	Yes	Yes	Yes
CAS / SDI	Yes	——	——	Yes	No	No	No
Boolean search	Yes / No	No	No	Yes	No	No	No
Union Catalogue	Yes	Yes	Yes	Yes	No	No	No
Z39.50 Server	Yes	Yes	Yes	Yes	No	No	No
Z39.50 Client	Yes	Yes	Yes	Yes	No	No	No
Price based	Yes	No	No	No	No	No	No

The above table shows that the features available in the open source library softwares are more or less very similar to purchased / proprietary softwares. Integrated library softwares have more common features with purchased / proprietary softwares whereas digital library softwares have less similarity with purchased / proprietary softwares features. This is only because digital library softwares serve the different purpose in comparison to integrated library softwares or purchased / proprietary softwares. This indicates that open source softwares can be successfully used by libraries and if necessary, can be modified accordingly.

8. PROS AND CONS OF OPEN SOURCE SOFTWARE

There are several advantages and disadvantages which are identified by software experts and researchers.[20]

The advantages of Open Source are:

1. It is a good way for business to achieve greater penetration of the market.
2. Open Source providers can establish an industry standard.
3. Helps in updation of technological developments.
4. Good way to promote companies' image.
5. Encourages the potential for a more flexible technology and quicker innovation.

6. Freely available, modifiable and redistributable to all.

The disadvantages of Open Source are:

1. No any final version available.
2. Every version has some changes which creates problem in exchanging data from one version to other.
3. Online assistance may take more time than purchased / proprietary software.
4. One have to pay proper attention for recent changes / facilities / shortcomings.
5. Sometimes advice / support is fee based.

9. CONCLUSION

Open source has paved his foot after the evolution of Unix. Eric Raymond has grown its wings in 1997 by an article "The Cathedral and the Bazar" and O'Reilly trained it to fly in the sky by his "Free Software Summit". Open Source Initiative (OSI) has started a movement in its favour. By this very efforts, today we have uncountable open source softwares and projects. The open source movement has influenced almost every field but computer software industry is totally affected by it. Now software developing companies are taking much interest in open source development. Library and Information Science field is also influenced by open source. There are various open source library softwares are available in this field. These open source library softwares have very common features which are similar to a purchased library software. This is the reason that open source library softwares have much installations than purchased softwares in very short time. In due short of time, more installations shows the bright future of open source library solutions. Librarians should frankly adopt open source library solutions for the automation & digitization of libraries as well as for digital archives.

REFERENCES

1. Open source. Available at http://en.wikipedia.org/wiki/Open_source (accessed on 10.12.2008).
2. Open Source Initiative. Available at http://www.opensource.org/ (accessed on 12.12.08).
3. The Open Source Definition. Available at http://opensource.org/docs/osd (accessed on 12.12.08).
4. History of the OSI. Available at http://opensource.org/history (accessed on 12.12.08).
5. Evergreen. Available at http://evergreen-ils.org/ (accessed on 15.12.08).
6. Georgia Public Library Service. Available at http://www.georgialibraries.org/gpls/about_us.pdf (accessed on 15.12.08).
7. Koha (software). Available at http://en.wikipedia.org/wiki/Koha_(software) (accessed on 16.12.08).
8. Koha. Available at http://www.koha.org/ (accessed on 16.12.08).
9. NewGenLib. Available at http://en.wikipedia.org/wiki/NewGenLib (accessed on 17.12.08).
10. NewGenLib Open Source. Available at http://www.verussolutions.biz/web/ (accessed on 17.12.08).
11. NewGenLib. In SourceForge.Net. Available at
12. http://sourceforge.net/project/showfiles.php?group_id=210780 (accessed on 17.12.08).
13. Greenstone digital library software. Available at http://www.greenstone.org/ (accessed on 18.12.08).
14. Greenstone (software). Available at http://en.wikipedia.org/wiki/Greenstone_Digital_Library_Software (accessed on 18.12.08).
15. DSpace. Available at http://www.dspace.org/index.php/ (accessed on 19.12.08).
16. DSpace. Available at http://en.wikipedia.org/wiki/DSpace (accessed on 19.12.08).
17. DSpace. In SourceForge.Net. Available at http://sourceforge.net/news/?group_id=19984 (accessed on 19.12.08).
18. Open Access and Institutional Repositories with Eprints. Available at http://www.eprints.org/ (accessed on 20.12.08).
19. EPrints. Available at http://en.wikipedia.org/wiki/Eprints (accessed on 20.12.08).

20. EPrints Files. Available at http://files.eprints.org/view/type/release.html (accessed on 20.12.08).

21. Open source software. Available at http://en.wikipedia.org/wiki/Open_source_software (accessed on 20.12.08).

22. Koha Users Around the World. Available at http://wiki.koha.org/doku.php?id=kohausers (accessed on 20.12.08).

22

Digital Information Awareness and Use of Internet Services by Faculty Members of Ch. Charan Singh University, Meerut, U.P., India: A Case Study

Krishna Kumar & Devendra Kumar

Faculty Member

Department of Library & Information Science,

Chaudhary Charan Singh University Meerut (UP), INDIA

E-mail: kkbhuvns@gmail.com

ABSTRACT

The study analyzed the use of Internet services by the users of faculty members of Chaudhary Charan Singh University, Meerut, Uttar Pradesh. A total of 60 well-structured questionnaires were distributed among faculty members of of Chaudhary Charan Singh University, Meerut, Uttar Pradesh. The questionnaires were checked, and 50 questionnaires were found fit for analysis, out of which 10 were considered unusable. The present study demonstrates and elaborates the various aspects of Digital information Awareness of IT, Internet usage, sources of getting information about Internet Web sites, favorite search engines, problems faced by the users in surfing the Internet, satisfaction with Internet for research purpose, and various facilities and infrastructure facilities available in the libraries. Suggestions have been given to make the service more beneficial in the of Chaudhary Charan Singh University, Meerut, Uttar Pradesh Meerut, U.P, India.

Keywords : Digital Information Awareness, Internet, User Study, Chaudhary Charan Singh University, Meerut, Uttar Pradesh.

1. INTRODUCTION

Society has been transformed by the rapid development and diffusion of information and communication technology (ICT) into fields such as education, business, health, agriculture, and so on. Information users may be bewildered by a variety of digitized information. The process of identifying and selecting information has become complex. It is critical to promote information literacy (IL) in the digital age. Computers have become a necessary part of this digital society, and skills for computer use are a common prerequisite on many job applications. The Department of Education, Training, and Employment (2001a) states:

To live and work in the technology-enabled world of the 21st Century, high-level skills in the use of information and communication technologies (ICT) are essential for all citizens. (DETE, 2001a, p.5)

With those objectives in mind, this survey was undertaken to study digital information awareness among faculty at Chaudhary Charan Singh University, Meerut, Uttar Pradesh and to set the priorities for promotion of digital information literacy among them.

Digital Information Awareness

Glister (1997, p. 290) defines digital awareness as, "a set of skills to access the Internet; find, manage and edit digital information; join in communications; and other wise engage with an online information and communication network. In simple terms, digital literacy is the ability to properly use and evaluate digital resources, tools and services and apply it to their life long learning process." The New Media Consortium (2005, p.2) states that digital Awareness, "includes the ability to understand the power of images and sounds, to recognize and use that power, to manipulate and transform digital media, to distribute them pervasively and to easily adopt them to new forms." The most essential aspect of digital literacy is the ability to make informed judgments about what is found online, for unlike conventional media, much digital information is unfiltered by editors and open to the contribution of all.

Digitally literate people are able to:

- Determine the extent of digital information needed;
- Access the needed digital information effectively and efficiently;
- Evaluate digital information sources and services critically;
- Incorporate selected digital information into one's knowledge base;
- Use of digital information effectively to accomplish a specific purpose; and
- Understand the economic, legal, and social issues surrounding the use of digital information access and use of this information ethically and legally.

Digital Information Awareness is a major component of information literacy. It helps users cope with information from a variety of electronic formats and provides techniques and methods of collecting digital resources. It creates awareness of issues like copyright and intellectual property rights in an electronic environment.

Internet

The Internet is an ocean of information and is used in every walk of life these days. It provides information on the fields of business science, education, government and nongovernmental organizations, etc. It is one of the facilities through which the information can be stored, arranged, and transmitted back to the users quickly, in a timely_fashion, and accurately. There are hundreds of millions Web pages, bibliographical databases, and full-text databases available on the Internet (*Prasher, 2003*).

2. OBJECTIVE OF THE STUDY

The purpose of this study was to investigate the digital information awareness and use of Internet services by the faculty members of Chaudhary Charan Singh University, Meerut, Uttar Pradesh, India. It specifically focused on the following objectives:

1. To determine computer literacy among Faculty members.
2. To identify their awareness about internet & its tools.
3. To study the present Internet services provided by Chaudhary Charan Singh University, Meerut, Uttar Pradesh.
4. To find out the different purposes for which the Internet is used by the users of Chaudhary Charan Singh University, Meerut, Uttar Pradesh.
5. To identify from which sources users get the latest information through Web sites and which Web sites are most used by users.
6. To know the favorite search engines used by users.
7. To identify the type of problems faced by users when using

the Internet services in Chaudhary Charan Singh University, Meerut, Uttar Pradesh under study.

8. To determine the satisfaction level of users regarding infrastructure facilities, membership fee, and location.
9. To find out the user satisfaction with the Internet services provided by Chaudhary Charan Singh University, Meerut, Uttar Pradesh under study.

3. METHODOLOGY

The study has been conducted through the case study method of research. A structured questionnaire was designed and used for collecting data. The sample for the study was selected purposefully because the investigators have been noticed in the internet lab more frequently. The questionnaires were distributed among 60 faculty member. Out of which as many as 50 filled in use able questionnaire were received back. The data so obtained was coded and analyses with the help of statistical package for social sciences.

4. DATA ANALYSIS AND INTERPRETATION

The present study was conducted on the use of Internet services by the faculty members Chaudhary Charan Singh University, Meerut, Uttar Pradesh. The collected data are organized and tabulated by using statistical methods, tables, and percentages.

Table 1: *Designation wise distribution of Questionnaire*

Designation	*No. of Respondents*	*% of Respondents*
Professor	10	20%
Reader	12	24%
Lecturer	28	56%
Total	50	100%

Above the table shows that the majority of respondents 28(56%) Lecturer 12 (24%) Reader and 10 (20%) professor.

***Table 2:** User awareness about computer knowledge*

Aware	*No. of Respondents*	*Percentage*
Yes	47	94%
No	3	6%
Total	50	100%

Table 2 reveals that 94% of faculty members aware about computer knowledge. while only 6% respondents not aware.

***Table 3:** User Awareness about IT/Digital information*

Aware	*No. of Respondents*	*Percentage*
Yes	45	90%
No	5	10%
Total	50	100%

Above the table shows that the majority of respondents 90% aware about IT/Digital information (10%) Respondent No.

***Table 4:** Type of IT Digital information knowledge*

IT-Digital information knowledge	*Yes*	*Percentage*
Internet applications	46	92%
MS Office/DTP Tools	31	62%
Multimedia	16	32%
Programming language	2	4%

Above the table shows that the most respondents 46(92%) have knowledge of internet application 31(52%) have knowledge MS Office/DTP Tools followed by, 15(32%) in multimedia but only 2(4%) have programming language applications. A majority of faculty who responded has acquired of internet application, but knowledge in other areas is less widespread.

***Table 5:** Purpose of internet use*

Purpose	*Frequency*	*Percentage*
Education/Research work	40	80%
E-Learning	10	20
Entertainment	7	14%
News	6	12%
E mail	23	46%
Discussion	3	6%
Sports	4	8%
Health	1	2%

One of the significant research questions was to explore the purpose for which they are using the internet. 40(80%) respondents used the internet for an educational/research work, 23 (46%) for the E-mail, 10(20%) E-learning, 7(14%) entertainment, 6(12%) for news, 4(8%) sports, 3(6%) used for it discussion, and 1(2%) for health.

***Table 6:** Experience of Internet use*

Experience of Internet use	*Frequency*	*Percentage*
Less than 6 months	7	14%
6 months to 1 year	12	24%
1 to 2 year	10	20%
2 to 4 year	6	12%
More than 4 year	15	30%
Total	50	100%

The question was asked to find out the facts such as when the faculty members using the internet did and how long they had been using the internet. It was found that 15(30%) of them had been using internet for more than 4 years, 12(24%) 6 months to 1 year, 1.(20%) 1 to 2 years, 7(14%) less than 6 months and 6(12%) respondents indicated having using it for 2 to 4 years. It is evident that the majority of respondents have been using internet an average for more than 4 years.

***Table 7:** Frequency of use Internet services*

Use Internet	*Frequency*	*Percentage*
Daily	27	54%
2-3 time a week	15	30%
Once in a week	3	6%
2-3 time a month	2	4%
Occasionally	3	6%
Total	50	100%

Above the table indicates that the majority of faculty members use internet service i.e. 27(54%) Daily followed by 15(30%) 2-3 time a week, 3(6%) once in a week, 3(6%) occasionally, and 2(4%) 2-3 time a month.

***Table 8:** Amount of time spent on the internet*

Amount the time	*Frequency*	*Percentage*
Less than 1 hours a week	9	18%
2-4 hours a week	22	44%
5-6 hours a week	12	24%
7-9 hours a week	4	8%
10-20 hours a week	No response	
Over 20 hours a week	3	6%
Total	20	100%

Above the table shows that the amount of time spent on the internet i.e. 22(44%) 2-4 hours a week, 12(24%) 5-6 hours a week, 9(18%) less than 1 hours a week, 4(8%) 7-9 hours a week, and 3(6%) over 20 hours a week.

***Table 9:** Method of learning internet skills*

Method	*Number*	*Percentage*
Trial and error method	27	24%
Guidance from collages & friends	21%	42%
Training from university/Department	10	20%
Self instruction	15	30%
External courses	7	14%

Faculty members were asked to indicate the methods used for acquiring the internet skills. It was found that most popular method of acquiring the necessary skills to use internet is via trial and error method. A majority of the respondents used this method with 27(54%) responses. A total of 21(42%) of them indicated that they took guidance from colleges & friends, 15(30%) of the respondents responses also acquired skill by self instruction method, 10(20%) of faculty learnt the internet through formal training offered by the university/department and 7(14%) participated in other courses such as external courses and workshops.

***Table 10:** Awareness of the services being provided on internet*

Service	*Yes*	*%*	*No*	*%*
E mail	42	84%	2	4%
www (World Wide Web)	23	46%	2	4%
Search engines (e.g. Google)	23	46%	2	4%
Remote log in (Telnet)	4	8%	5	10%
FTP (file Transfer Protocol)	4	8%	5	10%
Archie	3	6%	5	10%
List Serve/Discussion Group	3	6%	4	8%
BBS (Bulletin Board Service)	3	6%	4	8%
FAQ (Frequently asked question)	7	14%	4	8%
Chatting	8	16%	5	10%

Analysis of data regarding awareness of the service being provided on internet shows that 42(84%) faculty members aware E-mail, 23(46%) www (World Wide Web), 23(46%) search engines (e.g. google) 8 (16%) chatting, 7(14%) FAQ (Frequently asked questions 4(8%) Remote log in (telnet), 4(8%) FTP (File transfer Protocol), 6(6%) Archie, 3(6%) list serve/Discussion group.

Table 11: *Table of E-information/resources needed through internet*

Type of e-information	*Frequency*	*Percentage*
E-Journals	40	80%
E-articles	34	68%
E-thesis and dissertations	21	42%
E-databases	18	36%
E-books	16	36%
Mailing lists	7	14%
News groups	9	18%
Subject Gate ways	4	8%
E-archives	3	6%
Web resources	7	14%
Downloading services	21	42%
On line search	16	32%

Above the table shows that the majority resources needed through internet users were 40(80%) E journals, 34(68%) E-articles, 21(42%) E-Thesis and dissertation, 21(42%) downloading services, 18(35%) E-databases, 16(32%) E-books, 16(32%) on line search, 9(18%) news groups, 7(14%) Mailing list, 7(14%) web resources, 4(8%) subject gate-ways 3(6%) E-archives.

Table 12: *Most used web sites*

Category	*No. of Respondents*	*Percentage*
General Web sites	49	98
Discipline-based Web sites	38	76
Recreational Web sites	04	08

The above table reveals that a majority of the respondents (49 [98%]) perceive general Web sites as useful for all purposes; 38 (76%) and 4 (8%) respondents indicated that they have used discipline-based Web sites (i.e., access for specific subject) and recreational Web sites (i.e., entertainment, traveling in some historical places, etc.), respectively.

It is very interesting to note that a majority of respondents used general Web sites for accessing the latest information and the least number of users used recreational Web sites.

Table 13: *Which facility on internet use most for communication*

Communication Facility	*Frequency*	*%*
E-Mail	43	86%
Chat	3	6%
Net Phone	12	24%
None	1	2%

Above the table shows that the majority of faculty members 43 (86%) on internet use E-mail, 12(24%) Net Phone, 3(6%) chat, 1(2%) none.

Table 14: *Use the advance search facilities for retrieve information through internet*

Search Facility	*Frequency*	*%*
Boolean operators	19	38
Truncation search terms	2	4
Field searching	24	48
Type the web address directory	3	6
Use subscription data base	3	6
Phrase (To terms in a specific order	3	6
Other	-	-

According to analysis of data regarding to use the advance

search facilityes for retrieve information through internet most of the faculty members 24 (48%) were use field searching, followed by 19(38%) Boolean operators, 3(6%) type the web address directory, 3(5%) use subscription database, 3(6%) phrase to terms in a specific order, 2(4%) Truncation search terms.

***Table 15:** Evaluation Parameters for web resources*

Parameters	*Frequency*	*%*
Authentic	19	38 %
Reliable	29	58%
Objective	6	12%
Usable	10	20%
Less expensive	12	24%
Coverage all	7	14%
Comprehensive	5	10%
Accessible	9	18%

Table 16 reveals that most of the faculty members 29(58%) were answered Reliable is best evaluation parameters followed by 19(38%) Authentic, 12(24%) Less expensive, 10(20%) usable, 9(18%) Accessible 7(14%) coverage all, 6(12%) objective, 5(10%) comprehensive.

***Table 16:** Comparison of conventional documents & internet in your opinion*

Your opinion	*Frequency*	*%*
Time saving	40	80%
Time consuming	1	2%
More information	41	82%
Less informative	-	-
Less expensive	4	8%
More useful	34	68%
Less useful	-	-
More Preferences	24	48%
Less preference	-	-

Table 17 reveals that most of the faculty members 41 (82%) were answered Internet has more information than conventional documents followed by 40(80%) Time saving, 34(68%) more useful, 24(48%) more preferences, 4(8%) less expensive, 1(2%) time consuming

***Table 17:** Internet influence on academic efficiency*

Influence	*Frequency*	*%*
Use of conventional document has decreased	29	58%
Dependency on the internet has increased	25	50%
Expedited the research process	12	24%
Improved professional competence	23	46%

Above the table shows that the majority of respondents 29(58%) found use of conventional document has decreased, 25(50%) Dependency on internet has increased 23(46%) improved professional competence, 12(24%) expedited the research process.

***Table 18:** User satisfaction with internet facilities*

Satisfaction with internet Facility	*Frequency*	*%*
Fully	12	24%
Little	37	74%
Dissatisfied	1	2%
Strongly dissatisfied	-	-
Total	50	100%

Above the table shows that the majority of respondent 37(74%) little satisfied with internet facility, 12(24%) Fully satisfied, 1(2%) dissatisfied.

Table19: *Problems encountered while using internet*

Problems	*Frequency*	*%*
Slow access speed	34	68%
Downloading PDF files takes more time	16	32%
Lack of terminology	10	20%
Lack of command	5	10%
Privacy problem	1	2%
Overload of information the internet	4	8%
Difficulty in finding relevant information	7	14%

Above the table shows that the majority of respondents 34(68%) encountered the problem using internet slow access speed, 16(32%) lack of terminology, 7(14%) difficulty in finding relevant information 5(10%) lack of command, 4(8%) overload of information the internet 1(2%) privacy problem.

Table 20: *Use internet search engines*

Search Engines	*Frequency*	*%*
www.google.com	43	86%
www.yahoo.com	32	64%
www.excit.com	-	-
www.sify.com	-	-
www.virtual library	2	4%
www.answer.com	-	-
www.msn.com	-	-
www.altavista.com	-	-
www.scerus.com	-	-
Any other	-	-

Table 20 reveals that most of the faculty members 43(86%) used google internet search engine for their required information need followed by 32(64%) Yahoo, 2 (4%) www.virtual library.

FINDINGS OF THE STUDY

On the basis of responses received from digital information awareness and use of Internet by faculty members of Chaudhary Charan Singh University, Meerut, Uttar Pradesh India, the following important findings can be noted:

i. In view of analysis of data concerning user awareness about computer knowledge it appears that Majority of the faculty members 94% aware about computer knowledge and only 6% denied.

ii. Majority of the faculty members 90% aware about IT/ Digital information knowledge and 10% not aware.

iii. Majority of the respondents familiar with types of IT/ Digital information knowledge e.g. 92% Internet application, 62% MS-Office DTP tools, 32% multimedia, 4% programming language.

iv. Majority of the respondents 80% use the Internet for education/Research work followed by 46% E-mail, 20%, E-Learning, 14% entertainment, 12% News, 8% sports, 6% Discussion, and 2% Health.

v. Regarding location of use internet, Majority of respondents 94% used Internet at department, 24% at home, 16% at internet cafe, 8% at University library & only 2% at computer centre.

vi. Majority of respondents 30% have experience of internet use more than 4 year, 24% 6months to 1 year, 20% 1 to 2 year, 14% less than 6 months, 12% 2 to 4 year.

vii. Over half of the respondents 54% use Internet service daily for their information requirements, followed by 30% 2-3 time a week, 6% once in a week, 6% occasionally, 4% 2-3 times a month.

viii. About the response of respondents concerning the time spent by them on the Internet in searching specific information 44% respondents 2-4 hours a week, 24% 5-6 hours a week, 18% less than 1 hour a week, 8%. 7-9 hours a week, 6% over 20 hours in a week.

ix. Faculty members were asked to indicate the methods used for acquiring the internet skills. It was found that most popular method of acquiring the necessary skills to use internet is via trial and error method Over half of the respondents 54% favored this. Followed by 42% guidance from colleagues & friends, 30% self instruction, 20% training from university/department, 14% external courses.

x. Majority of respondents awareness of the services being provides on Internet 84% E-mail, 46% www (World Wide Web), 36% search engines (e.g. google), 14% FAQ (Frequently Asked Question), 8% FTP (File Transfer Protocol), 8% remote log in (Telnet), 6% Archie, 6% list serve/discussion group, 6% BBS (Bulletin Board Service).

xi. Majority of respondents about e-information /resources needed through Internet 80% needed E-journals, followed by 68% E-articles, 42% E-thesis and dissertations, 42% down loading services, 36%, E-databases, 32%, E-books, 18%, News groups, 14%, web resources, 14% Mailing list, 8% subject gate ways, 6% E-archives.

xii. Majority of the respondents 98% perceive general Web sites as useful for all purposes; 38 (76%) and 4 (8%) respondents indicated that they have used discipline-based Web sites (i.e., access for specific subject) and recreational Web sites (i.e., entertainment, traveling in some historical places, etc.), respectively

xiii. Majority of respondents about which facility on Internet use mostly 86% E-mail, 24% Net Phone, 6% chat, 2% none.

xiv. Majority of respondents about search facilities for retrieve information through Internet 48% field searching, 38%,

Boolean operators, 6%, type the web address directory, 6% use subscription database, 6% phrase (To terms in a specific order).

xv. Majority of respondents related to evaluation parameters for web resources 58% reliable, 38% authentic, 24% less expensive, 20% usable, 18% accessible, 19% coverage all, 10% comprehensive.

xvi. Majority of respondents' opinion related to conventional documents & internet 82% more information, 80% time saving, 68% more useful, 48% more preferences, 8% less expensive, 2% time consuming.

xvii. Majority of respondents' opinion about Internet influence on academic efficiency 58% says that use of conventional documents has decreased, 50% dependency on the internet has increased, 46% improved professional competence, 24% expedited the research process.

xviii. Majority of respondents about satisfaction with internet facilities 74% faculty little satisfied, 24% fully satisfied, 2% dissatisfied.

xix. Majority of respondents problems encountered about using internet 68% slow access speed, 32% downloading PDF files take more time, 20% difficulty in finding relevant information, 10% lack of terminology, 8% overload of information the Internet, 2% problems using Internet privacy problem.

xx. Majority of respondents about uses of Internet search engines 86% use google 64% yahoo 4% www.virtual library.

6. CONCLUSION AND SUGGESTIONS

This study gives a snapshot use of Internet by faculty members of Chaudhary Charan Singh University, Meerut, Uttar Pradesh, India. This study evaluated only Chaudhary Charan Singh University, Meerut, Uttar Pradesh. However with this snapshot it is clear that most of the library users use the Internet services daily and use the Internet for research and development purposes and to access information quickly. E-mail and search engines are the most used services by the faculty members. The present study indicates that a majority of faculty members use the Internet as one of their sources of information. The study also indicates that most users were satisfied with the information available on the Internet.

The present study puts forth the various suggestions to be implemented to improve Internet service in the library. Time slots should be increased, and printers should be made available to the faculty members. Faculty training programs are essential for the proper utilization of the Internet resources. Internet facilities should be improved, and upgraded PCs may be installed. CD–ROM/CD writers must be installed for data collections. Internet service should be provided around the clock. Broadband facilities should provide more journals online.

REFERENCES

1. Aggarwal, Y.P. (1986). *Statistical Methods: Concepts, Application, and Computation*. Sterling Publishers Private Limited; New Delhi ; p. 240
2. American Association of School Librarians (AASL) and Association for Educational Communications and Technology (AECT) (1988). *Information power: Guidelines for school library media programs,* Chicago: Author.
3. American Library Association Presidential Committee on Information Literacy (1989). *Final report.* Chicago: Author.
4. Anita, K. L. (1990). Information Literacy in the Electronic Age. *Research Strategies*; 8(1); 22-27
5. Bainton, B. et al. (2001). Information Literacy and Academic Libraries: the SCONUL approach (UK/Ireland). *67th IFLA Council and General Conference*. Aug 16-25; p. 312
6. Bansode, Sadanand Y. and Pujar, Shamprasad M. (2008). Use of internet by research scholars at Shivaji University, Kolhapur. *Annals of Library and Information Studies*, 55, 123-126.
7. Bawden, C.D. (2001). Information and Digital Literacies: A Review

of Concepts. *Journal of Documentation*; Chicago; pp. 22-33.

8. Behjgns, S. J. (1994). A conceptual analysis and historical overview of information literacy. *College and Research Libraries,* 55(4), 309-322

9. Birader, B. S., Rajshekhar, G.R. and Sampath Kumar, B. T. (2006). Astudy of internet usage by students and faculties in Kuvempes University. *Library Herald*, 44(4), 283-294.

10. Bundy, A. (2004). Information Literacy framework: Principles, Standards, and Practices. New Zealand Journal for Information Literacy; p. 240

11. Campbell, S. Defining Information Literacy in the 21 st Century (2004). 70th IFLA General Conference and Council; 22-27 August; Argentina; p. 234. Available at http://www.ifla.org.iv/ifla7/prog04.htm

12. Eynon, Rebecca (2005). The use of the internet in higher education: Academics' experiences of using ICTs for teaching and learning. *Aslib Proceedings: New Information Perspectives,* 57(2), 168 – 180.

13. Ghosh, B.N. (1992). *Scientific Method and Social Research*. Sterling Publishers Private Limited; New Delhi; p. 51-52.

14. Glister, P. (1997). Digital Literacy. New York: Wiley; p.67.

15. Kaur, A. (2000). Internet and libraries. *Library Herald,* 38 (1), 24-31.

16. Mahajan, Preeti (2005). Internet Use by Researchers; a Study of Panjab University, Chandigarh. *Library Philosophy & Practice.8* (2), 1-4.

17. Rajeev, K., & Kaur, A. (2005): A. Use of Internet by teachers and students in Shaheed Bhagat Singh College of Engineering & Technology: A case study. *Journal of Library and Information Science,* 29(1/2), 81-94.

18. Raju, N. Vasantha and Harinarayana, N. S. (2008). An analysis of usability features of library web sites. *Annals of Library and Information Studies,* 55, 111-122.

19. University (2004). Online Information Review, 28(1), 53-60. Available from: http://www.emeraldinsight.com/10.1108/14684520410522457

20. Singh, S. P. (2000). Internet and the role of libraries." Journal of Library and Information Science, 25(1), 26-37.

21. Srikantaiah,T. K., &Xiaoying, D. (1998). The Internet and its impact on developing countries: Examples from China and India. *Asian Libraries,* 7(9), 199-209. Available from: http://www.ingentaconnect.com/content/mcb/173/1998/00000007/00000009/

23

Major Initiatives for the Education & Development of the Rural Communities in the 21st Century: Indian Perspective

Nimai Chand Saha
Deputy Librarian , Central Library, Visva-Bharati
Santiniketan - 731235, Birbhum, W.B.
nimaichand.saha@visva-bharati.ac.in
Ajay Kumar Sharma
Assistant Librarian, Central Library, Visva-Bharati
Santiniketan - 731235, Birbhum, W.B.
ajaysharma.lib@visva-bharati.ac.in
Kanika Debnath
Assistant Librarian, Central Library, Visva-Bharati
Santiniketan - 731235, Birbhum, W.B.
kanika.debnath@visva-bharati.ac.in

ABSTRACT

We all know that to develop any nation the mission should be taken in such a way so that the effect should positively be percolates to all the community regardless of the geographical limitation. India is a developing nation and more than half of its population belongs from the rural villages and their earnings mainly depend on the agriculture, fisheries, weaving and physical labour etc. Even a great percentage of the peoples of India are still under illiteracy. So it is inevitable to activate some necessary action to eradicate such illiteracy from the rural communities. To facilitate the rural development efforts with particular emphasis and focus on the rural poor by improving the knowledge, skills and attitudes of rural development through some agencies of Government, NGO and corporate sectors. In view of the above the present paper would like to highlight the means of rural development, information needs of the rural communities, and the thrash area for the rural development. The paper also point out the role of LIS & IT Professionals for the educating the rural peoples by disseminating the information along with the initiatives taken up by the different agencies so far, for the all-wide development of the societies.

Keywords : Rural Community

1. INTRODUCTION

Immediate after the independence India being a sovereign country has trying to introduce and execute several initiatives for the betterment of the rural people. Planning has been one of the pillars for the welfare of the rural communities. The policies and programmes have been designed with the aim of alleviation of rural poverty & illiteracy, which have been one of the primary objectives of planned development in India. It was realized that a sustainable strategy of poverty alleviation has to be based on increasing accessibility of information in the process of growth itself. Elimination of poverty, ignorance, diseases, illiteracy and inequality of opportunities and providing a better and higher quality of life were the basic premises upon which all the plans and blue-prints of development were built. Rural development implies both the economic betterment of people as well as greater social transformation. In order to provide the rural people with better prospects for economic development, increased participation of people in the rural development programmes, decentralization of planning, better enforcement of land reforms and greater access to credit are envisaged.

2. RURAL DEVELOPMENT

Development refers to the process of progress and advancement in any field. In the context of a nation or a society 'development must …be conceived as a multi-dimensional process involving major changes in social structures, popular attitudes and national institutions as well as the acceleration of economic growth the reduction of inequality and the eradicating of absolute poverty. Development must (be) turn to diverse basic needs and desire of individual and social group". Development of any community or area involve:

Physical development i.e. development in the fields of communication, transport, sewage, irrigation, energy, forestry, environment and conservation of natural resources and livestock;

Economic development i.e. development in the fields of agriculture, animal husbandry, fishery, business and industry including Cottage and small-scale industries and trade;

Social development i.e. development in the fields of education, culture and political activities;

Health development i.e. development in the fields of nutrition, sanitation, community health, prevention of water and air pollution; and

Women development i.e. Raising consciousness about gender justice, self-help group for thrift, credit and self-employment, women employment generation.

Rural India is still lagging behind in almost all the above sectors. But exactly to what extent is possibly not known even to the government as it does not have sufficient information, some time for lack of efforts and some times lack of coordination among the concerned people. As a result, the development plans are often drawn either on the basis of presumptions, or on the basis of incomplete or outdated information. The outcome will be well imagined.

3. MAJOR INFORMATION NEED OF RURAL PEOPLE

- Agricultural and their related issue;
- Small-scale industries and their related issues;
- Employment;
- Education (courses offered by the institutions with fees., time and durations etc;
- Health and family welfare related;
- Credit and insurance facilities;
- Local communication (Train / Bus) timetable and contact number;
- Food and availability of cheap nutrition diet;
- Self-employment plans and programme;
- Animal husbandry; common diseases and their cure in animals;
- Public policy information: Govt. programmes, plans, projects, etc; and
- Legal aids and personal security.

Besides the above the rural people also need information on social welfare, village and cottage industries, housing, horticulture, local & political news etc.

4. COMMUNITY INFORMATION SERVICES (CIS)

The Community Information Centers has to conduct

surveys to know the information needs of the rural community in a particular area, collect information according to the needs, organize the information and then disseminate it as and when required. Its purpose is to –

- Educate the rural community to know and utilize the various schemes and programmes introduced by the Govt. (Insurance, Loan, Housing etc.);
- Develop a collection containing Govt. publication;
- Provide information about the schemes and training programmes available regarding agriculture, fisheries, cottage industries etc;
- Provide information of scientific method and techniques for better production, viz. weather reports, soil-testing report, use of improved seeds, fertilizers, plant protection chemicals etc;
- Inform about childcare and family planning; and
- Develop a local history collection of the particular area.

5. THRUST AREAS FOR COMMUNITY INFORMATION SERVICE

CISs must address the significant problems for the community. Designing and development of CISs should start with the identification and analysis of community information needs. Following are the may be regarded as thrust area for the requirement of the rural people:

- Agriculture
- Business
- Cultural activities
- Education
- Employment
- Finance
- Games and sports

- Government
- Health
- Housing
- Industry
- Infrastructure
- Legal
- Local events
- Local history
- Local news
- Marketing
- Natural disaster
- Organizations and groups
- Recreation
- Social service
- Weather

6. ROLE OF LIS PROFESSIONALS

In view of the new environment, library and information professionals manning information centers at different levels will have to play an important role in handling conventional and electronic resources for rural development. Extension oriented training programmes should be organized at regular basis with the following objectives:

- To understand the peoples need in a better way.
- To bring out new strategies to be formulated for different activities.
- To organize formal communication programme among rural people.

In addition the library professionals should involve themselves,

- Transition of print media based libraries to e-media based libraries.
- Changing passive users to active users.
- Networking of libraries.
- Developing information / knowledge resources focused on patron's need.
- Developing a cooperative and users centered culture; and
- Organizing the information resources on modern line.

They should have to aware of the following professional competencies to disseminate the service to its clientele:

- To have knowledge about content of the information resources available in both print and non-print formats.
- To have ability to apply appropriate Information Technology for information management and retrieval.
- To have ability to organize scientific and technical information in a systematic manner.
- To have ability to organize specialized information services to meet the various needs of the rural users community and
- To have ability to conduct users survey on regular basis.

7. ROLE OF IT PROFESSIONALS

Information Technology is a powerful tool for service to the rural people. IT professionals should aim at achieving sustainable and equitable development, with active participatory role for rural development.

- IT professionals should establish the viability of technologies and development.
- They must help rural people to come to terms with their own past.
- They have to create a situation in which every user has access to information.

- They have to encourage the convergence of existing and new development.
- They have to create a situation where every community is empowered to pursue its own vision.
- They should ensure people's participation in identifying their individual need / problem.
- They must avoid creation of a sense of inferiority in the people.

8. GOVERNMENT INITIATIVES

In some states the state governments or local self governments have set up information centers or Kiosks to disseminate the information required by the rural people of the area. Some instances of such effort are point out here:

8.1. Akshay Kendras : Kerala government is setting up information kiosks, named as 'Akshay kendras', in different villages. The government jointly with the Tulip IT services is setting up rural broadband wireless network eliminating the need of telephone lines to run Internet in this kiosks. The villagers can make payment of electricity bills to get birth certificate and contact police stations by e-mail, besides obtaining other information through these kiosks.

8.2. CLIC Project : The government of West Bengal has taken up a project of setting up in phases around 1500 Community Library and Information Centers (CLIC) in such villages where there are no Public / Rural Libraries. So far more than 100 such centers have been set up. Community Library Organizers (CLO) runs these. The centers, besides providing normal library services, specifically cater information relating to career and vocational opportunities, essential data needed for regional planning, and information pertaining to developmental activities being carried out by Village Panchayats.

8.3. Community Information Centers : In April 2000, the Ministry of Information Technology, Government of India, launched a project to establish Community Information Centers (CICs) in all Blocks in North-Eastern states of Arunachal Pradesh, Assam, Manipur, Meghalaya, Mizoram, Sikkim and Tripura to extend the reach of modern day technology even to the remote areas and difficult mountain terrains of these states in order to enable rapid socio-economic development and bring the area closer to the national mainstream.

8.4. Jana Mitra Scheme : Jana Mitra is a United Nations Development Programme (UNDP) – Government of India supported initiative. Under this scheme information kiosks have been set up in remote areas of Jhawalar District of Rajasthan. The scheme aims at providing access of information pertaining to government services and availing of many services on-line in remote pockets of the country.

8.5. Lokmitra project : Himachal Pradesh government has taken up 'Lokmitra Project' to provide the general public, specially those living in distant rural areas of the state, easy access to government information and the facilities of e-governnance at their door step. The project was first implemented in the Hamirpur District where a district wise intranet has been created. Lokmitra soochana Kendra have been set up in 25 panchayat areas, which are run by the unemployed youth.

8.6. NATP Project : Manage – National Institute of Agricultural Extension and Management, Hyderabad, under its National Agricultural Technology Project (NATP), has set up Internet kiosks in 24 districts of seven states, viz. Andhra Pradesh, Bihar, H.P., Jharkahnd, Maharasthra. Orissa and Punjab. Mutually Aided Cooperative Thrift and Credit Society (MACTCS) were given the responsibility to run the kiosks. These kiosks provides agricultural calendar, agricultural expert system for diagnosis of pest related problems, weather information, examination results to the people of the area.

8.7. NIRD Scheme : **N**ational **I**nstitute of **R**ural **D**evelopment (NIRD), Hyderabad has set up to public information kiosks with Internet connections, one at vikarabad in Ranga Reddy district and the other at Tenali in Guntur District (both in AP). The kiosks provides information about examination results, directories, agricultural prices, governmental forms, land records, educational opportunities etc. all services are nominally priced.

8.8. Raj Nidhi Scheme : Rajnidhi is a web enabled information kiosks system, developed jointly by the Rajasthan's department of Information Technology and Rajasthan state agency of computer services. From these kiosks, the citizens are able to access information or services relating to health, family planning, immunization schedules for children, employment, transportation, distance education, agriculture, water, electricity connection etc.

8.9. Wired Village project : Fifty four village information kiosks have been set up in Kolhapur district of Maharasthra under this project, implemented by a committee consisting of members from National Information Center Warna cooperative societies under the over all guidance of the collector of the district. The villagers are access to information in their local language about crops and agricultural market prices, employment scheme of the state government and educational opportunities through these kiosks.

8.10. HP I-Community, Kuppam : Hewlett Packard and the state of Andhra Pradesh, India to build an HP i-Community in kuppam, a community of 320000 people in rural villages.

9. NGO'S INITIATIVES

According to rough estimate, around one million NGOs are functioning in India, majority of which are working for the poor and the downtrodden. O some of the NGOs have taken initiatives in setting up information disseminating centers in rural areas. Some of the schemes are as;

9.1. Drishtee Project (http://main.edc.org/mosaic/mosaic7/india.asp) : Dridhtee has been described as "a platform for rural networking and marketing services for enabling e-governance, education and health services". It runs with the help of state-of-the-art software that facilitates communication and information interchange within a localized intranet between villages and district centers.

9.2. Gandoot Scheme (http://gyandoot.net/) : Under this scheme twenty villages in five blocks in the tribal area of Dhar district have been interconnected through an intranet owned by the community. Thirty-one villages wired centers are operational under the name of 'Soochanalayas'. Villages have bought computers and other required equipment themselves. The information served by them include agricultural product auction detail, commodity rates, career related information, government programme announcements, different forms required for government transactions, list of people covered under below poverty line criterion, details of marriageable boys and girls etc.

9.3. GRID Center : A rural information center called Tejas Samadhana Kendraor General Resources and Information Dissemination (GRID) center designed and developed by the Indian farmers and Industrial Alliances (IFIA) and the Federation of Farmers Associations, has come up in July 2004 Gummadidala Village in the Medak District of AP. It provides farmers with feedback and training in collaboration with local self-help groups including airing fortnightly forecasts on weather, crop activities and management techniques with the market trend of farm produce and other operational schemes.

9.4. Information Village : With a modest grant from IDRC, Canada, M.S.Swaminathan Rsearch Foundation,

Chennai, initiated in 1998 an imaginative experiment in electronic knowledge delivery in a cluster of villages and hamlets near pondichery, to meet the local needs using a mix of wire and wireless technologies and through a local website.

9.5. SARI Network (http://www.tenet.res.in/rural/sari.html): The Sustainable Access in Rural India (SARI) project, sponsored by Center for International Development (CID), Harvard University, media Lab at the Massachussettes Institute of Technology (MIT); TeNet group, Indian Institute of Technology, Madras and I-Gyan Foundation of the Internet Business Capital corporation (IBCC), is being implemented in the villages of the three blocks in Madurai District of Tamil Nadu.

9.6. TARAhaat Project (TARAhat.com) : Tarahaat, named after the all-purpose haat (meaning village bazaar), comprises " a commercially viable model for bringing relevant information, products, and services via the Internet to the unserved rural market of India". It won the Stockholm challenge award for the year 2001.

9.7. M S Swaminathan Research Foundation at Pondichery in Southern India.

9.8. Rural Development Through Educational System (RDES) in Pabal, Pune.

10. CORPORATE INITITATIVES

The motive of increasing market base has promoted several corporate houses to take up projects aimed at setting up information kiosks in rural area in different parts of the country.

10.1. Amul's DISK Net : The well-known dairy giant Amul of Anand, Gujrat has developed a network of Dairy Information System of Kiosks (DISK). Apart from milk accounts, the kiosks offer telephony, market intelligence, fund management, information on best practices etc.

10.2. Hindusthan Lever's iShakti : Hindusthan Lever Ltd., a corporate giant, has embarked upon a project, called iShakti – an IT based rural information services – to provide information and services to meet rural needs. The project has been set up of 1500 kiosks up to 2005. These kiosks remain open from 9am to 7pm six days a week.

10.3. ITC's e-chaupal : The International Business Division of another large corporate house, ITC, launched e-chaupal project in 2000 and has since set up around 2700such chaupals covering a population of around 1.2 million in five states viz.MP, Karnatak, AP, UP and Maharashtra. It offers services and information on subjects like weather and market prices, scientific farm practices, sale of input and purchase of product etc.

10.4. Ogilvy & Mather's Param : Param sponsored by Ogilvy & Mather, is an innovative initiative in rural connectivity. This project was originally conceived for marketing communications, but has evolved into a platform that can be shared by companies and government to reach out to villages. This electronic connectivity network can reach the remotest rural areas where no landline or media based communication is currently available.

10.5. Parry's Indiaagriline.com : EID Parry & Co has implemented a scheme in villages around Nellikuppam village in cuddalore district of Tamil Nadu, where the factory of the company is located, using CorDECT technology, developed by Indian Institute of Technology, Madras,which allows voce and data to be carried out simultaneously over a single pair of lines at cheaper rates. It offers Farm practices, farm business, farm advisory services, community details such as prices of different crops in nearby markets, detailed about crops grown in the area including banana, cashew, tapioca, ground nut etc.

10.6. Greenstar (http://www.greenstar.org) : Greenstar, a new consortium of companies from India and the United States launched its first solar powered Internet community center in pravatpur village, 150 kms from Hyderabad.

10.7. Ikisan.com (http://www.Ikisan.com) : Ikisan developed by the Nagarjuna group, offer weather forecasts, commodity news, online loan facilities, product availability etc.

11. ACTIVITIES OF THE DIRECTORATE OF LIBRARY SERVICES

With a view to strengthening the library services the state, the directorate of library services undertakes the various measures to make the libraries efficient in administration and their services

11.1. Career Guidance Center (CGC) : A new feature has been added by induction of CGCs in the State Central Library and 25 District Libraries of West Bengal. The objective of the scheme is to provide book support to the scholars and youths to prepare themselves for jobs.

11.2. Community library cum Information Center (CLIC): Under this scheme it has been provided to open one such center in the Gram Panchayat that do not have any public library.

11.3. Bibliographic Control : The directorate of library services used to publish a subject wise selected list of Bengali books to help the librarian to purchase books for their libraries. The directorate of library services arrange for bulk purchase of books for the matching programme with the Raja Rammohun Roy Library Foundation.

11.4. Co-operation with the Bengal Library Association (BLA) : The Bengal Library Association always played a leading role in the organization, management and extension of library services in the state. Since its establishment in 1925, it has been playing a very important role towards library movement In the state.

11.5. Organization of Book fair : Organization of book fairs has become a regular annual programme. Book fairs are organized in the district under the auspices of the respective local library authority.

11.6. Assistance to Non-Govt. and Non-sponsored libraries: Govt. rendered assistance to age-old non-government and non-sponsored libraries as a token of recognition of their service to common people. Such assistance could not be paid in 2000-01 but as assistance Rs.8.40 lakhs could be paid to such libraries in 2002-03.

11.7. Book assistance to selected govt. sponsored libraries in accordance with their performance.

11.8. Implementation of matching grant scheme of the Raja Rammohun Roy Library Foundation.

12. NEW CONCEPTS

Besides the above initiatives, two new concepts have been developed and or initiated which are also very useful in the context of information dissemination in rural areas.

1. Electronic Doorway Library : The Developing Libraries Network (DELNET) has floated a new concept of Electronic Doorway Library (EDL), which envisages a more comprehensive coverage. It has proposed to the planning commission the department of culture that such libraries are set up in rural India in a phased manner. As it is essential to offer such information to the people of rural India which they need and can use in improving their life, five subject areas have been identified, viz. health and welfare, agriculture, education, general information, and small scale industries, on which appropriate resources needs to be selected or developed a new.

2. Kiosk-on-wheel : The Indian Institute of Technology, Kanpur, has developed a mobile information kiosk for rural India. It is a dust proof unit on board a cycle rickshaw, called *infothella*. It will connect to the web through wireless system.

13. CREATION OF INFORMATION PRODUCTS

A scheme should be undertaken for creation of area profile based specific databases and other information products specifically needed in each village or region on the following aspects:

Healthcare : primary information on health & available facility, sanitation, water, environment etc.

Social welfare : Welfare schemes of the government and NGOs in the fields of eradication of poverty and illiteracy & mentally or physically handicapped persons, child and women development, insurance facilities etc.

Education : Literacy and adult education centers, local educational facilities, educational opportunities outside the region, scholarship and fellowship etc.

Agriculture : Information on crops, seeds, sowing time, pest control, cold storage, agricultural loan facilities, crop insurance, product marketing, pricing system and policy etc.

Animal Husbandry : Information relating to poultry farming, cattle rearing, pig raising, pisciculture, animal health and marketing animal produce etc.

Industries : information relating to local industries, specially handicraft and small scale industries, loan facilities for setting up a new small scale industries, raw materials, technology update, prices and marketing of products.

Finance & Investment : Banking and saving facilities, loan facilities, investment avenues etc.

Local libraries and or local panchayats may be given the responsibility to collecting necessary data and create the local databases or information product. All concerned officials and departments should be asked to cooperate in this scheme.

14. MAJOR PORTALS FOR RURAL DEVELOPMENT IN INDIA

The Internet based e-resources pertaining to rural development information and systems in India are highlighted below:

i) **Honduras :** SDNP a civil society's Information system, *http://www.sdnp.undp.org/it4dev/stories/honduras.html.*

ii) **ICRISAT** (*http://www.icrisat.org/*), data base containing 50000records on crops and resources of interest to farmers in semi-arid tropical areas.

iii) **India:** SKS-Smart Card (*http://www.sksindia.com*) delivering financial services to the doorstep of the poor.

iv) **India:** PlaNet Finance (*http://www.planetfinance.org*) supports organizations offering financial services to the very poor.

v) **India:** nLogue (*http://www.digitalpartners.org/nlogue.html*) wireless local loop a technology has been adapted that address the economic realities of rural India.

vi) **India:** AgriWatch (*http://www.agriwatch.org*) information on agricultural commodities trade.

vii) **India:** Drishtee (*http://www.drishtee.com*) creates model of rural distribution and promotion of consumer goods and basic services.

viii) **India:** Indian Villages (*http://www.cddc.vt.edu/knownet/article-ifa.html*) links thousands of villages with Internet kiosks.

ix) **India:** IT in weather forecasting in coastal villages, (*http://economictimes.com/today/04tech10.htm*).

x) **India:** Telemedicine service in pune primary health centers (*http://www.cddc.vt.edu/knownet/article/pune-telemedicine.html*)

xi) **India:** connecting rural India to the Internet: the challeges of Using V-SAT Technology (*http://sdgateway.net/webworks/case/da_vsat.htm*)

xii) **India:** communications revolution set to transform 1,000 Tamil villages, (*http://www.tenet.res.in/press/15022001.html*)

xiii) **India:** I.T.keeping track of water (*http://www.cddc.vt.edu/knownet/articles/it-water.html*)

xiv) **India:** toward a knowledge system for sustainable food security (*http://www.isoc.org/oti/articles/0401/balaji.html*)

xv) **India:** Asia's largest vegetables market goes on-line.

xvi) **India:** Information Technology and Disasters (*http://www.cddc.vt.edu/knownet/articles/india-it-disaster.html*)

xvii) **India:** telemedicine from Apollo.

xviii) **India:** empowering dairy farmers through a dairy information network and services kiosks (*http://www1.worldbank.org/publicsector/egov/diskcs.htm*)

xix) **India:** web site for aqua farmers launched (*http://www.cddc.vt.edu/*)

xx) **India:** Gyandoot (*http://www.gyandoot.net/gyandoot.intranet.html*)

xxi) **India:** e-post to be launched in six states (*http://cddc.vt.edu/knownet/articles/india-epost.html*)

xxii) **India:** Videoconferencing facility between Andhra Jails and courts (*http://cddc.vt.edu/knownet/articles/india/jail.html*)

xxiii) **India:** ITC to set up Net booths for coffee planters (*http:/*

/cddc.vt.edu/knownet/articles/coffeebooth.html)

xxiv) India: knowledge system for sustainable food security (*http://www.mssrf.org/information%20village/index.html*)

xxv) India: Innovative networking Solution for development organizations establishing remote areas networking through wireless radio modem (*http://xlweb.com/food/wireless/final.htm*)

xxvi) India: Soya Choupal (*http://www.soyachoupal.com*) the Hindi website providing information to the soyabean farmers.

xxvii) India: Andhra Pradesh (India) Electronic Governance Initiative (*http://apts.gov.in/twins/*)

xxviii) India. Health Library (*http://www.healthlibrary.com*)

15. MAJOR PROBLEMS

i. The number of Rural Library is not so sufficient to serve the remote rural people.

ii. The inadequate fund is the capital problem for offering rural library services.

iii. Most of the existing library suffering from common minimum infrastructure, viz. unplanned and unhygienic building better to say some of the libraries has no building, number of rooms, qualified and trained library staff, number of permanent library staff, lack of IT knowledge of the library staff & users also.

iv. Lack of library professionals participation in the policy formulation / decision-making process of the library services.

v. Lack of proper arrangement of Technology based training and workshop for the staff & users.

vi. There is huge number of casual and voluntary staff in the different sponsored and non-sponsored libraries. After providing voluntary service for a long period they have lost their motivation and interest to serve the library clientele.

vii. Psychological problem to cope with the modern technology.

viii. Language problem, as language of the people of India are voluminous so it is difficult to communicate one province to another even in the same state.

ix. The number of population is very high and their education as well as conscious level is very poor.

x. There is a lack of National Universal Information Policy in reality.

xi. Some technological products i.e. Mobile, TV, Computer (Internet/Game) etc attracted the youth society as a result the library has lost its users rapidly.

xii. Some times local political factor may be appeared as the problem to the library in its proper functioning.

xiii. Lack of electrical and telecommunication connection in the rural Indian villages it is not possible to serve them current information as per their requirement.

16. CONCLUSION

Ignorance is the greatest evil of the human being. Advance knowledge and information can broaden the mind and enlighten the intellectual outlook of the individuals leading / providing to ultimately to a better social life. Towards the beginning of 21st century, in India, we have witnessed at our disposal a technology of which our forefathers could only dream - a technology which can transform local happenings into global events and which can reverse the trends towards divergence. Rural Development has been an important area on which the government has been giving sustained emphasis since independence. Lots of initiatives have been made available to the rural areas to bridge the gap between urban and rural areas in terms of access to the information. The government, NGO and by the corporate sectors have been producing the vast amount of information which often do not percolate at different levels of the community due to the lack of awareness & availability of technology. So, proper awareness has to be created among the end users regarding the availability and usefulness of the facilities they can use for their development.

REFERENCES

1. Bandopadhyay, Amit Kumar (2008). Our Public Libraries: Evaluation of the Public Libraries in West Bengal, Burdwan: Smt. Ruma Bandopadhyay.
2. Chatterjee, Amitabha (2004). Information Support for Rural Development in India: Present situation and Future Strategies in 21st National Seminar of IASLIC on Information Support for Rural Development, 31st December 2004 to 03 January 2005, Jadavpur University. 1-14p.
3. Giri, J.S. Rao and Pattnaik, S.N. (2006), Technology for Rural Development Role of Telecommunication Media in India, Indian Media Studies Journal, 1(1).
4. Das, Binod Bihari and Khan, Salil Chandra (2003). Role of Librarians of Public Libraries as one of the grass root functionaries in Rural Development: The Present Scenario in West Bengal in 24th All India Conference of IASLIC on Knowledge Management in Special Libraries in Digital Environment.
5. http://rural.nic.in/i1.htm accessed on 18.12.2008
6. http://www.nird.org.in/ accessed on 18.12.2008
7. Das, Binod Bihari (2004). Information for beneficiaries and Functionaries of Rural Development: Perspectives for West Bengal Public Libraries in 21st National Seminar of IASLIC on Information Support for Rural Development, 31st December 2004 to 03 January 2005, Jadavpur University. 31-39p.
8. Mishra, Satyan (2003). Information kiosks in Rural India: Business Provides Franchise Opportunity for Young Entrepreneurs, Youth and Work: Young Entrepreneurs Share Their Stories, 5(1).
9. http: //main.edc.org/mosaic7/India.asp accessed on 17.12.2008.
10. Devi, Ch. Tanuja and Devi, Th. Madhuri (2004). Strategic Planning to support Information for Rural Development Through Public Libraries in 21st National Seminar of IASLIC on Information Support for Rural Development, 31st December 2004 to 03 January 2005, Jadavpur University. 15-19p.
11. Nanda, B.R. Libraries in a Developing Society in All India Library Conference, 1980, New Delhi.